Don't Go Upstairs!

Don't Go Upstairs!

A Room-by-Room Tour of the House in Horror Movies

CLEAVER PATTERSON

Foreword by David McGillivray

McFarland & Company, Inc., Publishers
Jefferson, North Carolina

Frontispiece: The real thing: No. 8 Cheyne Walk, Chelsea, London SW3. The house where Diana Dors meets her end in *Theatre of Blood* (1973), as seen today (author's photograph).

Library of Congress Cataloguing-in-Publication Data

Names: Patterson, Cleaver, 1968– author.
Title: Don't go upstairs! : a room-by-room tour of the house in horror movies / Cleaver Patterson ; foreword by David McGillivray.
Description: Jefferson : McFarland & Company, Inc., Publishers, 2020 | Includes bibliographical references and index.
Identifiers: LCCN 2019043673 | ISBN 9781476672977 (paperback) ∞
ISBN 9781476638041 (ebook)
Subjects: LCSH: Dwellings in motion pictures. | Horror films—History and criticism.
Classification: LCC PN1995.9.D84 P38 2020 | DDC 791.43/6164—dc23
LC record available at https://lccn.loc.gov/2019043673

British Library cataloguing data are available

ISBN (print) 978-1-4766-7297-7
ISBN (ebook) 978-1-4766-3804-1

© 2020 Cleaver Patterson. All rights reserved

No part of this book may be reproduced or transmitted in any form or by any means, electronic or mechanical, including photocopying or recording, or by any information storage and retrieval system, without permission in writing from the publisher.

Front cover images © 2020 Shutterstock

Printed in the United States of America

*McFarland & Company, Inc., Publishers
Box 611, Jefferson, North Carolina 28640
www.mcfarlandpub.com*

To "B"
who knows more about film than I ever will...

Table of Contents

Acknowledgments ix
Foreword by David McGillivray 1
Introduction 3

1. The Hallway and Landing 9
2. The Living Room 24
3. The Library and Study 39
4. The Dining Room 56
5. The Kitchen 71
6. The Cellar 87
7. The Bedroom 102
8. The Nursery and Schoolroom 118
9. The Bathroom 131
10. The Attic 145
11. The Conservatory and Greenhouse 159
12. The Grounds 174
13. The Spare Room 189

Appendix: Abner Pastoll on the Importance of the House as a Film Character 203
Chapter Notes 215
Bibliography 219
Index 223

Acknowledgments

In the early 1980s, I went on a school trip to the Isle of Man where I found in a local news agent shop a copy of the film magazine *The House of Hammer*. I can only imagine I got away with buying it because our accompanying teachers weren't aware of what I'd discovered. In it was a feature on the British horror film *Satan's Slave*, directed by cult filmmaker Norman J. Warren and written by prolific author and film critic David McGillivray. *Satan's Slave*—and one notorious scene in particular involving a Satanic black mass and a metal nail file—stuck in my mind, and still haunts me to this day. When I at last got to see the film, I'm glad to say that particular scene did not disappoint. Skip several decades and I was delighted when I got the opportunity to interview Norman for the horror magazine *We Belong Dead*. Who could imagine such a warm and friendly, unassuming gentleman was responsible for helming that marvelously diabolical and depraved film?

A couple of years later when I was deciding who to approach to contribute a foreword to this book, one name came to mind that, more than any, fit the bill perfectly: David McGillivray. Not only had he penned *Satan's Slave* but he'd also written a number of other classic British chillers from the 1970s, including the over-the-top *Frightmare* which I've included in the films covered here. Who better to share his thoughts on a book about houses in horror? To my delight, David agreed and I could not have asked for a more insightful addition.

At London's Frightfest Film Festival in 2015, I saw British writer-director Abner Pastoll's *Road Games*, which excited me with both its originality and ability to saturate the viewer's subconscious. When I came to write this book, I decided it would be pertinent to feature some firsthand observations on the importance of the house in horror films, from someone actually involved in the filmmaking process. As *Road Games* has a house at its core, I thought I could find no one better than its director to share his views. My interview with Abner has provided a unique insight into the process a filmmaker undertakes when sourcing a physical building in which to house his cinematic vision and I'm indebted to him for his willingness to talk to me and contribute to the book.

In the years since I started in earnest to write on film, contributing on the subject to various books, magazines and websites, several people have encouraged me, provided opportunities and opened doors which would likely have otherwise remained closed. David Miller, one-time editor of the now defunct horror magazine *Shivers*, gave me my first writing opportunity on that publication, for which I will always be in his debt. The late, great Ingrid Pitt, who contributed a regular column to *Shivers*, gave me my first major interview, published in *The Sunday Times Magazine*, an opportunity for which I owe her much. Thanks too to Robin Yacoubian, founder of the film website *Flickfeast* to which I am an occasional contributor, for giving me the chance to see films I would likely have otherwise missed, and Eric McNaughton, editor of *We Belong Dead* magazine and its spin-off books, for letting me air my opinions through his publications.

I'd like to thank my family for their support, especially my late parents Adrian and Pat Patterson, who I know would have been proud of my achievement, and my friends Charlie Brown, James Fox, David McFarland, Winnie Magee, Tony McGrath, Nesta Morgan, Rosemary Stephens and Darren Wassell. I realize horror may not be your subject but all of you have, over the years, shown interest in my writing, for which I'm grateful.

When not writing, I am known to put in some hours at Foyles bookshop in Central London. Numerous colleagues there, past and present, have been regaled with regular updates concerning my literary endeavors, for which I can only apologize. I'd particularly like to thank Cristina Rey Aliseda, Chris Banks, Jen Bell, Clare Bolton, Abi Bryant, Chloe Coles, Charlotte Colwill, Paul Davis, Jim Elliott, Elspeth Henderson, Ben Morgan, Nick Morgan, James Munroe, Sarah Myers, Rupert Osborne, Gary Perry, Marion Rankine, Thesy Surface, Gianni Washington, Laura Wearden, Mark Whelan, Christian Whitehead and Patrick Wray. Special thanks must also go to Samier Al-Jaibechi and Mark Dicker who made several apt suggestions as to the structure of this book.

To Maureen Kincaid Speller, who cast her critical eye over the book's finished manuscript, thank you. I may have only met you by email, but I feel I know you, and your assistance has been invaluable.

And Nina Allan. In the years since we first met, you have shown enthusiasm for and interest in my writing, far beyond the call of duty. I hope you realize how important your friendship is to me.

Finally, and most of all, "B"—your support means the world to me. On the frequent occasions when I wanted to give up, you encouraged me to stick at it. Without your humor, patience and willingness to read yet another rough draft, I can truly say this book would not exist … thank you.

Foreword by David McGillivray

Today, more than ever, it seems that every aspect of the horror film has been written about. There is a community of gorehounds able to share information more easily than at any previous time on forums and blogs and at the horror film festivals that no self-respecting crossroads is now without. Fans pick over every new film, even the rubbish that goes straight to DVD; also every classic going back to the dawn of cinema; and every piece of minutiae concerning the lowliest stuntman or makeup artist. What is there left to add?

Well, it turns out there *is* something to add and here it is in *Don't Go Upstairs!* Perhaps it's a book that should have been written long ago. After all, the haunted house, the house of horror and the old dark house are endemic to the genre. A director for whom I worked, Pete Walker, embarked on a series of what he called terror films, most with "house" in the title. Perhaps he might still be making them today had he not, somewhat surprisingly, decided to pack it in after *House of the Long Shadows*.

But be prepared. This is not a comprehensive account of every house in every horror film. That tome might be un-liftable. This is a novelty survey of just 65 films, released between 1933 and 2011, chosen at the whim of hard-working author Cleaver Patterson, who seems to have watched a lot of films and decided which rooms have been best represented in houses you wouldn't want to visit after dark. Thus *The Picture of Dorian Gray* is discussed in terms of its attic. The prominent part of the house in *The Texas Chain Saw Massacre* is, *pace* Patterson, its hallway.

This approach opens up a kind of alternative horror film universe in which the high point of Joan Collins' career is her murder in the living room of *Tales from the Crypt*. Focus tends to switch from the director, the writer and the cast to the art director. There are some distinguished but by no means household names mentioned here, among them Charles D. Hall, Wilfred Shingleton, John Barry and Cedric Gibbons.

Foreword by David McGillivray

Patterson's survey draws attention to some little-known films of which readers may not be aware. Personally I'm tempted to track down *Murders in the Zoo*. I'm also pleased to see the inclusion of a film I've championed for decades, *Corruption*, the work of some terrible old hacks that still manages to achieve a fine sense of Grand Guignol. And what a surprise to find mention of the rarely screened *The Ones Below*, highly recommended. Although it has echoes of many previous thrillers, it builds to a deliciously horrible climax.

The book is likely to provoke argument because of the titles omitted. The cellar section does not include *The Beast in the Cellar*. Probably one of the most enduring images of horror cinema is of the "corpse" rising from the bath in *Les Diaboliques*. But you won't find the French classic in the bathroom section. Perhaps there are enough omissions to warrant another book.

Recently I had the pleasure of seeing sections of the masterpiece *The Clock*, Christian Marclay's 24-hour–long compilation of filmclips showing clocks and watches. I knew instinctively that I never again would see a cut-away of a dial or a digital display without thinking, "I wonder if he knows about that one?" *Don't Go Upstairs!* is likely to have the same effect the next time I see a dining room or a greenhouse in a shocker on late night TV.

Writer, critic, actor and producer David McGillivray rose to prominence during the 1970s as assistant editor of the BFI periodical The Monthly Film Bulletin, *for which he was also a regular reviewer. It is his collaborations during this same period with horror directors Norman J. Warren and Pete Walker on such classics as* Satan's Slave *(1976) and* House of Mortal Sin *(1976) for which he is best remembered.*

Introduction

You've seen the film, you've read the book. You know the one—there've been so many: The young couple find the home of their dreams, the wife's ecstatic, the husband's happy but more controlled; they move in, the kids (usually one of each) tear around the empty rooms. But we know there's something sinister about the place, because we've read the blurb and paid our money. Slowly, THINGS start to happen. There's something nasty in the locked room at the top of the old creaky stairs; something lurks in the cellar below, which is possibly itself the Gateway to Hell. You know the story.
—*The Magic Cottage*, James Herbert (1986)

Like fear itself, a house such as that in James Herbert's bestselling *The Magic Cottage* is something everyone can relate to. After all, whether we rent an inner city apartment or own a stately country pile, most of us live in some kind of house. So it makes the perfect setting for a horror film, whether as the central core around which the action revolves, or simply as somewhere for the madman with an axe and hockey mask to hole up while he awaits his next victim. Whatever its purpose, a house makes horror real.

But why use the presence of the house in horror films as the foundation for a book? There are several reasons. Firstly, having written on both topics for various publications over the years, films, particularly horror films, and houses and their interiors have always intrigued me. Two of my favorite films, the chilling *Frightmare* (1974) directed by Pete Walker, and the cult shocker *Satan's Slave* (1976), directed by Norman J. Warren, both from prolific writer and critic David McGillivray, stand out for the isolated Home Counties houses they take place in as much as for the gruesome deeds they feature.

Secondly, fear (read horror) and the need for somewhere to live are two basic elements of life that everyone understands. Why not combine these components, with film, to create a real-estate guide to houses in horror films? To the best of my knowledge, this has not been done before.

Just as fear manifests itself in multitudinous forms, so too do the

Something nasty in the woodshed: Dorothy Yates (Sheila Keith) and her daughter Debbie (Kim Butcher) drive home their point in the deranged shocker *Frightmare* (1974).

houses that appear in horror films, being as varied and individual as the people who inhabit them. The houses I've included appear in films as wide-ranging as James Whale's *The Invisible Man* (1933), from Hollywood's Golden Age of Horror, to contemporary shockers such as the Columbian chiller *The Hidden Face* (2011). The choice of films was difficult but, as far as possible, those which made the cut did so because they had specific rooms which stood out from the rest of the house.

There are numerous horror films where the house as a whole—as opposed to individual rooms—takes center stage. As its title infers, in the James Whale classic *The Old Dark House* (1932) the remote, storm-lashed mansion is what really frightens viewers and the unfortunate travelers who seek shelter there. Equally, in *The Amityville Horror* (1979), it's George and Kathy Lutz's home as a complete entity that one remembers as much as its internal layout. On the other hand, films from cinema's silent period were often shot throughout a house, seldom having one specific room that stood out. *Frankenstein* (1910) and *Nosferatu* (1922) featured interiors that were horrific as a whole, not because of their individual parts. This is why I have not included any films from the silent era in this guide.

If you go down to the woods today: devilry from the prolific pen of writer David McGillivray and director Norman J. Warren in *Satan's Slave* (1976).

Those films that are included are memorable for a particular scene, in a specific room, against which much of the rest of the film's action pales. Take, for example, the home of Michael and Claire Bartel, in Curtis Hanson's distressing psycho-thriller *The Hand That Rocks the Cradle* (1992). Its actual exterior lies in the American city of Tacoma in Washington State. Though the interiors of the house are like something from *Architectural Digest*, once the garden's greenhouse is thrown into the equation, little else matters.

There are, of course, exceptions. A wonderful example of American gothic architecture, the mansion belonging to the twisted Dr. Freudstein in Lucio Fulci's notorious *The House by the Cemetery* (1981), is superbly macabre throughout, although, as we'll see, its hallway features one of the most sustained depictions of violence to ever appear on screen, and it stands out for that reason. In the same way, although the kitchen scene is significant in *Poltergeist* (1982), the Freelings' house is, as a whole, equally disturbing.

And what of houses to come? How might we see them depicted in horror movies 20 years from now? Analyzing more recent films, the eagle-eyed viewer could well deduce the way in which houses will appear in the horror genre in the future. The gruesome *Thir13en Ghosts* (2001)

Fireside stories: Philip Waverton (Raymond Massey), Sir William Porterhouse (Charles Laughton) and Philip's wife Margaret (Gloria Stuart) hang on every word of their host Horace Femm (Ernest Thesiger) in *The Old Dark House* (1932).

leaves little doubt that hi-tech homes such as the one created by the late eccentric Cyrus Kriticos will place an inventive array of home security options at every property owner's disposal. Although living on distant planets may remain the stuff of fantasy, longterm survival on ships in space, as in the case of the International Space Station, already happens. Intergalactic craft in which people are required to live for months, even years, at a time, are in fact little more than automated houses floating in space, complete with dining rooms, kitchens, laboratories and bedrooms, as imagined in Ridley Scott's nightmare space epic *Alien* (1979).

Some will disagree with the films I have chosen to represent each room. As far as possible, I avoided the obvious, deciding, for instance, against including the bathroom scene from *Psycho* (1960)—which, strictly speaking, takes place in one of the Bates Motel cabins, not the Bates house—and Regan's room in *The Exorcist* (1973) as an example of the bedroom. Both films appear elsewhere in the book. My criteria for selection were that the film featured the room in question, and secondly, that the

Introduction

Under the influence: George Lutz (James Brolin) and wife Kathy (Margot Kidder) regret their real estate purchase in *The Amityville Horror* (1979).

scenes should be memorable and, most importantly in my opinion, fun. I took particular delight in including films that I hope will surprise all but the most devoted horror fan. I am reasonably confident that the wonderfully atmospheric ghost story *The Uninvited* (1944) and the bizarre chiller *The Ballad of Tam Lin* (1970) will be new to many, but they warrant inclusion thanks to the incredibly ostentatious houses at their core. Films—like individual houses, unless you happen to live in them—will reveal previously unexplored corridors and hidden rooms with each successive visit, all of which is part of the allure of the medium itself.

Finally, if my selections in the book make you want to visit these houses, by watching the films (all of which are available on DVD, Blu-ray or via the Internet), or by taking a trip to the actual locations, so much the better. There are a few points to remember, however. Many of the buildings and their rooms were little more than movie sets and are long gone. Some, though, were the authentic thing, with the locations used being real homes or public buildings. Places like the ubiquitous Oakley Court (now a deluxe hotel) in Berkshire, England, and the Stanley Hotel in Colorado (inspiration for the Overlook Hotel in Stephen King's *The Shining*) are open to the public during normal hours. Others were, and

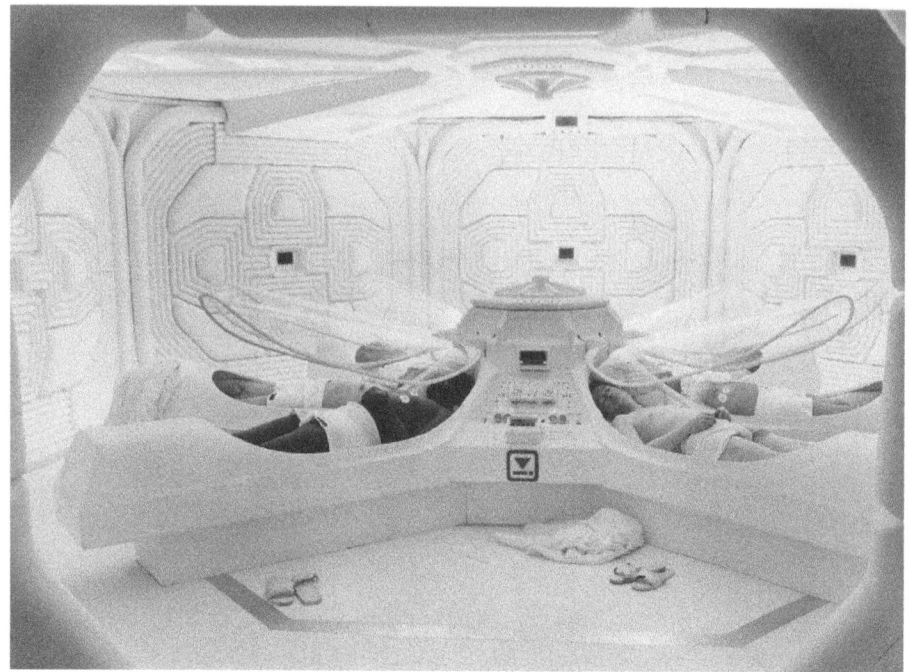

Up and at 'em: The crew of the *Nostromo* space tug are woken from hypersleep in *Alien* (1979).

still are, private property. You may, with a little research, be able to find these but please bear in mind that they are people's homes, and behave accordingly.

So now, turn the key, open the door and enter these houses of horror at your own risk.

1

The Hallway and Landing

When you create those characters that people love and care about and put them in a dark hallway, already the audience is on edge, and they feel empathy for that character. Then it's up to me to decide what jumps out in that hallway. So I think laying that foundation of strong characters and strong story is the most important thing in a horror film.

—James Wan, Director of *Saw* (2004)
and *The Conjuring* (2013)

The hallway is perhaps the most obscure room in any home though—if cult horror director James Wan is to be believed—it would appear as suitable as any other in the house for the setting of horrific manifestations. The black sheep of any dwelling, the hallway is neither one thing nor the other, without any distinct purpose beyond leading people to another place. A room which magnifies transience, from which people are either welcomed into the house or sent on their way, it is rarely a place where anyone lingers. In the same way, the landing, which can seem like a continuation of the hallway below, is often devoid of life, merely providing a connection between one room and the next, or from one staircase to another.

But hallways and landings feature marvelously in films of the macabre, frequently providing the ideal means with which to make a dramatic entrance—as in *The Exorcist* (1973)—or exit—*The Texas Chain Saw Massacre* (1974). The following motley collection from notorious houses of horror proves if nothing else that hallways are rooms you ignore at your peril.

The Exorcist (1973)

There are no experts. You probably know as much about possession than most priests. Look, your daughter doesn't say she's a demon. She says she's the devil himself. And if you've seen as many psychotics as I have, you'd know it's like saying you're Napoleon Bonaparte.

Stairway to Hell: Sharon (Kitty Winn), Willi (Gina Petrushka), Chris (Ellen Burstyn), Father Karras (Jason Miller) and Father Merrin (Max von Sydow) are stopped in their tracks in *The Exorcist* (1973).

Director: William Friedkin
Written by: William Peter Blatty (novel and screenplay)
Starring: Ellen Burstyn, Max von Sydow, Lee J. Cobb, Kitty Winn, Jack MacGowran, Jason Miller, Linda Blair, William O'Malley, Barton Heyman, Peter Masterson, Rudolf Schündler, Gina Petrushka, Robert Symonds, Arthur Storch, Thomas Birmingham, Vasiliki Maliaros, Titos Vandis, John Mahon, Wallace Rooney, Ron Faber, Donna Mitchell, Roy Cooper, Robert Gerringer, Mercedes McCambridge (Demon voice)

Chris MacNeil (Ellen Burstyn) is an actress living in Georgetown, Washington, D.C., while working on her latest film. Renting a beautiful period property in the city, she lives there with her young daughter Regan (Linda Blair), a seemingly content and happy 12-year-old. Regan finds an old Ouija board in the basement of the house and plays with it—then starts to act oddly. As her daughter's behavior becomes increasingly bizarre, Chris is forced to face the disturbing reality that Regan has summoned an ancient evil of Biblical proportions, intent on destroying the child and anyone who tries to help her.

William Friedkin's *The Exorcist* raises several unanswered questions, which make for an ultimately puzzling viewing experience. Take the undeveloped connection between the archaeological work in the Middle East carried out by the priest Father Lankester Merrin (Max von Sydow), and the eventual exorcism he is asked to perform on Regan during the film's hell-and-brimstone climax. Or the underdeveloped character of Regan's absent father, clearly estranged in some way from her mother, Chris. Such perplexities aside, there is no denying the shock value of one of cinema's most notorious films, even though now, over 40 years since its first release, it is difficult to decide whether it really deserves its reputation as one of the most terrifying films ever made. In an age of technological wizardry, when we can see people sliced apart in full anatomical detail, does Regan's 360° head-spin, or spouting of pea green soup over the unfortunate Father Karras (Jason Miller), still have the ability to frighten any but the most susceptible viewer? In fact, when looked at closely, the film's blasphemous and anti-religious undercurrents are, in truth, more shocking than the special effects, no matter what era they're being watched in.

That's not to say the film doesn't contain disturbing scenes, with one in particular standing out. It prominently features the staircase of the mansion where Regan and Chris live. There was every chance this segment, fondly referred to as the "spider" scene, would remain unseen by the general public. Involving, as it did, cables to support stuntwoman Ann Miles (standing in for Blair) as she walked, bent over backwards, down the stairs, there was no way to remove these supports from the finished print, until they were digitally erased for the film's 2000 re-release. The result is a scene not only frightful in its unexpectedness but one that also highlights the tranquility and beauty of the house, especially the staircase against which the possessed Regan is juxtaposed.

Despite further questions which arise concerning the things found in the house—for example, Chris' seemingly laid-back attitude to Regan's discovery and use of the Ouija board, and the obvious connection between this and her future possession—there is no denying that the building itself is gorgeous. The sense of decadence and good taste which it emanates, is a clear reflection of Chris who, like many pampered film stars, wants for very little materially. From the outside, the house looks like many others in the well-heeled Washington, D.C., suburb of Georgetown: black, wrought-iron gates guard the entrance to a red brick, Old World mansion whose sedate and reserved outer appearance hides a comfortable and luxurious retreat where Chris can escape the tensions of life on a film set.

As in many houses, the staircase forms the focal point of the house: it's the first thing viewers see when characters enter the house, or move from room to room. Dominating the left-hand side of the entrance hall, its white wooden balustrades frame a flight of stairs covered in thick-pile, biscuit-colored carpet, backed by a wall artistically scattered with choice pictures. At the top of its majestic sweep is the first floor landing, from which the bedrooms lead off. It is on these stairs that Chris and others on several occasions hear noises and disturbances from Regan's bedroom, leading them to race to the girl's assistance, only to discover scenes of increasing horror. From the hall below and the galleried landing above, everyone in the house is afforded an unobstructed view of the stairs and anything that happens there, including the incident now infamous in the annals of horror cinema.

In the "spider" scene, the possessed Regan comes down the staircase in a fashion both startling and nauseating in its originality and shock value. It's not only Chris—just come through the front door—who stares in open-mouthed horror as her daughter descends, bent backward like a crab, only to spout a torrent of blood from her mouth when she reaches the bottom. Shot from the side and then from the bottom of the staircase, the full length of Regan's descent is captured in startling detail; its culmination is simply the bloody icing on the cake.

An early appearance of Chris has her filming a scene—in the film within the film—as a protestor on the entrance steps of a university, while two characters in the main story meet their ends at the bottom of a flight of steps outside Chris and Regan's home. Inside, stairs top and tail the house itself, leading both to the attic and the cellar where a number of old-fashioned yet effective shock sequences play out. It is nonetheless the main staircase, and Regan's remarkable descent, that remains one of the most disturbing and arresting images not just in the film but in cinema as a whole.

The Texas Chain Saw Massacre (1974)

> *The film which you are about to see is an account of the tragedy which befell a group of five youths, in particular Sally Hardesty and her invalid brother Franklin. It is all the more tragic in that they were young. But, had they lived very, very long lives, they could not have expected nor would they have wished to see as much of the mad and macabre as they were to see that day. For them an idyllic summer afternoon drive became a nightmare. The events of that day were to lead to the discovery of one of the most bizarre crimes in the annals of American history, The Texas Chain Saw Massacre.*

Director: Tobe Hooper
Written by: Kim Henkel (story), Kim Henkel and Tobe Hooper (screenplay)
Starring: Marilyn Burns, Allen Danziger, Paul A. Partain, William Vail, Teri McMinn,

1. The Hallway and Landing

Edwin Neal, Jim Siedow, Gunnar Hansen, John Dugan, Robert Courtin, William Creamer, John Henry Faulk, Jerry Green, Ed Guinn, Joe Bill Hogan, Perry Lorenz, John Larroquette, Levie Isaacks

From its opening titles until the final credits, *The Texas Chain Saw Massacre*, one of the most infamous films in the history of the medium, has a surreal, frequently heavy atmosphere about it. Which, when you think about it, is hardly surprising considering its subject matter.

Sally Hardesty (Marilyn Burns) and her disabled brother Franklin (Paul A. Partain) are traveling through Texas—along with their friends Jerry (Allen Danziger), Kirk (William Vail) and his girlfriend Pam (Teri McMinn)—to visit the grave of their grandfather, amid reports of vandalism and grave robbing in the area. After visiting the grave, they decide to stop by the old Hardesty family home nearby, where they become stranded after running out of gas. Leaving Sally, Franklin and Jerry at the house, Kirk and Pam head off to a local farm to borrow some fuel. There they meet the owners of the farm, resulting in a nightmare in which only the unlucky ones are left alive.

He's coming to get you: Leatherface (Gunnar Hansen) makes his entrance in *The Texas Chain Saw Massacre* **(1974).**

If the final 20 minutes of this film amount to a protracted chase sequence as Sally, the sole survivor among the five friends, attempts to escape from the murderous character Leatherface (Gunnar Hansen) and his family, then the first half-hour is the polar opposite. An opening sequence, concerning the crimes of real-life murderer Ed Gein, is followed by a brief spell when Sally & co. pick up a shifty-looking hitchhiker who attacks them in their camper van. The same man is revealed to be part of Leatherface's extended family when he makes a later reappearance. These scenes aside, however, the film's otherwise uneventful introduction, following the young people on their camper trip through rural Texas in search of Sally and Franklin's old family homestead, lulls the viewer into a false sense of security. So deceptive is this part of the film, that when Kirk and Pam meet their end as Leatherface's first victims, we are taken aback by the sudden and unexpected brutality of the attack, to the extent that it takes some moments for what we've just witnessed to sink in.

From outside, the house looks like any other Texan farmhouse—white clapperboard with a two-seat swing in the garden, where Pam waits when Kirk goes to look for the owners. His initial meeting with the masked Leatherface, at the far end of the house's hallway, remains one of horror cinema's most effective shock moments, no matter how often you see it. It is outside again, when Pam gets up from the swing to search for her boyfriend, that the viewer is confronted with an unexpectedly beautiful yet discomfiting image. Despite its initial apparently welcoming appearance, the house, shot from behind Pam, and at a low angle, against a piercing blue sky, looms over her with a sinister air. Her halter-neck top and red cut-off jeans draw attention to Pam's flawless skin, which will later be seen in a whole new light, once the viewer discovers the horrors to come. The fact we already know what has happened to Kirk—now a convulsing wreck thanks to a hammer blow to the head, courtesy of Leatherface—adds to the palpable terror which will soon set in, and then not stop until the film ends.

The hallway of Leatherface's family home is the perfect setting for the chase and capture of Pam by this butcher with a taste for human flesh. This corridor, by comparison to the rooms of the farmhouse, looks relatively normal. It may be dark, with what appears to be paper hanging from the walls and ceiling giving it an odd, unsettling appearance, but its comparative ordinariness simply highlights the macabre sitting room, complete with caged chickens, human bone furniture and a knee-deep carpet of bird feathers and excrement. What could be worse, save the makeshift abattoir where, once captured in the hallway by Leatherface, Pam is dragged to meet her end alongside the now lifeless Kirk. Bookended by two doors, one that leads to the bright safety of outdoors, and the other leading to

Leatherface's slaughterhouse, the hallway between them could be seen as a way of concealing the horrors which lie throughout the remainder of the house.

The hallway may, in reality, be small—the house itself is not big—but when Pam is pursued by the monstrosity that is Leatherface, the passage extends to nightmare proportions. The safety and freedom of the bright day beyond the front screen door juxtapose harshly with the nightmare world behind the sliding steel doors separating Leatherface's domain from the hallway and the world outside, and which clang shut with resounding finality once he pulls Pam inside.

The Texas Chain Saw Massacre, in its original form, is one of the best examples of inference in horror cinema. When the unfortunate Pam is eventually trussed up by Leatherface, an ugly, razor-sharp meat hook rupturing her flawless back, and forced to endure the spectacle of the unconscious Kirk being sawn up by a chainsaw, the viewer will likely swear blind that they have, just like Pam, seen every gruesome moment. Fortunately—unlike in the film's inferior 2003 reimagining, where every gory detail was lovingly drawn out—the camera cuts away before the saw does, allowing the imagination to take over. As the best filmmakers know, this always gets better results.

The Omen (1976)

"Have no fear, little one.... I am here to protect thee."

Director: Richard Donner
Written by: David Seltzer
Starring: Gregory Peck, Lee Remick, David Warner, Billie Whitelaw, Harvey Stephens, Patrick Troughton, Martin Benson, Robert Rietty, Tommy Duggan, John Stride, Anthony Nicholls, Holly Palance, Roy Boyd, Freda Dowie, Sheila Raynor, Robert MacLeod, Bruce Boa, Don Fellows, Patrick McAlinney, Dawn Perllman, Nancy Manigham, Miki Iveria, Betty McDowall, Nicholas Campbell, Burnell Tucker, Ronald Leigh-Hunt, Guglielmo Spoletini, Ya'ackov Banai, Leo McKern

The Omen is a stylish yet very disturbing exercise in filmmaking. Not that the thriller, which launched the trend for the high-octane, glossy horror that has saturated the market since its release in the mid–1970s, is overtly frightening. Its storyline seems to exist simply to link one set-piece death with the next. Even the film's most spectacular deaths (of which there are several) are carried out in such a sanitized manner, that only the hyper-squeamish could possibly be offended. No, what is really sinister about the film when it is looked at more closely is its passing off of the story's basis (if you believe in such things) as a contemporary fable,

Hang in there: Kathy Thorn (Lee Remick) holds on for dear life, while her son Damien (Harvey Stephens) watches in *The Omen* (1976).

and certainly not as something that modern people should be overly concerned about.

It is the film's glossy "Hollywood" approach to its more horrific elements that is its most disturbing as well as most intriguing aspect. Never has a film looked more slick, almost dreamlike in parts, making its viewing, if not pleasant, then at least a more engaging experience than that created by many similar genre entries. Central London—where the main action unfolds—and its surrounding environs, as far out as Putney and Windsor, look beautiful in a glamorized, picture postcard fashion, while the house in which Robert and Kathy set up home is the kind the outside world appears to believe most British people live in, but which in reality exists only in a few well-heeled pockets on the outskirts of the metropolis. Befitting the

1. The Hallway and Landing

status of the American ambassador to Great Britain—or 'The Court of St. James,' as Robert pompously calls it—the period home they rent makes Buckingham Palace look like a suburban semi. It comes complete with paneled library, nursery wing and mile-long staircase and landing.

Though several rooms are seen periodically throughout the action, it is the building's stairs and the galleried landing wrapping around them, that are the setting for several of the pivotal scenes including, perhaps, its most shocking. Initially, the staircase forms the dramatic backdrop for a stand-off between Kathy and Mrs. Baylock (Billie Whitelaw), Damien's new nanny, when her attempt to dissuade the boy's parents from taking him to a church wedding falls on deaf ears. "Excuse me for speaking my mind, ma'am, but do you really think that a five-year-old will understand the goings-on at an Episcopal wedding?" Aside from this dramatic showdown between the film's two principal female characters, the accident which later befalls Kathy at the top of the same stairs, at the hands—or rather the wheels—of her energetic offspring, may not be the film's worst, but it is certainly shocking, and amongst the most likely to leave a lasting impression on the viewer.

Like many of horror's best moments, *The Omen*'s most memorable scenes—including Kathy's fall from the landing—come upon the viewer unexpectedly, with little or no fanfare and a subdued, almost laid-back build-up. Here, stuck in the house because of bad weather, the bored Damien has been getting on his mother's nerves. He is banished from her presence in an almost Victorian fashion; the demonic glare the little boy gives her as he is being escorted from the room, though wholly understandable, leaves the viewer to ponder whether the curly-haired poppet is as innocent as he looks. Later, as he rides his tricycle around the nursery, his ever-watchful nanny from Hell opens the door, allowing her devilish charge to trundle off and wreak revenge upon the unsuspecting Kathy, now fixing a hanging plant on the landing outside. The sparseness of the landing's decor, save for a couple of potted ferns and a fishbowl—the breaking of which, after it's knocked into the hallway below, adds more drama to Kathy's fall—and the grandeur of the ornate white staircase which leads to the hall simply emphasize the horror to come. The wisdom of Kathy's use of a side table to reach the plant above may seem, in retrospect, questionable. However, who in the same situation would imagine any inherent danger? As Damien makes his way towards Kathy, the significance of the landing takes on Biblical proportions, intensifying Damien's squeaky advance and the sudden horror of the inevitable collision. The importance of the bannister and the staircase's long and dominating run only now becomes clear. A small or enclosed flight of stairs would never have worked—this is an accident which needs an expanse in which to create an impact, which it certainly does when Kathy hits the parquet flooring with a sudden and resounding finality. The use of dolly carts, false walls and slow motion photography to achieve the shot is well documented, and the resultant sight of an unconscious Kathy lying on the floor, blood seeping from her mouth, while a startled Damien watches through the bannisters above, makes for a truly arresting image. Though Kathy survives the accident, she eventually goes on to meet an even more spectacular death at the hands of her child care nemesis, Mrs. Baylock. However, not even this has the impact of her descent from the landing.

The Biblical authenticity of the film's storyline may be open to debate, depending on your point of view. Its entry in the 1996 edition of the *Variety Movie Guide* highlighted the fact that the requirement on the viewer's part of any "religious commitment … is minimal; the only premise one must accept is that the fallen Lucifer remains a very strong supernatural being."[1] This aside, there is no denying that it forms the basis for a marvelously lush and atmospheric viewing experience, giving cinema one of the most stunning housebound "accidents" ever committed to celluloid.

The House by the Cemetery (1981)

> *In this house what you don't know will hurt you. It was to be a getaway dream. It's become a runaway nightmare. He's been awaiting the arrival of his new guests. One by one they are disappearing. One by bloody one. When you move to this house, before you get locked in, read the fine print. You may have just mortgaged your life.*

Director: Lucio Fulci
Written by: Lucio Fulci, Giorgio Mariuzzo, Dardano Sacchetti (screenplay), Elisa Livia Briganti (story), H.P. Lovecraft (inspiration [uncredited])
Starring: Catriona MacColl (as Katherine MacColl), Paolo Malco, Ania Pieroni, Giovanni Frezza, Silvia Collatina, Dagmar Lassander

Houses feature in many horror films, but seldom are they honored with top billing in the title. When they are, as with the house at the center of the schlock masterpiece *The House by the Cemetery*, it often feels like they have become characters in their own right.

The House by the Cemetery contains some of the most haunting and surreal imagery ever created by director-writer Lucio Fulci, the Italian filmmaker responsible for many of horror cinema's most disturbing entries including the notorious *Zombie* (1979) and *The New York Ripper* (1982). Its plot revolves around stories of a mysterious Dr. Freudstein (read into that name what you will) who carried out sinister experiments in a deserted mansion outside Boston. It's pure, hardcore Fulci, with enough gore

1. The Hallway and Landing

Putting her foot in it: Real estate agent Laura Gittleson (Dagmar Lassander) gets the point in *The House by the Cemetery* (1981).

and mutilation to warrant the film's inclusion on the infamous Video Nasties list of the 1980s.

Dr. Freudstein's makeshift abattoir lies in the basement of the neglected house, and other rooms in the mansion also feature occasional bloody manifestations of evil. But what the characters refer to as the hallway features in one of the film's most graphic and disturbing murders. Here is a room which—like the house generally—has an air of abandonment, with faded wood paneling, decaying furniture and dust-covered floors. It also features a tombstone—one of the film's weirdest elements, which is saying something when you consider the house as a whole. Fulci thrived on the ambiguous and unexplained, which adds to his films' otherworldliness, though not necessarily their coherence, as highlighted in *The House by the Cemetery* entry in *The Overlook Film Encyclopaedia / Horror*:

> Fulci has acquired something of a cult following, but narrative cohesion is certainly not his strong point, and the fact that this film, like ... *E Tu Vivrai new Torrore! L'Aldil*a [*And You'll Live in Terror! The Beyond*] (1981), is nominally set in America tends to underline this shortcoming.[2]

Fulci was renowned for the unhurried set-piece deaths which littered his films: with everything from electric drill lobotomies in *City of the Living Dead* (1980) to acid face-melts in *The Beyond* (1981), nothing was off-limits for the man who took hardcore gore to unprecedented levels during the early 1980s. Where American, British and even some European directors knew that cutting away just when things get nasty is frequently more disturbing than showing everything full-on, Fulci was clearly not a fan of "less is more." In *The House by the Cemetery*, the death of the unfortunate Mrs. Gittleson (Dagmar Lassander), the estate agent who lets Freudstein's house to a young academic and his family, must rate as one of the most unpleasant in cinema. It's not that the means of murder—stabbing with a poker—is particularly bad, but the fact that it is shown in slow, loving detail, played out for twice as long as is necessary. Arriving at the seemingly empty house, she is startled by an unseen adversary. As she tries to make her escape, the tombstone in the hallway inexplicably cracks open, trapping her foot as her would-be killer bears down on her, poker in hand. Nothing is left to the imagination, as Fulci closes in on the poker's first thrust into Gittleson's ribcage, then into her breast and heart, before it is finally forced into her neck, from which blood erupts in a sticky crimson fountain. Fortunately, viewers aren't made to endure what is done to Gittleson's face, though they do have to watch as her body with its eyeless head is dragged toward the kitchen and into the basement, leaving a bloody trail along the hallway floor.

Look, if you can, however, beyond Fulci's trademark splatter and you will find—particularly in the mansion where the action plays out—a masterpiece of otherworldly beauty and disarming tranquility. Everything, from the exterior of the remote house—a perfect example of American Victorian gothic set amidst a forest of lifeless vegetation and crumbling tombstones—to the dusty grandeur of its down-at-heel interiors, is captured in a palette of faded grays and autumnal hues. These muted tones serve to heighten the viciousness of the graphic horrors which color the screen when you least expect it.

Like the authenticity of the occurrences at the heart of the story—its air of ambiguity emphasized by the blurring of the lines between this world and the next during the enigmatic ending—Freudstein's home is open to interpretation by the viewer: Beautiful? Forlorn? Menacing? Whatever your conclusion, there is no denying that the house by the cemetery is one of horror cinema's most atmospheric and beguiling abodes.

Opera (1987)

> *Why should I trust you? You could be the maniac.... No, you're fooling me. Go away. Go away. Hey, I've seen you before. I know you. No, not the gun, I want to see your face again.*

1. The Hallway and Landing

All cut up: Cristina Marsillach's distorted image stares from a trade magazine ad, promoting writer-director Dario Argento's disturbing masterpiece *Opera* (1987).

Don't Go Upstairs!

Director: Dario Argento
Written by: Dario Argento (screenplay and story)
Starring: Cristina Marsillach, Ian Charleson, Urbano Barberini, Daria Nicolodi, Carolina Cataldi-Tassoni, Antonella Vitale, William McNamara, Barbara Cupisti, Antonio Iuorio, Carola Stagnaro, Francesca Cassola, Maurizio Garrone, Cristina Giachino, György Győriványi, Bjorn Hammer, Peter Pitsch, Sebastiano Somma, Elizabeth Norberg-Schulz (Lady Macbeth, soprano singing voice), Michele Pertusi (Macbeth, bass singing voice)

Dario Argento's *Opera* (aka *Terror at the Opera*) is widely considered to be the last of his great "masterpieces," and watching it you can understand why. The plot is typically weak—storytelling was never Argento's strong point—and the characters largely two-dimensional, including the obligatory addition of a "big name" star, in this case Scottish actor Ian Charleson). But visually the film contains all the hallmarks for which this master of the giallo genre is best known: sumptuous photography, the use of primary block colors to emphasize shock, bizarrely striking settings and, of course, gore. As critic Head Cheeze says in their summation of the film on the website *horrorview*:

> [T]he story once again takes a backseat to Argento's beautiful camerawork, bloody violence, and lush lighting and visuals, and for me, that's fine. I don't pop in an Argento film expecting *Schindler's List*, I pop into an Argento film and expect Hitchcock as channeled through a music video director with a large portion of his budget allotted to blood, gloves and retractable knives.[3]

The various murders within the film are, even by Argento's standards, pretty gruesome stuff. The killing which stands out, however, does so more for its originality, that it happens so quickly, and for the fact that it's more than a little unexpected. It's a real blink-and-you'll-miss-it showstopper.

Much of the action plays out within the main auditorium and backstage rooms of an undisclosed opera house, where Betty (Cristina Marsillach), a young operatic understudy, is performing in her first lead role. As with the legendary tale "The Phantom of the Opera," fate plays a hand in Betty landing the role of a lifetime as Lady Macbeth in a production of Verdi's *Macbeth*. However, someone hovering in the wings has other plans for Betty's blossoming career. Though the opera house provides ample gloomy corners for some typically over-the-top Argento moments, it is the hallway of the young Betty's bohemian flat that provides the setting for the film's most memorable death scene. Here we find the perfect backdrop to highlight two of Argento's most frequently repeated characteristics, his use of color blocking to emphasize stark horror, and an unexpected killing. The victim in this case is Betty's friend and agent Mira (Daria Nicolodi).

This scene involves just three people (we see only the chest and hand of one of them) and it's set within the confines of a narrow room. But it is

1. The Hallway and Landing

one of the film's most arresting and expansive scenes. When Mira quarrels with the person on the other side of the front door—whom she and Betty believe to be the murderer—and puts her eye to the peep-hole, demanding to see the face, the viewer is aware that something shocking is about to happen.

However, the way in which Mira's death unfolds is both unexpected and disturbing in its brevity and (quite literal) impact. Claiming to be a policeman, the person on the other side of the door brandishes a pistol at the peephole as Mira puts her eye to it for a better view. The image of the gun, and the journey of the bullet in slow motion down the apparent endless passage of what is in fact mere millimeters of peephole, before it passes through the eye and head of the unfortunate Mira, makes for a shot which, once seen, will sear itself forever on the viewer's memory.

Seldom has the hallway of a home looked as beautiful as that in Betty's flat, yet been so deadly. Lit by a Japanese-style, circular window by the front door, the bohemian art deco vibes which suffuse the rest of the apartment are carried through to this connecting corridor from which all the rooms lead off. Furnished with wooden, feature-piece furniture (straight-backed, formal chairs, a standard lamp, ornate desk and solid parquet floor), much of this long room is cast in shadow. All the better to emphasize the double entrance door at the far end—bathed in shades of green, red and yellow light reflected from the aforementioned window—through which Mira meets her end. The hallway's floor across which the distraught Betty, cowering by a wall, has tried to drag a telephone to call for help, becomes seemingly elongated as she then escapes along it to the sound of death threats from the murderer. Her ensuing flight from the killer through the darkened apartment, to the strains of Maria Callas singing "Casta Diva" from Bellini's *Norma*, is a truly mesmerizing piece of cinema, beautiful yet chilling in equal measure.

Argento went on to make his own typically grisly vision of *Phantom of the Opera* in 1998, a version more faithful to the original Gaston Leroux tale. However, *Opera* remains a rare feat within the world of horror cinema: a contemporary chiller which used the essence of a well-known story to create a fresh and altogether original modern classic.

2

The Living Room

Then, on entering the drawing-room again, I began to feel somewhat uneasy, the long curtains were gently rustling in the evening breeze and sombre shadows were slowly creeping across the walls and floor. It was as if the tenuous veil of everyday reality was gradually being withdrawn from the darkening room, and that its ghostly inhabitants were about to reveal themselves to me.
—*Phantoms of the Isles*, Simon Marsden (1990)

Living room, drawing room, sitting room, lounge. Call it what you will, this room comes in all shapes and sizes, though probably few are as grand as the drawing room of Skyrne Castle, in Ireland's County Meath, as described by photographer and ghost-hunter Simon Marsden.

There is no denying that this room is the hardest to define, as what you call it often speaks volumes about your social aspirations. It is also a room required to straddle both the formal and informal, used not only to entertain visitors but also as a place where the family can relax and unwind. Like the human characters in horror films, the depiction of this room runs the gamut from posh, as in the segment "The Elemental" from Amicus' terror compendium *From Beyond the Grave* (1974), to the run-down living-cum-dining room seen in *The Evil Dead* (1981). However you look at it, the room and the activities which unfold there are guaranteed to be the focal point of any social gathering.

The Invisible Man (1933)

Are you satisfied now, you fools! It's easy, really, if you're clever! A few chemicals mixed together. That's all. And flesh and blood and bones just ... fade away.

Director: James Whale
Written by: R.C. Sherriff (screenplay), H.G. Wells (novel)
Starring: Claude Rains, Gloria Stuart, William Harrigan, Henry Travers, Una O'Con-

2. The Living Room

nor, Forrester Harvey, Dudley Digges, E.E. Clive, Dwight Frye, Walter Brennan, John Carradine

James Whale's big-screen visualization of H.G. Wells' sci-fi–horror novella *The Invisible Man* remains a novelty in the world of classic Hollywood horror.

Wells' story was first published in 1897 in installments by *Pearson's Weekly* magazine, and collected in novel form later the same year. The movie version was a surprising hit in a genre where everything depended on what was seen on the screen: Here instead was a film where the central character—a true "anti-hero"—remained unseen, except during the film's closing frames. Even in the early 1930s, cinema—though it had been established for some 30 years—was still considered relatively new. As a result, the medium relied strongly on the image seen on the screen, especially where the subject of horror was concerned: Boris Karloff's Monster and Bela Lugosi's nocturnal nobleman Dracula depended heavily on visual impact for their chilling effect.

Parlor games: Dr. Jack Griffin (Claude Rains) concocts a potion in *The Invisible Man* (1933).

But here in *The Invisible Man* was a character who derived terror from the fact that he couldn't be seen, an aspect which *New York Times* critic Mordaunt Hall highlighted in his November 18, 1933, review:

> No actor has ever made his first appearance on the screen under quite as peculiar circumstance as Claude Rains does in [*The Invisible Man*].... Other players have, it is true, been thoroughly disguised by weird makeup, but in this current offering Mr. Rains' countenance is beheld for a mere half minute at the close of the proceedings. The rest of the time his head is either completely covered with bandages or he is invisible, but his voice is heard.[1]

The Invisible Man was Rains' American screen debut. Like many of the genre greats, including Karloff and Christopher Lee, Rains created impact by his mere presence. Although, as noted, you barely see the actor "in the flesh," given he spends most of his time swathed in bandages or prancing around in a literal state of nothingness, his character is everpresent, lurking somewhere in the background.

Rains' character, Jack Griffin, may journey far afield from the safety of the remote village and the public house where he initially takes refuge, and to which he returns periodically, but the living room of this establishment—or sitting room, as its landlady Mrs. Hall (Una O'Connor) calls it—is the perfect foil to his transparency and the mayhem which follows him. Here is a room high up in the eaves, far removed from the establishment's public bar, approached by a long flight of stairs, all of which adds to the apprehension felt by any character visiting Griffin in his makeshift lair. Seemingly as big as the bar downstairs, the living room—decked out in typically cluttered, Old World style, complete with bookcases, open fire and a table big enough to seat half the village—is where viewers and many of the film's extended cast first properly encounter the half-crazed Griffin. It is also from here—once the invisibility potion begins to affect his mind as well as his physical make-up—that Griffin sets out on the murderous escapades that build to the film's climax.

He is on the run, initially from his scientific colleagues, and then the police, after he creates his fantastical invisibility potion. It is not long before Griffin's nefarious activities and increasingly moody demeanor arouse suspicion amongst the villagers and especially the curious Mrs. Hall. After her inquisitiveness gets the better of her—does he really require the mustard she forgot to put on his dinner tray?—she catches Griffin with his guard (and bandages) down, resulting in a particularly memorable encounter which sees the poor woman leaving the room in the most spectacular style. Later, once Griffin has been hidden away for some weeks, the villagers, police and viewer enter the living room to discover a homemade laboratory he's created to aid his research into an antidote to the invisibility process. Here, flasks, tubes and burners have encroached on every spare surface, making Mrs. Hall's once homely parlor into a madman's retreat rivaling that of Baron Frankenstein.

In fact, watching the film, the ambience which unfolds on screen has a gothic air to rival that of the area in which the baron lived: from the lonely lane down which you see Griffin approach the village in the opening scenes, to the village itself which looks more like Central Europe than middle England, and the public house with its welcoming living room, the film has the unmistakable feel of pure Hollywood horror. This is not so surprising once you realize that the film's appearance was the responsibility of Oscar-nominated art director Charles D. Hall and cinematographer Arthur Edeson, both of whom had worked with Whale on *Frankenstein* two years previously.

The film is now remembered as much for its secondary features—its humor and groundbreaking special effects—as for its horror, as pointed out in *The Oxford Companion to Film*: "The magical ending has the Invisible Man's body gradually reappearing as life is leaving it. James Whale's film is notable for its superb trick effects and its humor bordering on the slapstick."[2] Which is perhaps a shame as, beneath its surface of atmospheric whimsy, is a classic from Hollywood's Golden Age which retains an ability to chill as much for what wasn't seen as for what was.

Tales from the Crypt (1972)

> We interrupt this programme for a special announcement. A man described as a homicidal maniac has escaped from the hospital for the criminally insane. He is six foot, three inches tall, two hundred and ten pounds, dark eyes, bald and may be wearing a Santa Claus costume taken from a shop in Burley. All residents of the county are warned to be on the lookout for this man, and to phone the police if they see him. We now continue our programme of carols for Christmas Eve.

Director: Freddie Francis
Written by: Milton Subotsky (screenplay), Al Feldstein, Johnny Craig and based on stories by William M. Gaines.
Starring: Joan Collins, Oliver MacGreevy, Chloe Franks, Martin Boddey, Robert Rietty, Peter Cushing, Roy Dotrice, Richard Greene, Ian Hendry, Patrick Magee, Barbara Murray, Nigel Patrick, Robin Phillips, Ralph Richardson, Geoffrey Bayldon

"This initial episode sets the tone and flair of the whole film which combines the inextricable humor and violence, clear outlines and bold colours, of the comic strip style, with overtones of Nineteenth Century Christmas 'chain' stories and popular literary allusions."[3]

In her review of Amicus' classic portmanteau horror *Tales from the*

Cry for help: Joanne Clayton (Joan Collins) realizes her number's up in *Tales from the Crypt* (1972).

Crypt, Margaret Tarratt identified what made the film's first story "And All Through the House" not just the highlight of the film, but also one of the best examples of a style the company had indisputably made their own.

Amicus started making these horror anthologies the previous decade with *Dr. Terror's House of Horrors* (1965) and *Torture Garden* (1967); by the early 1970s they were producing one such film a year, with the lurid titles *Asylum* (1972), *The Vault of Horror* (1973) and *From Beyond the Grave* (1974). Like the popular American pulp horror comics, Amicus' hit series connected several stories with one over-arching tale, in films which sanitized their heavily stylized gore and shocks with a darkly comic edge, allowing some genuinely nasty content to get past the stringent censorship of the day.

Amicus' terror anthologies regularly featured such stalwarts of 1960s and 1970s British horror as Geoffrey Bayldon and Peter Cushing, but it was frequently the other stars, and the stories in which they appeared, that stood out. Donald Sutherland in "Vampire," from *Dr. Terror's House of Horrors* (1965), and Barbara Parkins in "Frozen Fear," from *Asylum* (1972), are two examples of the "A" list names the studio attracted in order to spice up the public appeal of what were, if we are honest, rarely little more than second features. The fourth in the series, *Tales from the Crypt*, is widely considered the best of the studio's portmanteau shockers, and it's not hard to understand why. From the opening sequence, where viewers are led through the overgrown grounds of North London's Highgate Cemetery to the eerie strains of Bach's Toccata and Fugue, we know we are in for some deliriously macabre entertainment. This is the film in which all the elements of Amicus' previous compilation outings gelled, from the setting of the connecting story (a group of visitors, lost during a tour of the catacombs deep beneath the ancient cemetery, are told their futures by a mysterious monk [Ralph Richardson]), to the tales themselves, derived from strip features which had appeared during the 1950s in the controversial EC horror comics. Though the cast as a whole, including well-known names Ian Hendry, Patrick Magee and Barbara Murray, was above par, it was without doubt Joan Collins who made the biggest impression, as Joanne Clayton, a murderous suburban housewife who gets her just deserts in the festive offering, "And All Through the House."

Collins was destined to play scheming, vindictive women who met their comeuppance in a variety of nasty ways. She is best known now as Alexis, the archetypal corporate bitch from the 1980s soap opera *Dynasty*. The career of the actress, regularly touted in the 1950s as Britain's most promising young starlet, was in the doldrums during the 1970s. Before American prime-time TV came calling, she appeared in a series of largely forgettable roles in such lurid titles as *I Don't Want to Be Born* (1975) and *The Bawdy Adventures of Tom Jones* (1976). She also appeared in "Neck" (1979), a wildly camp episode of the British cult TV series *Tales of the Unexpected*.

None of these roles came close to her stylish portrayal of the cold and sadistic Mrs. Clayton, who heartlessly dispatches her innocent husband, only to find herself in turn cornered by a vicious murderer, escaped from the local lunatic asylum, and dressed as a mad-eyed, salivating Father Christmas. Collins' masterful performance is a largely solo affair, showing her as an actress, if not of award-winning caliber, then at least a level above that of the average celluloid scream queen. Her portrayal of Joanne Clayton's disintegration from cool-headed killer—clearly having planned her husband's death to the last detail, in order to make it look like an accident—to becoming the victim of a serial killer herself is a master class in subtle hysteria. Her mounting frenzy as she runs from door to window, frantically checking that she and her daughter Carol (played by British child star Chloe Franks) are safe from the madman stalking the outside of her house, is a chillingly effective example of ratcheting up the tension before ramming home a shock finale by means of an unexpected twist. That Carol plays an unwitting role in her mother's demise lends the closing scenes an added sense of poetic justice.

In his bestselling novelization of *Tales from the Crypt* (published by Bantam Books in April 1972, to coincide with the film's American release), Jack Oleck made much of the reasoning behind Joanne's murder of her seemingly devoted, if insipid, husband Richard (Martin Boddey): Clearly nothing came between a doting older man and his spoiled, money-grabbing young wife, except perhaps his hefty life insurance policy. However, those behind the story's celluloid visualization had equal fun imagining the scene of the ensuing murder and mayhem: the Claytons' kitsch, state-of-the-art designer home. Being set at Christmas allowed Amicus' resident art director Tony Curtis to go to town on the living room where Joanne's life, and the story's main action, quickly and violently unravel. White carpets and cream sofas, gleaming brass and glass embellishments, and a towering tree standing amidst wrapped gifts, not only showed that this was the house of a family where money was no object, but also provided a wonderfully pristine backdrop against which the blood flows. The surprisingly clinical foundation of the set-piece room simply emphasizes the cartoonish gore which abounds when Richard's wife brings a showpiece poker crashing through his cranium. Though the majority of the story—including both murders—takes place within the living room, a surprising amount of the remaining house sneaks in an appearance: From kitchen to cellar, and Carol's bedroom to landing and hallway, the viewer is given the sense of an opulent, contemporary family home in which Joanne's night of Christmas carnage takes place.

In the *Fangoria* website's evaluation of the film's Scream Factory Blu-ray release, Chris Alexander could not have praised Amicus' stylishly disturbing offering any higher: "[F]rom its first frames to its invasive final shot, this classic British creeper offers an unrelenting study in the art of the macabre."[4] High praise indeed for a film which will surely go down in horror history as not just one of the high points of Ms. Collins' somewhat patchy acting career, but also one of the best examples of the pulp anthologies at which Amicus excelled.

The Beast Must Die (1974)

> *This is the werewolf break. Have you guessed who the werewolf is? Is it Paul Foote? Jan? Davina? Dr. Lundgren? Caroline? You have 30 seconds to give your answer.... Made up your mind? Let's see if you're right!*

2. The Living Room

Director: Paul Annett
Written by: Michael Winder (screenplay), Paul Annett, Scot Finch (uncredited), James Blish (story "There Shall Be No Darkness") (uncredited)
Starring: Calvin Lockhart, Peter Cushing, Marlene Clark, Charles Gray, Anton Diffring, Ciaran Madden, Tom Chadbon, Michael Gambon, Sam Mansary, Andrew Lodge, Carl Bohen, Eric Carte, Valentine Dyall, Annie Ross

Though dismissed by many genre experts as below par even by the standards of Amicus Productions, a company *not* renowned for intellectual horror fare, *The Beast Must Die* remains a surprisingly stylish and atmospheric viewing experience. Film historian Kim Newman describes it as "trashy fun of the first order,"⁵ an accurate summation of a film which never tries to be anything but an exercise in mad hokum, aimed at providing slick entertainment spliced with the occasional grisly shock.

Likened to a reimagining of Agatha Christie's classic *And Then There Were None*, with the addition of werewolves, the film's premise follows mil-

Are we sitting uncomfortably: Prof. Christopher Lundgren (Peter Cushing) is interrogated by Tom Newcliffe (Calvin Lockhart), observed by [in foreground from left] Tom's wife Caroline (Marlene Clark), and guests Davina Gilmore (Ciaran Madden), Paul Foote (Tom Chadbon) and Davina's husband Jan (Michael Gambon), in *The Beast Must Die* (1974).

lionaire megalomaniac and big-game hunter Tom Newcliffe (Calvin Lockhart), who invites guests to a house party on his island estate, in the hope of discovering which one of them is a werewolf. Unlike many films within the horror genre, *The Beast Must Die*, despite its sluggish spots, has stood the test of time by appealing as much to our intellect as to our somatic senses.

Most of the real action takes place outside Newcliffe's palatial home. An extended opening scene has the host tracked by some soldiers through the woods surrounding his home, which are rigged with cameras and microphones to detect any movement, human, wolf or hybrid of both, ending in a wonderful disruption to his houseguests' afternoon tea on the lawn. However, despite this incident and others like it—including a lengthy chase where the werewolf is pursued by Newcliffe through his estate's moonlit grounds—it is several scenes set within the house itself which provide the most thought-provoking moments, unexpectedly deep for this kind of film. The interiors, including a conservatory, dining room and the living room—which, considering the setting, might be more appropriately referred to as a drawing room, and is where one of the film's best shocks takes place—reveal a house decked out like a sumptuous Victorian hunting lodge, where guests want for nothing and their every whim is catered to, at the mere tinkle of a silver hand bell.

Throughout the film there are what appear to be several red herrings, simply adding to the overall feeling of a country house murder mystery, with a werewolf as the killer. The addition of a "Werewolf Break"—where the film freezes and a stopwatch is superimposed over the faces of Newcliffe's various guests, giving viewers time to decide who they think the beast is—is derided by many horror connoisseurs, though it is a feature which other fans describe as one of the film's highlights. This, however, along with a pass-the-parcel dinner game played with a silver candlestick, the touch of which Newcliffe hopes will accelerate the transformation of the wolf, are simply false starts before the real showdown takes place over coffee and brandy in the drawing room.

And what better place for the disclosure? The comfort of an open fire, deep leather armchairs and subdued lighting, add to the soporific atmosphere, lulling the characters (and viewers) into a false sense of security, from which they are soon rudely awakened. Here, after a member of the party—the mysterious Dr. Lundgren, an academic of undisclosed Eastern European origins (played with characteristic panache by Peter Cushing), whose hobby is the study of lycanthropy—reveals the essential elements required to trigger a man (or woman's) werewolf transformation, the scene is set for an original and unique method for revealing the beast within. It having been explained that the cursed person's skin could have been protected from contact with the silver candlestick by a synthetic coating such as nail varnish, each guest must place a silver bullet in his or her mouth, eventually revealing the identity of the wolf, to the horror of the remaining party. That this may—or may not—be the end of the story, allows for several more twists and murders before a poignant climax, which simply emphasizes the fact this is a film with more depth than the average prowl-and-ghoul horror show.

The location of this crucial scene within the intimate after-dinner setting of an elegant drawing room is another element which raises the production above the level of your average werewolf film. An outstanding cast (Cushing, Charles Gray, Anton Diffring and Michael Gambon, who clearly took the preposterous business seriously), and the wise use of a real dog as the werewolf instead of a man in a dodgy disguise (this was, remember, before the days of CGI and computer trickery), serve to make this a film which plays as much on the reasoning and suffering behind the curse of lycanthropy as it does on the havoc caused by the person inflicted.

In an interview, director Paul Annett discussed this rarity in the world of horror, a film that caters to the thinking person as much as to the gorehound: "Though the whole film was about werewolves, I concentrated on the actors as much as I possibly could, and I was very blessed by having such a good company. I think we got away with it."[6]

From Beyond the Grave (1974)

> *Dark foul thing from down below, get thee hence or I'll bestow a curse upon your hardened soul and turn your black heart into coal.*

Director: Kevin Connor
Written by: Raymond Christodoulou, Robin Clarke, R. Chetwynd-Hayes (stories)
Starring: Peter Cushing, Ian Carmichael, Margaret Leighton, Nyree Dawn Porter, David Warner, Donald Pleasence, Angela Pleasence, Ian Ogilvy, Lesley-Anne Down

The production of Amicus' compilation horror films lasted for almost a decade, starting in the mid–1960s. It was an extremely successful attempt by the company to beat Hammer at their own game. Where Hammer had cornered the market in gothic horror, Amicus caught the public's imagination with what were, for all intents and purposes, a series of short and punchy potboiler stories placed in modern settings.

One of the films' most striking aspects—apart from the genuine creepiness of their stories—was an intrinsic "Britishness" which colored everything on screen. This was even more surprising when you consider that many who worked behind the scenes at the company—from

We're not alone: Reginald (Ian Carmichael) and Susan (Nyree Dawn Porter) receive an unwelcome house guest, as seen in this Mexican lobby card for *From Beyond the Grave* (1974).

co-founders Max Rosenberg and Milton Subotsky to regular story contributor Robert Bloch—were American.

The stories in their other compilation films frequently exude funky contemporary vibes. The Joan Collins vehicle "And All Through the House" from *Tales from the Crypt* featured a house furnished in a modish style. *From Beyond the Grave* breaks with that tradition. Although set in the 1970s, the houses which form the backdrops for its various stories appear stuck firmly in the past, quite literally in one case. The film is composed of four stories by the popular British horror writer R. Chetwynd-Hayes, each featuring a living room in some form, connected by a tale where "The Proprietor" (Peter Cushing), a sinister antiques dealer, sets in motion the fates which befall various unscrupulous customers. However, although the rooms featured in the accompanying tales, for the most part, appear dark, drab and brooding, the one in the third installment, "The Elemental," is positively disconcerting in its gentrified English tweeness. It is the room in which the main action of the story plays out, embodying the secret of Amicus' strength: the simple ordinariness and everyday familiarity of their film's environments and characters. Okay, so Reginald (Ian Carmichael) and Susan (Nyree Dawn Porter) might be posh, Madame Orloff (Margaret Leighton), the medium who helps them in their hour of need, completely off the radar, and their house expensive, but everything is familiar to the audience watching, giving the ensuing horrors an added edge of reality.

Here is a typically detached house somewhere in London's commuter belt, with chintzy decor that wouldn't look out of place in *House & Garden*. Watch carefully, though, and the purpose of the room's over-the-top fussiness—decorative plates on the walls, fake brasses over the mantle and a profusion of lamps and knickknacks covering every available surface—soon becomes clear.

The story charts the terrifying experience which befalls the unfortunate Reginald and Susan, after he becomes the reluctant host to an Elemental (a particularly malevolent offspring of the poltergeist family) which latches onto his shoulder during his nightly journey home from town. Once wacky clairvoyant Madame Orloff makes her appearance, under the guise of helping the couple rid themselves of their unwanted guest, a scenario is established, the action of which patently requires a room to be destroyed with the utmost visual impact. So follows an exorcism the likes of which would shake the faith of even the most devout Vatican priest, let alone an unassuming English housewife and her stiff-necked, businessman husband. Curtains are rent, cushions burst, china and glassware explodes, and poor Reggie and Susan are, by the end, left as quivering—though Elemental-free—wrecks.

As with many of the stories from Amicus' anthologies, "The Elemental" appears to be largely set-bound. Apart from Reginald's antique shop visit and his initial meeting with Madame Orloff in a train carriage, the remainder of the action plays out in two rooms of the Warrens' house, the kitchen and the living room. Where this restriction in *mise en scène* may have appeared claustrophobic in any other production, here—where the story unfolds as a miniature one-act drama—such confinement plays in the film's favor, allowing the three cast members the space to come alive on screen. However, though Carmichael and Porter are authentically uptight and melodramatic respectively, Leighton as the eccentric spiritualist steals the show. The English actress had the kind of screen presence which demanded attention, even when she wasn't hamming it up as she does here: Leighton's glittering Tony- and Oscar-nominated career was cut tragically short when she died from multiple sclerosis in 1976, aged just 53. *New York Times* film critic Richard Eder observed, the third story, and Leighton's performance in it, stood out:

> By far the best is "The Elemental," and the reason is the late Margaret Leighton. In yellow wig and dark glasses, Miss Leighton has—and bestows—a hilarious time wrestling the spirit all over a prim and proper Surrey cottage, filling the air with feathers, smashed crockery and outraged exclamations.[7]

Having seen Leighton's embodiment of Madame Orloff, complete with floppy-brimmed hat, floating chiffons, beads and crucifixes, who could have blamed even the most vindictive of spirits for taking flight?

As is often the case with the stories featured in the Amicus anthologies, "The Elemental" does not end on a happy note when—as is frequent in real life—evil apparently conquers good. Here, a shock twist provides the story with one last moment of sustained and surprisingly brutal horror, sprung upon you when, just like Reginald and Susan, you think the worst is past. Then, as with all the best horror, everything returns to normal. All is silent tranquility, leaving viewers to question whether what they've just seen really happened at all.

The Evil Dead (1981)

> *I know now that my wife has become host to a Kandarian demon. I fear that the only way to stop those possessed by the spirits of the book is through the act of ... bodily dismemberment.*

Director: Sam Raimi
Written by: Sam Raimi
Starring: Bruce Campbell, Ellen Sandweiss, Richard DeManincor, Betsy Baker, Theresa Tilly

> [T]here was no electricity, no running water and no telephone service in the cabin. Cattle had had the run of the place and had managed to deposit nearly four inches of manure in every room. There were no doors, the rooms were very small and the ceilings were claustrophobically low. This sucker needed work—a lot of it. Art Director Dart reckoned it would take about a week of pretty hard work to get it in shape.[8]

If Bruce Campbell's memories of the cabin used during the filming of *The Evil Dead* are correct, then it wasn't hard for him and the other cast members to get into character. Still considered amongst the most influential horror films of modern times, *The Evil Dead* may seem tame in the light of the torture porn and graphic mutilation found in much contemporary genre fare. Even so, it still proves a chilling experience, with a sense of isolation and desperation that sets in the moment the opening credits roll. No sooner does Campbell's all–American college kid and his four friends turn their car off the high road, heading deep into the forests of rural Tennessee, than viewers know they are in for a visual experience quite unlike anything before or after in the annals of horror cinema.

The fact the film was the first major outing for many of the cast and crew undeniably shows; the roughness around its edges cannot be escaped. From the cast's performances to the relentlessly horrific effects and

2. The Living Room

the dilapidated cabin itself, nothing of what's on show has the slick, plastic finish of a big-budget Hollywood production. This, though, plays in the film's favor, its grimy earthiness adding to the disturbing realism of its horrors playing out on screen.

As with many of the best horror films that take place in and around a central building, the cabin takes on the virtual persona of an extra cast member. It helps, of course, that the building's living room is not only the place where the major internal action plays out, it is also the core of the house. Other rooms—bedrooms, bathroom, cellar and outhouse—play host to various incidents as the bloody mayhem unfolds, but only ever fleetingly and never to the detriment of the living room, the heart of the cabin and its troubles. This is the room where decisions are made, truths laid bare, and the gore-soaked thriller comes to its climax.

The sparseness with which the living room is kitted out merely emphasizes the intensity of the killings. Stabbing with knives and pencils, eye-gouging, burning, and chopping by axe are only a few examples of the visceral nastiness on show. It was one of the titles in Britain's notorious "Video Nasties" scare; the film's violence is undoubtedly hard to watch. This, though, may be due as much to its unrelenting intensity, as to the graphic nature of the horrors on show, which are largely risible thanks to their obvious fakeness.

Though the room is scant in content, nothing in it goes to waste. The cellar—reached through a trapdoor in the center of the living room floor—is where the kids find the notes and tape recordings of an archaeologist, along with a copy of the *Naturom Demonto* (a Sumerian version of the Egyptian *Book of the Dead*), all of which he'd brought to the cabin to study, and which the kids unwittingly use to wake a host of demons which proceed to terrorize and kill them. A rustic fireplace with open hearth serves as a roasting pit for one of the group once they've become demon-possessed. Various doors and windows, once broken, do little to protect the dwindling group of friends from the evil spirits which have been hiding in the woods surrounding the cabin, and are now intent on destroying all—human and otherwise.

The living room is also the place where the most gruesome violence takes place. Apart from an infamous forest scene during which one of the girls is savagely and graphically attacked by some animated vegetation, and a later decapitation which again takes place outside, the scenes which caused most controversy all take place within the confines of the cabin's main room, as most of the characters meet their end here. Much of the film's (undeniably) most atmospheric footage—an autumnal forest setting, swirling mists and a huge harvest moon suspended above the cabin—occurs in the area surrounding the cabin. As *Variety* highlighted in their December 31, 1982, review, the film had its fair share of guts and gore but it achieved its strongest sense of atmosphere when it suggested more than director Raimi showed:

> While injecting considerable black humor, neophyte Detroit-based writer-director Sam Raimi maintains suspense and a nightmarish mood in between the showy outbursts of special effects gore and graphic violence which are staples of modern horror pictures. Powerful camerawork suggests the lurking presence of the huge-scale demons in the forest.[9]

When the action relocates to the living room, however, very little is left to the viewer's imagination. Here limbs are cut off and people are beaten, kicked and thrown about, burned, stabbed and reduced to little more than quivering masses of gooey pulp. And everything is doused in so much fake blood, most of which Campbell has claimed ended up on him, that it's hard by the end to determine exactly who, if any, of the cast have actually survived intact.

Few films retain their ability to unsettle the viewer, even after almost 40 years, quite as much as *The Evil Dead*. What works in the film's favor, lending it a universal appeal, is the fact that it doesn't take itself too seriously: The film is little more than a dark—and admittedly sick—joke on the part of a group of young filmmakers barely out of college. As *The Overlook Film Encyclopaedia—Horror* pointed out, it was hard, as with many of its kind, "to see how anyone could take the film seriously, though some arbiters of public morals appear to have done so."[10] Many more enlightened people, though, saw Raimi's virtuoso production as his introduction to a career in which he became one of the most original and influential purveyors of the fantastical, of his—or any other—generation.

3

The Library and Study

Every bit of the walls was lined with shelves and every bit of the shelves was full of books. A fire was burning in the grate (you remember it was a very cold wet summer that year) and in front of the fire-place with its back towards them was a high-backed armchair. Between the chair and Polly, and filling most of the middle of the room, was a big table piled with all sorts of things—printed books, and books of the sort you write in, and ink bottles and pens and sealing-wax and a microscope.
  —*The Magician's Nephew*, C.S. Lewis (1955)

Who hasn't wished they lived in a house big enough to warrant its own library or study? A room dedicated to the pleasure of books, reserved for quiet contemplation, or simply to escape to. Somewhere like the secret study of Digory's Uncle Andrew, hidden beneath the eaves of a nondescript London terrace, in C.S. Lewis' allegorical fantasy *The Magician's Nephew*, where you can hide from the world and work in privacy without fear of prying eyes.

As with the other rooms portrayed in horror films, the library-study comes in many shapes and sizes, and serves many purposes. Whether home to an ornate desk used to conceal nefarious secrets, as in the disturbing *Murders in the Zoo* (1933), or a secret passage with hidden horrors, as in the creepy *The Cat and the Canary* (1939), no two depictions of the room are the same.

However, as Patrick Magee and Adrienne Corri discover in *A Clockwork Orange* (1971), inviting strangers into your inner sanctum is simply asking for trouble.

Murders in the Zoo (1933)

Beasts? I love them. They're honest in their simplicity, their primitive emotions.... They love, they hate, they kill.

Don't Go Upstairs!

Director: Edward Sutherland
Written by: Philip Wylie and Seton I. Miller
Starring: Charlie Ruggles, Lionel Atwill, Gail Patrick, Randolph Scott, John Lodge, Kathleen Burke, Harry Beresford

Wealthy eccentric Eric Gorman (Lionel Atwill) likes to hunt game—of all shapes and sizes. Although his primary interest is in obtaining specimens of rare and dangerous animals for a zoo in America, he also has a keen interest in tracking down any unwary predator who sets his sights on his attractive young wife Evelyn (Kathleen Burke). Returning from one particularly fruitful collecting expedition, Gorman discovers Evelyn has started a relationship with Roger (John Lodge), for whom she intends to leave him. Infuriated, Gorman plans a terrible revenge on his unfaithful wife and her unfortunate lover.

> Lionel Atwill as the insanely jealous husband is almost too convincing for comfort, and Kathleen Burke as the wife suggests the domestic terrors of her life capably. Judged by its ability to chill and terrify, this film is a successful melodrama.[1]

Given the brief summation of director Edward Sutherland's chiller-thriller *Murders in the Zoo* in Andre Sennwald's *New York Times* review (April

Strike a pose: Kathleen Burke, John Lodge (center) and Charlie Ruggles feature on a lobby card for *Murders in the Zoo* (1933).

3. The Library and Study

3, 1933), you may be forgiven for asking why you've never heard of a film which sounds like it should be up there with the classics. With a top cast, featuring horror king Lionel Atwill and Hollywood heartthrob Randolph Scott, exotic locations—the film kicks off in the jungles of Indochina before transferring to an American city zoo—and some spectacularly realistic and disturbing murders, it seems an injustice that the film is not as revered as some of its contemporaries. (In the same year, 1933, audiences shuddered at such lauded films as *Mystery of the Wax Museum* and *The Invisible Man*.)

Perhaps some aspects of *Murders in the Zoo* were too much even for early 1930s, pre–Code Hollywood, where generally pretty much anything went. As William K. Everson pointed out in his in-depth study *Classics of the Horror Film*, the film suffered at the hands of the censor for many years. "*Murders in the Zoo* is sometimes quite grim stuff; on its original release, many local and state censor boards removed chunks of footage, including the villain's climactic death; later, television showings usually made cuts as well."[2]

Though barely lasting an hour—its 66 minutes was a pretty tight running time, even for films of the period—it still manages to pack in three murders, an attempted murder, another death and a couple of extramarital affairs. It's the quality and originality of the deaths—and the sharp storyline connecting them—which makes the film stand out. It opens in a jungle clearing, with Gorman performing DIY surgery on a man who messed with Evelyn, and then leaves the wretch to his fate at the jaws of some wild beast. The sight of the poor victim staggering through the undergrowth, his hands bound and lips sewn together, is enough to freeze the blood. When Evelyn asks Gorman what the missing man said when he last saw him, Gorman simply replies, "He didn't say *any*thing!" This being 1930s Hollywood, the film's victims are mainly up to no good, meaning that the violence of their deaths could be excused as just retribution for their dastardly deeds: even so, being fed to crocodiles, poisoned with deadly snake venom and being crushed to death by a boa constrictor did make for some particularly gruesome on-screen imagery.

Grisly activities aside, one of the film's most memorable scenes does not directly involve death. Instead, following a showdown with Gorman, after she confronts him with her suspicions about his involvement in Roger's sudden death, Evelyn fools Gorman by locking herself in her bedroom. Then, hitching up her evening dress, she clambers out the window and edges her way along the balcony to her husband's study next door, where she makes a shocking discovery which ultimately seals her own fate.

Gorman's study offers a marvelously arresting environment onscreen,

Caged animals: Charlie Ruggles, John Lodge and Kathleen Burke (pictured left to right) fall prey to Lionel Atwill and his jungle friends in an atmospheric poster for Paramount's grisly shocker *Murders in the Zoo* (1933).

providing a sumptuously decadent retreat for the big game hunter when he returns from his latest jungle adventure. Fitted out in the romantic style favored by artistically inclined establishment figures of the period—think late Victorian pre–Raphaelite with an art deco edge—the explorer's lair is all deep armchairs, shaded lamps and heavy wooden desks. Added depth is given to the interior by its juxtaposition with a cityscape of brightly lit skyscrapers lying just beyond the window, as well as its contrast with the architecture and settings elsewhere in the film. Roger's apartment, seen earlier in the film, is the last word in bachelor-boy modernism, while the laboratory of the zoo for which Gorman provides animals, is colored by the mad scientist vibe so favored by 1930s horror.

Her husband's study is the perfect setting for Evelyn as she struggles to pry open the drawer of his desk, before discovering the evidence she hopes will put him away for good. With it being right next to her bedroom, her desperation to find the incriminating evidence is given extra urgency as she hears, with mounting dread, as do viewers, the sounds of Gorman breaking down her bedroom door. That both she—and, eventually, Gorman—come to unfortunate ends is neither here nor there. It's the couple's luxuriously bohemian lifestyle—as seen through their travels in far-flung lands, and the lushly appointed home to which they periodically return—which lingers in the mind's eye.

Stand-out murders and atmospheric settings aside, *Murders in the Zoo* was ahead of its time for another interesting reason. Made during an era when women, on the whole, were still seen and not heard—unless, like Fay Wray, they found themselves in perils which required them to scream at the top of their voices—the film's female cast had surprisingly meaty roles. Evelyn and Jerry Evans (Gail Patrick)—whose father, Prof. Evans (Harry Beresford), owns the zoo, while her fiancé Jack Woodford (Randolph Scott) is its head scientist—are women unafraid to take on men at their own game. Evelyn, when pushed, isn't scared to confront her husband, who is quite clearly mentally unhinged, while Jerry is Jack's assistant, equally involved in the day-to-day running of the zoo's laboratory. With this display of early onscreen feminism to the fore, it's perhaps time this unfairly neglected gem from Hollywood's Golden Age of Horror was embraced by a whole new generation of horror enthusiasts.

The Cat and the Canary (1939)

> THE PSYCHOLOGY OF FEAR—*What happens when a cat is allowed to come close to a canary in a cage? The bird, seeing the terrible eyes of its enemy so close, is often frightened to death.*

Director: Elliott Nugent
Written by: Walter DeLeon and Lynn Starling (screenplay), John Willard (based on the stage play by)
Starring: Bob Hope, Paulette Goddard, John Beal, Douglass Montgomery, Gale Sondergaard, Elizabeth Patterson, Nydia Westman, George Zucco, John Wray, George Regas, Willam Abbey, Milton Kibbee, Charles Lane, Frank Melton, Nick Thompson, Chief Thundercloud

> Panels slide as menacingly as ever; Paulette Goddard's screams would part a traffic snarl in Times Square; the lights dim and an eerie wail rises when the hopeful legatees assemble in the manse in the bayous for the reading of Uncle Cyrus' will. Over them all broods Bob Hope, with a chin like a forehead and a gag line for every occasion.[3]

As with most people at the time—critics and public alike—the pairing of perennial screen comic Bob Hope and Hollywood beauty Paulette Goddard could seemingly do no wrong in the eyes of *The New York Times'* Frank S. Nugent. In fact, they were such a success in Elliott Nugent's masterly retelling of playwright John Willard's classic horror comedy, *The Cat and the Canary*, that Paramount would repeat their winning formula a year later with *The Ghost Breakers*.

It is ten years to the day since reclusive millionaire Cyrus Norman died, leaving his estate to one lucky relation. Now, with the members of his family—including the perpetually flippant Wally Campbell (Hope) and feisty beauty Joyce Norman (Goddard)—gathered for the reading of his will, the scene is set for a night of mayhem as a hidden killer sets out to murder Norman's sole inheritor and steal the fortune.

In truth, *The Cat and the Canary* really shouldn't have worked as well as it did. Though fun and genuinely scary, the truth is that many aspects of it are so cliché-ridden that the whole production should, by rights, have fallen flat. A remake of the 1927 silent film version of the play—considered by many a classic of its kind—the retelling has everything one might expect from a haunted house creepy: a mansion complete with failing lights, secret passages and mist-shrouded grounds, an assortment of guests who nearly all hate each other, a sinister housekeeper, and the ubiquitous murderer on the loose from the conveniently local lunatic asylum.

All this, however, is possibly the reason the film worked so well, both on its initial release and even now, 80 years later. Sometimes the public simply wants what they are familiar with, and that is what they get here. The fact that the whole thing is carried off so effortlessly by the cast, and imbued with such atmosphere and realism by the filmmakers, adds to the sense that you're watching a beautifully effective and believable melding of horror and humor. A comedic twist—which often grates with modern viewers—was frequently added to film chillers during the 1930s and '40s, possibly to leaven the fear for the more susceptible members of the audience, as well as for the ever-vigilant censor. Here, though, it doesn't jar, be-

3. The Library and Study

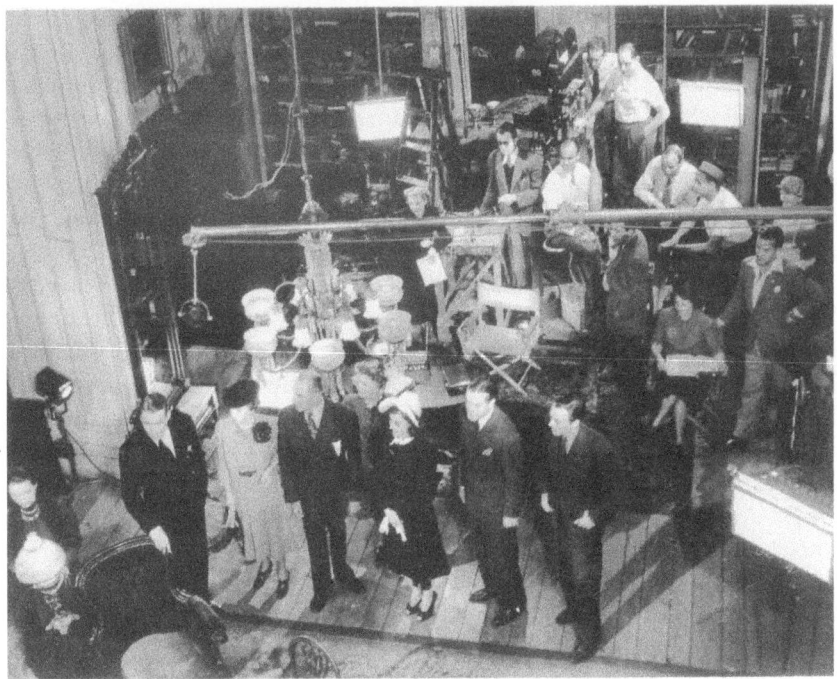

Set piece: (Left to right) Gale Sondergaard, Douglass Montgomery, Elizabeth Patterson, George Zucco, Nydia Westman, Paulette Goddard, Bob Hope and John Beal gather for the reading of a will in a behind-the-scenes shot from *The Cat and the Canary* (1939).

cause much of it grows from a natural reaction to the events taking place. Many of the jokes could be made by anyone in a similar situation, instead of as a condition of the actors' contract.

Once the cast members make their way through the Louisiana swamps to the home of the late Cyrus for the reading of his will, they, and the story, are confined to the dilapidated mansion for the film's duration. This allows the wonderfully decayed building to become a character in its own right. From the creeper-clad outer facade and columned porch to the peeling wallpaper and creaking floorboards within, everything gives the impression that the house itself is alive, a breathing, pulsating being. Little is seen of many of the mansion's actual rooms: In watching the film, the restrictions of its settings does remind you that it was originally intended for the stage. Those that do feature, though, are marvelously fleshed out. The spacious hallway, with a grand staircase which sweeps away to unseen floors above. The bedroom where Joyce, having been named as Cyrus' heir, attempts to spend the night before being rudely disturbed by the hand of an unseen intruder. (It emerges that the assailant is after a priceless necklace belonging to Cyrus, which Joyce and Wally found and subsequently hid beneath her pillow.) And then of course, there is the study...

The study, where many key scenes take place, including the reading of the will which sets in motion the chain of events which will leave more than one of the guests dead. The study, with its musty air of comfortable decay, furnished with overstuffed armchairs, open fire and floor-to-ceiling shelves stuffed higgledy-piggledy with numerous antiquarian volumes. The study where, once she has been revealed as the sole heir to Cyrus' fortune and the rest of the disgruntled family members have gone to bed—Joyce is left with Cyrus' solicitor Crosby (George Zucco), who insists that he has to tell her something of great importance. Of course, he is dispatched before he can, providing the film with a scene of genuine terror: As Joyce sits in an armchair, her back to the bookcases, one of them swings away from the wall, revealing a hand that grabs the unsuspecting Crosby and pulls him behind the wall while Joyce, blithely unaware, continues to talk to a now empty room. The result is a wonderfully effective and chillingly realized exercise in suspense.

It goes without saying that everyone gets their just deserts by the end of the night, but not before Joyce is given plenty of opportunity to show her gutsier side, along with the occasional and largely ineffectual assistance of Wally. From being pursued along cobweb-hung secret passages, to emerging from a trapdoor into the mist-shrouded garden—creating an effectively horrific image to rival the best from Hollywood's Golden Age of Horror—Goddard revealed an underused talent as a prototype for the modern scream queen.

Like the mists encroaching relentlessly upon the melancholy Norman estate from the surrounding swamps, one can't help but remain impressed by the palpable dread which saturates this masterpiece of comic horror.

The Wolf Man (1941)

> *Even a man who is pure in heart, and says his prayers by night; May become a wolf when the wolfbane blooms and the autumn moon is bright.*

Director: George Waggner
Written by: Curt Siodmak (original screenplay)
Starring: Lon Chaney, Jr., Claude Rains, Ralph Bellamy, Warren William, Patric Knowles, Bela Lugosi, Maria Ouspenskaya, Evelyn Ankers, Fay Helm, J.M. Kerrigan, Forrester Harvey

The libraries or studies of a home come in various shapes and sizes, serve multiple purposes, and are found anywhere in the house. Take, for

3. The Library and Study

instance, Talbot Castle, the Welsh ancestral home of aristocrat and amateur astronomer Sir John Talbot (Claude Rains), father of Larry Talbot (Lon Chaney, Jr.), the unfortunate lycanthrope in Universal's *The Wolf Man*. Situated at the top of the stately pile, the room—with glass roof, multiple windows and raised platform on which sits Sir John's impressive telescope—offers a bird's eye view over all of Sir John's land and the adjoining village. It also houses his extensive book collection and charts on science and astronomy, as well as a desk, and armchairs where he can relax and entertain guests. This is truly a man-lair of the highest order, and one which comes in handy when Talbot's estranged son returns home to live with him.

For a horror film, *The Wolf Man* contains very little visceral horror. Previous entries in Universal's monster cycle, such as their realization of Frankenstein's Monster, Count Dracula and the Mummy, all featured (for the period) a fair degree of graphic unpleasantness. This, however, was largely missing from their vision of the werewolf. Apart from a couple of prolonged and savage forest-based scenes, where Larry initially contracts the lycanthropic curse through an attack from a werewolf gypsy called Bela (a significant though fleeting appearance by Bela Lugosi), then later—following his own wolf transformation—where he is beaten to death by his father, any violence shown is remarkable tame. This is a point picked up by writer William K. Everson: "Its horror content was not strong, perhaps because this time the stress was more on characterization than on plot, and in order to keep the Werewolf (played by Lon Chaney, Jr.) a sympathetic lead character throughout, his forays into nocturnal prowling were short and relatively restrained."[4]

This increased room for characterization allowed for extended play on the relationship between Larry and his father. Their establishing scenes play out in Sir John's beautifully appointed study. Though much of the film's action takes place outside of Talbot Castle—in the neighboring village and surrounding woodlands—the scenes which take place within the Talbot home itself are pivotal to the storyline and development of various central characters. Hardly has Larry stepped across the threshold—returning home, having lived abroad for several years after falling out with his father—than Sir John takes him up to the study. This is when we see Sir John's study-cum-observatory for the first time in all its glory. The telescope, reached by a ladder, overlooks a massive desk and a book-lined wall, lending the room the air of a captain's "great cabin" aboard a sailing ship. Here, Sir John—impressed by his son's knowledge of mechanical things, picked up when abroad—asks Larry to fix the new attachment to the machine, encouraging him to use the telescope to spy out the surrounding lands. As we are still in the days—at least in Hollywood's fantasy version of them—when a British gentleman held feudal sway over the villages on his estates, Sir John urges his son to get to know the people who live in them; "*your* people" as he puts it.

It is from here—once Sir John has gone—that Larry uses the telescope to spy on the village, and in particular on the beautiful Gwen Conliffe (Evelyn Ankers), whose father owns the local antique and curio shop. Later, when Larry visits Gwen in the shop and reveals facts about her which he couldn't possibly know, he is forced to admit that he was spying on her from his castle-top aerie, much to the young woman's annoyance. Larry, of course, quickly charms the defensive Gwen into submission, inviting her to come out with him that night, a date predictably culminating in disaster.

The unspoken sense of heavy richness which colors Sir John's study continues into other areas of the house seen throughout the film—for example, its grand reception hall and Larry's bedroom—and later, to a lesser degree, the local village. Everything retains the air of decayed opulence which many outsiders believed depicts reality in rural Britain, particularly those who wanted to bring it to the screen in Hollywood in the 1930s and 1940s. In this imaginary land, the gentry all live in baronial manor houses, while village life is played out in surroundings which look like a European fairy tale crossed with Cotswold romanticism. Perhaps this shouldn't be so surprising considering that the village scenes in *The Wolf Man* used the same Universal backlot which had appeared in most of the studio's other monster horrors from the 1930s.

The werewolf as a character in Hollywood horror would return several times during the remainder of the 1940s: Chaney, Jr., reprised the role four times for Universal, while studios like Twentieth Century–Fox and Columbia tried to recreate *The Wolf Man*'s box office magic with *The Undying Monster* (1942) and *The Return of the Vampire* (1944) respectively. None of them, however, quite managed to recapture the atmospheric magic which makes *The Wolf Man* stand out as a classic from Hollywood's golden era of monster movies.

The Mummy (1959)

Seems I've spent the better part of my life amongst the dead.

Director: Terence Fisher
Written by: Jimmy Sangster (screenplay)
Starring: Peter Cushing, Christopher Lee, Yvonne Furneaux, Eddie Byrne, Felix Aylmer, Raymond Huntley, George Pastell, Michael Ripper, George Woodbridge, Harold Goodwin, Denis Shaw, Gerald Lawson, Willoughby Gray, John Stuart, David Browning, Frank Sieman, Stanley Meadows, Frank Singuineau, James Clarke, John Harrison, Frederick Rawlings, Roy Stewart

3. The Library and Study

As is often the case with Hammer's interpretations of horror's unholy triumvirate—Dracula, Frankenstein's Monster and the Mummy—their first attempt was the best, except perhaps in the case of Dracula where their next vampire outing, *The Brides of Dracula* (1960), certainly equaled if not surpassed the original *Horror of Dracula* (1958). The seemingly endless follow-ups slowly deteriorated with each successive visit. The truth is, once introduced, there are few places you could take the monsters without the accompanying storyline becoming increasingly convoluted and far-fetched: there are only so many times you can resurrect these creatures (supernatural powers or not) without them becoming farcical. So it is that Hammer's first take on the mummy legend remains one of their better attempts at resurrecting Egypt's past.

The eminent Egyptologist Stephen Banning (Felix Aylmer)—along with his son John (Peter Cushing) and brother-in-law Joseph Whemple (Raymond Huntley)—has, after many years' work, uncovered the tomb of the legendary Egyptian princess, Ananka. In the process they have also unwittingly woken the mummified body of her guardian, the High Priest

Study in terror: The Mummy (Christopher Lee) and John Banning (Peter Cushing) battle it out in *The Mummy* (1959).

Kharis (Christopher Lee), who, under the guidance of a devout follower of Ananka called Mehemet Bey (George Pastell), follows the archaeologists to England to wreak a terrible revenge upon the desecrators of his mistress' tomb.

The Mummy was the archetypal example of what went on to become Hammer's trademark: making something believable and authentic-looking from the minimum resources. Here is a film which—though traveling across continents from Egypt to England, while lending an air of authentic Victorian lushness to the proceedings—utilized between 10 and 15 sets, interspersed with occasional stock footage or authentic location shots.

Among the sets, John Banning's study dominates. It is furnished in the style typical of a rich, educated, scientific Victorian. An archaeologist who has traveled and worked with his father in Egypt, Banning is clearly well read and equally well heeled; his study is really more of a working drawing room. Complete with comfortable chairs and roaring log fire, it is flanked at one end by an enormous desk in front of well-stacked bookcases and littered with books and paraphernalia on Egyptology, history and hieroglyphics, while the opposite features a raised dais with three floor-to-ceiling windows leading outside, which in time provide a dramatic entrance for the Mummy.

All of which make it the perfect setting for much of the action to take place in, playing host to many of the prime movers and the plotline's pivotal confrontations. Banning, his wife Isobel (Yvonne Furneaux), Joseph, Police Inspector Mulrooney (Eddie Byrne), Mehemet Bey *and* the Mummy all pass through the study at some point during the proceedings. Its comfortable surroundings are perfect when—following the death of Stephen at the hands of the Mummy—John, with Joseph's help, starts to go through his father's papers in the hope of finding a clue to his unexplained death. Later, after Mehemet Bey sends the Mummy to kill him, John has his first confrontation with the creature, complete with attempted stabbing by an ornamental spear from the wall behind his desk. This potentially deadly conflict is ended when Isobel rushes in, stopping the Mummy in his tracks. Isobel reminds him of Ananka—to whom Isobel bears a conveniently uncanny resemblance—whom he'd loved and had been condemned to guard in embalmed form for eternity. The Mummy's attention is distracted, and he retreats via the windows he had smashed his way through a few minutes earlier. A further opportunity for revelations between Banning and Inspector Mulrooney takes place—in what has now, in the eyes of the viewer, become the principal room of the Bannings' house—before the final climactic battle between the main protagonists, initiated once again in Banning's comfortable retreat, spills out into the neighboring countryside with a suitably dramatic conclusion. As is the

3. The Library and Study

Come to Mummy: The Mummy (Christopher Lee) is stopped in his tracks by Isobel Banning (Yvonne Furneaux), when they come face to face in *The Mummy* (1959).

case with many Hammer films, the study's elaborate, almost over-the-top appearance, complete with a profusion of books, paintings and china, and created by resident production designer Bernard Robinson, allowed ample opportunity for Lee's creature to cause havoc and destruction on a grandiose scale.

Beautifully visualized though the film is, its other main strength—the characterizations, which create three-dimensional individuals that the viewer actually feels something for—is also one of its weaknesses. An extended sequence in which Banning explains how high priest Kharis became a mummy, slows the action unnecessarily. Though striking to watch, its running time of over ten minutes seems drawn-out, while the cartoon garishness of its colors jar harshly with the Victorian palette of the remaining film.

The scenes here also contained *The Mummy*'s few concessions to gore which, for a Hammer production, were remarkably tame. As Derek Conrad pointed out in the British magazine *films and filming*:

Another in the long and seemingly endless line of Hammer horrors, *The Mummy* is a far more competent thriller, even if it misses the mark as a chiller, than their previous efforts. At last the boys at Bray have followed fairly successfully the golden rule of suspense: It is not what you see, but what you don't that stimulates the imagination and provides the excitement.[5]

What horrors there are—a tongue ripped out, beheadings, people buried alive—while mostly taking place off-screen, retain an unpleasant air though they sit somewhat uncomfortably with the more sedate murder methods of strangulation, shooting and stabbing which are the order of the day when the action returns to England of the nineteenth century.

Concluding his review, Conrad gave what would have been considered high praise for a production from a genre not generally held in much regard by those in the film world ... though his opinion of its audience was clearly not so great. "Hammer's highly organized team have given the film enough gloss to satisfy its undemanding customers, and enough thrills to keep them half-way to the edge of their seats."[6]

A Clockwork Orange (1971)

> *She was very badly raped, you see! We were assaulted by a gang of vicious young hoodlums in this house! In this very room you are sitting in now!*

Director: Stanley Kubrick
Written by: Stanley Kubrick (screenplay), Anthony Burgess (novel)
Starring: Malcolm McDowell, Patrick Magee, Michael Bates, Warren Clarke, Jon Clive, Adrienne Corri, Carl Duering, Paul Farrell, Clive Francis, Michael Gover, Miriam Karlin, James Marcus, Aubrey Morris, Godfrey Quigley, Sheila Raynor, Madge Ryan, John Savident, Anthony Sharp, Philip Stone, Michael Tarn, David Prowse, Carol Drinkwater, Richard Connaught, Cheryl Grunwald, Katya Wyeth

It can be said of few filmmakers in the history of the medium that their entire *oeuvre* is worthy of classic status. Alfred Hitchcock? Possibly. Stanley Kubrick? Definitely. Whether his jarring, frequently surreal style of filmmaking is to your taste or not, there is no denying that his work constantly stirs and provokes the viewer. Though none of his films are anything less than controversial, one in particular has caused significant debate since its release: *A Clockwork Orange*. Shocking and, in places, downright obscene, this film is so chock full of images designed to disturb, its overall ability to upset those of a sensitive disposition is uniquely effective.

3. The Library and Study

One scene, taking place early in the film and pivotal to what follows, stands out. Generally referred to as the "rape scene," the vicious attack in their isolated, modernist mansion on academic Mr. Alexander (Patrick Magee) and his wife (Adrienne Corri) by the protagonist Alex (Malcolm McDowell) and his gang of "Droogs," as he calls his thuggish friends, makes for a thoroughly harrowing viewing experience.

Much has been written on the subtle nuances, underlying messages and hidden meanings behind Kubrick's *enfant terrible*. There is no denying however that watching it is an emotional experience which retains the power to shock the viewer out of any apathy they may feel towards the horror genre, a feeling highlighted by the *New York Times* critic Clayton Riley when he pointed out that "as a horror show, *A Clockwork Orange* has few peers."[7]

A lot of *A Clockwork Orange*'s real horror works so well because it derives from a fear which everyone can relate to. Being physically at-

What a wind-up: Alex (Malcolm McDowell, center) shows off his fancy footwork, as Dim (Warren Clarke), Mrs. Alexander (Adrienne Corri, on Clarke's shoulder), her husband (Patrick Magee, lying on floor) and Georgie (James Marcus) enjoy the spectacle in *A Clockwork Orange* (1971).

tacked—especially in your own home, as is the case with Alexander and his wife—is something which you can imagine might just possibly happen. The physical brutality to which the couple are subjected to may seem bad enough—Alexander is confined to a wheelchair because of injuries he sustains in the attack, while his wife later dies from the effects of being raped by Alex. However, the wanton destruction and vandalism of the couple's house by the gang is equally traumatic on a psychological level, in a way which leaves scars which often cannot heal.

Mr. Alexander is busy at his desk, surrounded by books and papers, most of which are likely irreplaceable—this does, after all, take place in a pre-computerized era. His wife is reading, relaxing—if that's possible—in the most extraordinary pebble-shaped chair. Though their house is extremely modernist verging on the austere, there is nonetheless a sense of comfort and intimacy provided by the pale wooden flooring and doors which softens the severity of the futuristic, set-piece furniture. Here also, the film's use of Beethoven—seen mainly through Alex's obsession with the composer and his music—is highlighted as the Alexanders' doorbell, which alerts the couple to the presence of Alex and his gang, plays the opening bars of the composer's Fifth Symphony. The doorbell calls Mrs. Alexander up a double flight of wide, shallow stairs which serve not only to prolong her journey from the lounge to the hallway but also provides a spectacular backdrop for Alex and the Droogs to prance down once she has unwittingly invited them in.

The almost clinical emptiness of the house's main living area—with its clean lines, white walls and acres of polished wooden floors—is emphasized in an understated way by production designer John Barry, who went on to win an Oscar for *Star Wars: Episode IV—A New Hope* (1977): There is little in the way of additional decor, apart from the occasional random seat, coffee table or piece of statement art, all of which magnifies the chaotic, "mad professor"–like quality of Alexander's study sitting off to one side of the lounge. The cluttered appearance of this area—typewriter and papers littering the desk with the surrounding industrial shelving crammed to bursting with academic volumes—makes for the perfect environment not just to emphasize the severity of the rest of the house but to provide Alex with plenty of material for destruction once he begins his rampage.

And so unfolds one of the most distressing house attacks seen on film, all to a soundtrack of *Singin' in the Rain*. As McDowell himself pointed out in 2011, in a *BBC Breakfast News* interview, there "was not a lot of blood" in it, with the violence being more "psychological."[8] That said, who needs blood when a husband is gagged and kicked repeatedly in the ribs by someone young enough to be his son, while being forced to watch his wife being defiled and his life's work destroyed wantonly in front of him.

The remainder of Kubrick's sordid fantasy is a confection of often hard-to-stomach excess, its orgy of violence seemingly never-ending. But none of what follows comes close to capturing the shock—physically, mentally and visually—of what the Alexanders endure at the hands of their unwelcome houseguests.

4

The Dining Room

> "The dinner-table is often the terrain of critical conversations, for it is there one has the better of one's interlocutor. There is no escape without scandal, there is no turning aside without self-betrayal. To invite a person to dinner is to place them under observation. Every dining-room is a temporary prison where politeness chains the guests to the laden board."
> —*The Hands of Orlac*, Maurice Renard (1920)

In his fantasy novel *Les Mains d'Orlac*, French author Maurice Renard captures perfectly the essence of the dining room as it has appeared in horror films.

As Renard points out, this room acts as an area of confinement, where characters and storyline return periodically, drawn to gather round a table or elaborate fireplace and reveal further points pertinent to proceedings. Whether the setting for an interrogation in the starkly minimal *Son of Frankenstein* (1939*)*, a *tête-à-tête* between two lovers in French cinema's majestic masterpiece *La Belle et la Bête* (1946), or sinister revelations in Hammer's vampire classic *Dracula—Prince of Darkness* (1966), the dining room proves to be the place for anything but a cozy get-together.

Son of Frankenstein (1939)

> "Is it the old legendary monster of my father's time, or am I supposed to have 'whipped' one up ... as a housewife whips up an omelette?"

Director: Rowland V. Lee
Written by: Willis Cooper (screenplay), Mary Shelley (suggested by the story written in 1816)
Starring: Boris Karloff, Basil Rathbone, Bela Lugosi, Lionel Atwill, Josephine Hutchinson, Donnie Dunagan, Emma Dunn, Edgar Norton, Perry Ivins, Lawrence Grant, Lionel Belmore, Michael Mark, Caroline Cooke, Gustav von Seyffertitz, Larimer Johnson, Tom Ricketts

4. The Dining Room

Tea and sympathy: Baroness Elsa von Frankenstein (Josephine Hutchinson) and her husband Wolf (Basil Rathbone) entertain Inspector Krogh (Lionel Atwill) in *Son of Frankenstein* (1939).

It is many years since Baron Wolf von Frankenstein (Basil Rathbone) lived at the castle where his father Henry created a monster. Now, returning to the ancestral home with his wife Elsa (Josephine Hutchinson) and young son Peter (Donnie Dunagan), memories of the past—along with something else—are awoken within Wolf, with disastrous results.

> Yes, sir, Castle Frankenstein is the showplace of the neighborhood. At dinner in the great hall Josephine Hutchinson seems justified in remarking to Basil that the front-door knocker "gets on her nerves," inasmuch as each stroke is equivalent to the Independence Day explosion in San Francisco.[1]

Whoever wrote the anonymous *New York Times* review of this Universal chiller was clearly impressed by the sheer on-screen scale of the latest incarnation of the Frankenstein family home: Everything about the film speaks of the ominous building's remoteness, its vastness and its cavernous interior. Obviously removed from the local town—Baron Wolf von Frankenstein, his wife Elsa and young son Peter have to reach it by car when they arrive at the local railway station—this is a home built with the clear intention of inspiring awe within the local populace, or anyone else who should come calling. Within hailing distance across a ravine is Frankenstein's father's mountaintop laboratory (looking like a jagged alien spaceship that's landed within some windswept, rocky landscape) but little is seen of the castle's exterior, save a rain-lashed front door on the stormy night that the baron and his family arrive. The inside of the building appears only slightly less inhospitable.

Though the film is inspired by a novel written by Mary Shelley during England's late Regency period, Hollywood's visualization of Frankenstein and his creation—even in the earlier *Frankenstein* (1931) and *Bride of Frankenstein* (1935)—was clearly more than a little inspired by the impressionistic and art deco styles popular in so many genre films of the 1930s, a look which comes into its own in the castle dining room in *Son of Frankenstein*.

Film historian Leslie Halliwell spoke glowingly of the film's on-screen appearance, "Jack Otterson's interior design of the 'castle,' with its crooked open stairways and medieval bosses meeting over the dining table, is already bidding fair to be the best thing in the picture…."[2] With sets created by multi–Oscar-nominated Otterson, and dressed by Oscar-winning set decorator Russell A. Gausman, the austere appearance of the castle's interior falls between baronial gothic and concrete brutalism. Its bedrooms and library are the only rooms which allow some concession to coziness, with comfortable beds, armchairs and a profusion of books lining the walls. However, even here, the reasoning behind the decor seems to be primarily for dramatic effect: In the library, great windows fill one side of the room, allowing Wolf and Elsa to experience the full force of the storm as they look out.

It is in the castle's main public rooms where the film's sense of visual bleakness, highlighting the storyline's theme, comes into its own. In the entrance hall, twisting open staircases of slatted wood climb past towering gray, stone-slabbed walls, free of adornment, while in the dining room, sinister shadows are cast over featureless monochrome expanses. Strangely though, in two key scenes set within the dining room, the space also retains a degree of intimacy despite its seemingly measureless dimensions.

On the first morning in their new home, Wolf and Elsa take breakfast in the room with nothing but a table and two armchairs, overshadowed by two beast-headed corbels protruding from above the twin fireplaces, looking down on the table from high overhead. It is here that Elsa catches her first glimpse of her late father-in-law's abandoned laboratory, and where Wolf hints at his excitement about going to explore it for the first time.

Later in the film, Inspector Krogh (Lionel Atwill) of the local police is given tea by Elsa, in front of one of the dining room's great fireplaces, as he awaits the return of Wolf. Here again, the room is virtually bare apart from a lone sideboard, an ornate high-backed armchair set against a wall, the dining room table and a couple of chairs and low tea table where Krogh and Elsa are seated. When Wolf joins them, the scene is set for Krogh to quiz him on his activities at his father's ruined laboratory, a discussion which merely reinforces the inspector's suspicions that something strange is again taking place within the confines of the castle and its estate. His misgivings are of course proven right, with devastating results for everyone.

In the years since its release, the film has joined the pantheon of classics from the closing years of the 1930s, the period considered by many to be the Golden Age of Hollywood horror, as much—as we've seen—for its look as for any real horror content. David J. Skal summed it up: "The film is visually stunning, and arguably one of the most visually ambitious American films before *Citizen Kane*."[3] High praise indeed for an example from a genre not generally commended for its aesthetic or artistic sensibilities.

La Belle et la Bête (1946)

> *Belle, you mustn't look into my eyes. You needn't fear. You will never see me, except each evening at 7:00, when you will dine, and I will come to the great hall. And never look into my eyes.*

Directors: Jean Cocteau, René Clément (uncredited)
Written by: Jean Cocteau (dialogue, screenplay, story), Jeanne-Marie Leprince de Beaumont (story)
Starring: Jean Marais, Josette Day, Mila Parély, Nane Germon, Michel Auclair, Raoul Marco, Marcel André, Jacques Marbeuf, Jean Cocteau (voice of Magic, uncredited)

A once-successful French merchant (Marcel André) now fights to make ends meet, having lost most of his goods at sea. Embarking on yet another business trip, the merchant asks his three daughters what each would like him to bring back. The two older ones, haughty and vain, demand expensive gifts, while Belle (Josette Day), his beautiful youngest daughter, requests a simple rose as there are no longer any in their own garden.

Returning home the merchant loses his way and finds himself on the grounds of a beautiful chateau in which grow the most entrancing roses, and he plucks one for Belle. Suddenly, as if from nowhere, appears the chateau's owner—a truly fearful beast (Jean Marais). He claims that his roses mean more to him than life itself, and demands a terrible price from the merchant for his theft: either he, or one of his daughters, must return to the castle and forfeit their lives.

La Belle et la Bête, French filmmaker Jean Cocteau's fantastical cinematic interpretation of the macabre fairy tale "Beauty and the Beast," is a film which, while lacking in the generally accepted trappings of violence, nonetheless stirs an equally disturbing feeling within the viewer. Save for the occasional scene which conjures up moments of real shock—such as when the Beast at one point appears in a state of semi-undress, having succumbed to the darker side of his nature—much of the horror here comes from the endless array of surreal settings and imagined environs within which the storyline unfolds. From Belle's father's shabby house— the home of a once rich family now down on its luck—to the mysterious, ornate chateau where the melancholic Beast idles away his days in decadent grandeur, everything about *La Belle et la Bête* has the surreal touch of its mastermind, Jean Cocteau.

The manor house of Rochecorbon in Touron doubled as Belle's family home and captured perfectly the idea of a rustic French idyll, while the overgrown estate of Louis XVIII's Chateau de Raray near Senlis, with its many statues, was tailor-made for the rambling, dreamlike environs of the Beast's isolated castle.

An artist, writer and filmmaker, Cocteau reveled in immersing himself in every part of the moviemaking process. Not only did he direct and write the film, but he also voiced one of the lesser characters. His vivid imagination takes over in the recreation of the legendary French fairy tale with, at times, slightly disturbing results. On one occasion, when Belle is given leave by the Beast to visit her father who is ill, one of her sisters attempts to steal a string of pearls that Belle is wearing, only to have them transform into a vine-like rope in her hands. At another time, when the Beast appears to Belle—having just succumbed to his baser instincts and killed an animal off-screen—he begs her forgiveness, proffering outstretched paws around which the smoke of death swirls ominously.

It is inside the Beast's dreamlike lair, however, where Cocteau's sense of the grotesque really has free rein. The chateau's interior has a real air of the sinister, its lack of furnishings and decor simply heightening the film's surreal atmosphere: the darkened corners of rooms appear to open into boundless voids, gardens encroach at the edges of reality. It is a look that Cocteau felt to be more than a little menacing, as seen by his description of Belle's bedroom in the Beast's chateau, in his diary entry marked December 15, 1945:

> I'd like to hear this room described by Edgar Allen [sic] Poe; for it is, as it were, isolated in space with the remnants of the forest set on one side, and the beginnings of the stream set on the other. With the result that bushes can be seen through its walls of net, suggesting a whole incomprehensible landscape behind it. Its carpet is of grass and its furniture in the magnificent bad taste of Gustave Doré.[4]

4. The Dining Room

The entrance hall–dining room of the Beast's home is most unsettling. Its lack of definition through pictures, etc., on the walls—where there are only disembodied arms holding candlesticks—and absence of furniture save for a refectory table and two high-backed dining chairs, gives the sense of a room set alone, suspended in darkness. The theme of bodiless arms as servants is carried through to the table, groaning under the weight of sumptuous feasts, laid out when the merchant initially enters the chateau, and then for Belle each evening at 7:00 when she sits to dinner with the Beast. And all this under the baleful glare of the living statues ornately cast into either side of a massive fireplace which looms over proceedings at the side of the room.

This is the room where the weary merchant receives his first experience of the Beast's magical hospitality, as well as where Belle and the Beast lay the ground rules for their burgeoning relationship. He will attend her each evening at dinner, but remain unseen behind her chair so that she never looks him in the face. She does, of course, as time goes on. However, their early encounters—played out within touching distance of each other, yet out of sight—add an extra tension to the film's sense of supernatural horror.

As with much of the film, it's the details that matter in the dining hall. The room may be bare in essence, but this simply highlights such minutiae as the carved animal heads on the arms of Belle's chair—brought into close focus to emphasize the roaring arrival of the Beast at dinner. Or the hand which, earlier in the film, slaps away that of the merchant, when he sits at the grand table and tries to pour wine from a jeweled decanter, before proceeding to fill the shocked man's glass itself.

The story ends well for Belle and the Beast, but not so for its other characters. The Beast, now transformed into a handsome and courtly prince, reveals to Belle the future for her family which, in keeping with the often dark conclusions of early fairy tales, may not be altogether happy. Viewers, on the other hand, can relax, knowing they have enjoyed the work of a true genius of the cinema of the fantastique.

Dracula—Prince of Darkness (1966)

> *Oh, why not? Ten minutes ago we were stranded in the cold, miles away from anywhere. Now we're warm. We're going to be fed. And if that man's master is anything like I think he's going to be, we're going to be entertained as well.*

Director: Terence Fisher
Written by: Jimmy Sangster (screenplay—as John Sansom), Anthony Hinds (idea—as John Elder), Bram Stoker (characters)

Don't Go Upstairs!

Starring: Christopher Lee, Barbara Shelley, Andrew Keir, Francis Matthews, Suzan Farmer, Charles Tingwell, Thorley Walters, Philip Latham, Walter Brown, George Woodbridge, Jack Lambert, Philip Ray, Joyce Hemson, John Maxim

"It is hard to ring variations on the basic elements of vampirism and the story here is routine and dull even though Terence Fisher's staging is more than competent. The shock and horror moments have to justify the rest, and for my money they don't add up to enough."[5]

Allen Eyles' summation of Hammer's wonderfully lush *Dracula—Prince of Darkness* may seem harsh. Perhaps, for a public still recovering from the shock of the groundbreaking *Horror of Dracula* (1958), its equally arresting follow-up *The Brides of Dracula* (1960) and the highly regarded *The Kiss of the Vampire* (1963), anything subsequent was going to be a letdown. Looked at in retrospect, however, Hammer's fourth vampire outing (the second to feature Lee as the bloodsucking nobleman) is quite simply one of the most exquisite examples of the golden age of British horror cinema. Even the most cynical viewer would be hard put to find complaint with Terence Fisher's masterly direction of vampiric nastiness

Dinner is served: Count Dracula's butler, Klove (Philip Latham), stirs up trouble for the Kent family (Suzan Farmer, Francis Matthews, Barbara Shelley and Charles "Bud" Tingwell, clockwise from left) in *Dracula—Prince of Darkness* (1966).

amidst the Carpathian Mountains, starring Lee as Dracula, and Francis Matthews, Charles Tingwell, Suzan Farmer and Barbara Shelley as the unfortunate English tourists ensnared in his web of evil.

Charles Kent and his brother Alan (Matthews and Tingwell) and their respective wives, Diana and Helen (Farmer and Shelley), are touring a remote region of Eastern Europe. Staying the night in a local inn, they fall into conversation with Father Sandor (Andrew Keir), a priest from a nearby monastery. Mysteriously, without explaining why, Sandor warns them against staying too long in the area and particularly in the vicinity of the town of Karlsbad and its infamous castle. The following night, after an incident involving their coach and its reluctant driver, the Kents ignore Sandor's advice and accept an offer of hospitality at the castle. It's not long before they discover why it is that local inhabitants refuse to acknowledge the existence of the castle and its mysterious owner, Count Dracula.

An unofficial sequel to *Horror of Dracula*—right down to its pre-credits reuse of that film's breathless denouement between Lee's count and Peter Cushing's Van Helsing—*Dracula—Prince of Darkness* was, and still is, the perfect embodiment of everything which made Hammer not only Britain's premier film company during the 1960s, but the main purveyors of gothic horror worldwide. Involving a host of Hammer stalwarts, including Lee and Shelley, in front of the camera with director Fisher and screenwriter Jimmy Sangster behind the scenes, the production had all the qualities that audiences had come to expect from the studio: sumptuous and atmospheric settings, sharp dialogue and actors who approached the proceedings, no matter how preposterous, with the utmost seriousness. One can only sit and wallow in the sheer nostalgia of this superior frightfest, particularly when the four tourists first enter Dracula's castle and are welcomed at the dining table by his faithful retainer, Klove (Philip Latham).

And what a beautiful room it is where the Kents sit down to dine, an open area—as in many European castles—serving a multitude of purposes: entrance hall, dining room and sitting room, complete with armchairs, sofas and roaring fire capacious enough to take a small tree trunk. Richly decorated with heavy oak furniture, oil paintings and ornate candlesticks, the room resembles the dining hall of some elaborate and decadent hunting lodge. From above it is overlooked on one side by a colonnaded gallery, from which a grand staircase descends, and along which the vampire count himself will make his entrance at a later stage.

The room's versatile layout usefully highlights key points in the story which take place within it. Not perhaps viscerally graphic, these scenes are nevertheless dramatic, and vital to the plotline. It is here where the four guests arrive—having been brought to the castle by a driverless carriage—

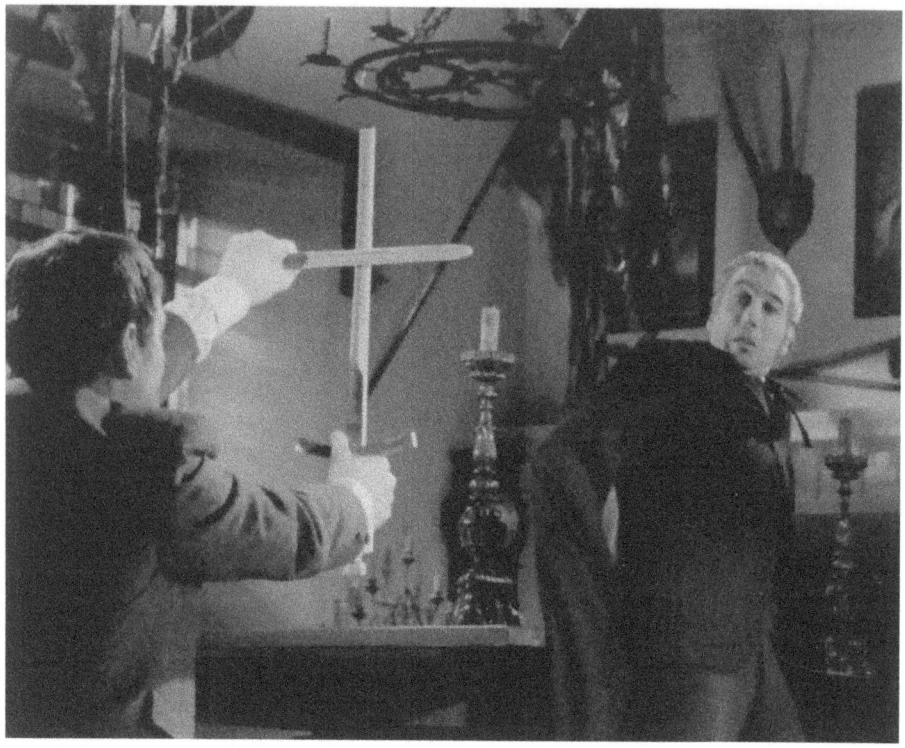

Cross purposes: The decadence of Castle Dracula's entrance-cum-dining hall is evident in this still capturing the initial confrontation between Charles Kent (Francis Matthews) and Count Dracula (Christopher Lee) in *Dracula—Prince of Darkness* (1966).

to find a table laid for dinner, as though they had been expected. It is also where Dracula's footman Klove reveals himself before serving their meal. He explains to the bewildered group that his late master had left orders that the castle be kept in perpetual readiness should guests ever happen by.

Later, after Alan has unfortunately been used by Klove in the rebirth of his master, and Helen defiled by the lusty count, Charles and Diana face a dramatic confrontation and stand-off with their one-time sister-in-law and the resurrected Dracula, before making a swift escape from the castle.

After Charles and Diana's departure, the interior of the castle is not visited again, although the film's climax does take place within its bleak and ice-bound grounds. It is an austere exterior which belies the luxurious surroundings of the extended dining hall within, doubtless still kept in readiness for the next traveler unfortunate enough to stumble across Count Dracula's mountain retreat.

Twins of Evil (1971)

The Devil has sent me twins of evil!

Director: John Hough
Written by: Tudor Gates (screenplay), J. Sheridan Le Fanu (characters)
Starring: Peter Cushing, Dennis Price, Mary Collinson, Madeleine Collinson, Isobel Black, Kathleen Byron, Shelagh Wilcocks, Damien Thomas, David Warbeck, Harvey Hall, Alex Scott, Judy Matheson, Luan Peters, Katya Wyeth, Inigo Jackson, Roy Stewart, Maggie Wright, Kristen Lindholm, Peter Thompson

Critic and screenwriter David McGillivray—the man behind such sleaze classics as *Frightmare* (1974) and *Satan's Slave* (1976)—has never been one to mince his words. Take his thoughts on Hammer's *Twins of Evil*: "The only novelty of the story lies in the twins of the title, one good, one bad, one to be fatally drawn to Karnstein Castle, the other to be mistaken for her vampire sister. Everything else churns away as it has done for the past 15 years."[6] True, but also harsh, as the familiarity of Hammer's films was often the factor which made them one of cinema's most successful production companies.

Hammer produced three films in the early 1970s—*The Vampire Lovers* (1970), *Lust for a Vampire* (1971) and *Twins of Evil*—based around characters from author Sheridan Le Fanu's vampire tale, *Carmilla*, and which became known as the Karnstein Trilogy. *Twins of Evil* bore the least resemblance to the novel, though it is sometimes considered a prequel as its set and costumes are strongly eighteenth-century in tone, with the first two films clearly taking place later.

Following the death of their parents, twins Maria and Frieda Gellhorn (Mary and Madeleine Collinson) travel from Venice to live with their puritan uncle and aunt, Gustav and Katy Weil (Peter Cushing and Kathleen Byron). Gustav and Katy live in a village high in the Carpathian mountains, in the shadow of the home of vampire acolyte Count Karnstein (Damien Thomas). And once Karnstein sets his sights on the newly arrived Maria and Frieda, all Hell (quite literally) breaks loose.

The trilogy's screenplays, by Tudor Gates, who was responsible for writing Jane Fonda's cult vehicle *Barbarella* (1968), all feature some degree of lesbianism, though in *Twins of Evil* this is more inferred than seen. The third film more than makes up for this shortcoming, however, with an equally disturbing, if not downright distasteful, underlying theme, child molestation: Maria and Frieda are no more than teenagers when Karnstein attempts to have his wicked way with them. This aside, the film, with its fast pace and disturbing originality, simply rollicks along. From the opening scenes, where the Devil—in the form of Karnstein, a sexually charged vampire nobleman, who lords it over the local townsfolk, while

Teenage tearaways: (Left to right) Identical twins Maria and Frieda Gellhorn (Mary and Madeleine Collinson) prove double the trouble for their kindly aunt, Katy Weil (Kathleen Byron), and puritanical uncle, Gustav (Peter Cushing), in *Twins of Evil* **(1971).**

subjecting the surrounding countryside to his reign of terror—is pitted against God—in the guise of Bible-wielding Weil and the combined force of the town's officials and schoolmaster. Until the usual gory Hammer climax, the action never lets up.

While good use was made of Buckinghamshire's Black Park Country Park, Wexham, for most of the film's exteriors, its main interiors were filmed at Pinewood Studios, Iver Heath, Buckinghamshire and the Centralni Filmski Studio Kosutnjak in Belgrade, Serbia. And what marvelously atmospheric interiors they were, created under the guidance of production designer Dragoljub Ivkov and art directors Roy Standard and Vladislav Lasic. From a woodcutter's hut in a mist-shrouded forest clearing, where Karnstein has his first confrontation with Weil and his merry band of Bible-bashers, to the cavernous hall of the nobleman's mountaintop fortress, everything about the sets imbued the action with a sense of authenticity, but nowhere more so than in the dining room-entrance hall of Weil's Spartan home. In keeping with its owner's puritan lifestyle, the interior of the house he shares with his wife is stark, almost clinical, especially when juxtaposed with the lavishness of Karnstein's castle: a bare wooden staircase and beams, along with a scrubbed wooden table and bench seating, ensure the focus of any visitor remains on things above, and not the worldly trappings of everyday life.

As with most houses of the period—whether grand or simple—the dining room in Weil's home also serves as its main living and entertaining area. Here is where Weil is first introduced to his headstrong young wards shortly after their arrival—and where he makes plain his opinion of their fine city clothing, which leaves little to the imagination.

It is also here, once their nieces have retired to bed, that Katy warns her husband against antagonizing the powerful Karnstein, whom Weil is determined to bring to heel. The starkness of the room in which they discuss the possible dangers of his intended actions, merely emphasizes the coldness of their own relationship, and the fact that Weil would rather spend time routing out evil with his religious zealot friends than with his own wife. And it is here that Frieda, the more troublesome of the two sisters, eavesdropping on Weil and Katy's conversation from her bedroom above, first hears of the debauched parties at Castle Karnstein, which she determines to visit for herself, with disastrous repercussions for her family.

> Let's say that Mary and Madelaine Collinson, the actual identical-twin actresses of *Twins of Evil*, are nobly endowed enough to keep any red-blooded boy interested in vampirism. The rest of the costumed crew, led by that veteran horror hand, Peter Cushing, as the twins' witch hunting uncle, who chases the fanged Count and his retinue, hardly give *Twins of Evil* a good name.[7]

So, any shortcomings there may have been with the production were not as a result of its visualization. Nor the caliber of its cast, though *New York Times* critic A.H. Weiler's comments regarding Mary and Madeleine Collinson, that the sisters were most likely chosen for their similarity and physical attributes, is probably true. However, with Cushing and Byron—of *Black Narcissus* (1947) fame—as their uncle and aunt, alongside horror veteran Dennis Price as Karnstein's right-hand man Dietrich, there was a level of professionalism amongst the principal cast members that elevated the production.

Released in the U.K. on October 3, 1971, with an X rating—likely due to the sexual emphasis and, even by Hammer's standards, some particularly graphic violence—and distributed by Universal as an R in the U.S. in June 1972, *Twins of Evil* met with mixed reviews. There's no denying, however, that through its evocation of eighteenth century Carpathian mayhem, the film is a wonderfully atmospheric, if slightly bonkers, romp.

You're Next (2011)

Grab anything that might make a good weapon.

Director: Adam Wingard
Written by: Simon Barrett
Starring: Sharni Vinson, Nicholas Tucci, Wendy Glenn, AJ Bowen, Joe Swanberg, Margaret Laney, Amy Seimetz, Ti West, Rob Moran, Barbara Crampton, L.C. Holt, Simon Barrett, Lane Hughes, Larry Fessenden, Kate Lyn Sheil, Calvin Reeder

Paul and Aubrey Davison (Rob Moran and Barbara Crampton) call their four children—and the children's respective partners—to their country mansion to celebrate their wedding anniversary. As the family gathers, sibling rivalries simmer beneath, ready to explode with devastating effect. At least, that is, until some uninvited guests gatecrash the party, hell-bent on making this a night to remember for all the wrong reasons.

> Everybody knows family reunions can be a drag, but even enduring Uncle Roger's blow-by-blow account of growing his prizewinning tubers would be preferable to the fate that awaits the party guests in Adam Wingard's delightful slasher romp.[8]

Jeremy Kay, writing for *The Guardian*, was spot on in his summation of this horror-thriller: Many people hate a family reunion, but seldom would this result in the all-out carnage that occurs here. Just when the modern horror movie appeared in danger of losing its way, with the appeal of the post–*Scream* slasher film fast waning, director Adam Wingard came along and battered the genre back to life (or death) with an adrenalin show which feels like an extension of the break-in scene from Stanley Kubrick's *A Clockwork Orange.*

Reimagining the old premise of a group trapped in a secluded mansion being picked off by unseen assailants using increasingly gruesome methods, the film unfolds like a retelling of Agatha Christie's *And Then There Were None*, but with few of her gentrified British subtleties. Filmed in a stunning mock–Tudor mansion—if Americans do one thing better than the British, it's fake British period architecture—its wood interior, complete with heavy oak furniture and dark paneled rooms, provide the ideal setting for a twist on the classic country house murder mystery, complete with violence intensified for the twenty-first century.

You're Next makes good use of the extended house but one room stands out. Not only setting the scene and tone from which the remaining action will take its cue, the initial gathering in the dining room and subsequent visits to the wood-paneled room reflect the coziness of a family dinner, the comfort of its familiarity belying the darkness to come: As with most families, nothing in this film is as it initially seems.

Apart from a shock pre-credit opening sequence, *You're Next*—like all the best horrors—lulls its viewers into a false sense of security, from which they awake with a jolt, to then sit on the proverbial edge of their seat for the next 90 minutes. It would be unfair to provide much detail about how each member of the Davison family is dispatched, as the various murder methods and their timing in the plot clearly create the film's best shocks. Suffice to say, once the first member of the clan is unexpectedly offed—just after the family has settled down for dinner—things go downhill quickly.

As the house is still very much a work in progress—Paul bought it as a project to occupy his retirement—much of the action takes place in rooms devoid of furnishings. However, the constantly dwindling cast of characters uses the dining room as a place to reconvene between each murder, before heading off again to inevitably meet with some grisly end. The room itself is ideally positioned—just off the hallway, and with large windows looking onto the front driveway—to leave those in it vulnerable to attack, while its sparse furnishings—a simple polished wood dining table and assorted chairs—allow for little or no protection once the deadly siege begins.

This doesn't mean those under attack can't—or don't—fight back, although many family members crumble under pressure and as a result are soon gone. Crampton in particular: As Aubrey, the matriarch, she plays the woman-in-peril character, on which she had built a solid career, to the hilt. One of those present does use ingenuity to resist, giving rise to some of the film's more inventive and cringe-inducing moments. Everything from chairs, used for protection from an avalanche of crossbow bolts—the favorite weapon of destruction throughout the film—to the good old-fashioned knife in the neck for downing your adversary, are deployed to suitable effect. One method for stopping the murderer's entry through a window, involving nothing more sophisticated than strips of wood embedded with nails, is particularly unpleasant, even though viewers can see what is coming long before the victim does.

It's appropriate that the film reaches its climax in the room where it all began. This is where the family initially met and, in a scene typical of many family gatherings, tensions boiled, with the true feelings of those present rising to the surface. It is also where, while hiding in fear, one member overhears a conversation which reveals what has really been going on, before being forced into a final confrontation, with predictably devastating consequences.

The trailer for *You're Next* must be one of the most mesmeric in recent horror cinema. Lou Reed's 1972 hit "Perfect Day" rings out against scenes from the unfolding carnage of the Davisons' disastrous family reunion. The dulcet, dream-like tones of the song stand in stark contrast with, yet perfectly complementing, the events of Wingard's beautifully disturbing shocker.

5

The Kitchen

He added that if she had no other business with him she could return to her duties, and henceforth would be well advised to stay clear of the kitchen.
—*The Cook*, Harry Kressing (1965)

As Conrad—the mysterious new cook in the darkly humorous fantasy novel of the same name by American writer Harry (Ruber) Kressing—warns the Hill family's housekeeper to keep out of his domain, so people, especially in horror films, would be well advised to give kitchens a wide berth. All manner of foul and murderous things take place there, few if any of which have to do with cookery, though many require culinary skills and dexterity with a well-sharpened knife.

Frequently referred to as the heart of a house, the kitchen is much more than a place simply for meal preparation. Often, this is somewhere for families to get together and bond—as Anthony Perkins' Norman Bates did with his long-lost mother in *Psycho II* (1983)—or acquaintances to rekindle dead passions like Susannah York's Cathryn and Hugh Millais' Marcel do, in Robert Altman's exquisite *Images* (1972).

Equally, the kitchen—as Conrad makes clear—can be a place best avoided, as it harbors all sorts of hidden dangers. Like Drew Barrymore's Sidney in *Scream* (1996), who simply wanted some TV nibbles, or Alexandra Dane's unsuspecting Sandy, looking for an illicit snack in the schlocky British potboiler *Corruption* (1968), characters often get more than they bargained for when they enter the kitchen in a house of horror.

Corruption (1968)

No woman will dare go home alone after seeing Corruption. *Therefore no woman will be admitted alone to this super-shocker!*

Don't Go Upstairs!

Director: Robert Hartford-Davis
Written by: Donald Ford and Derek Ford (screenplay)
Starring: Peter Cushing, Sue Lloyd, Noel Trevarthen, Kate O'Mara, David Lodge, Anthony Booth, Wendy Varnals, Billy Murray, Vanessa Howard, Marian Collins (Girl in the Flat, International version), Jan Waters (Girl in the Flat, U.K. version), Phillip Manikum, Alexandra Dane, Valerie Van Ost, Diana Ashley, Marianne Morris (Topless Girl in the Flat, uncredited)

You know when the star of a film states they regret making it that there must be something of interest to it. But when that person is the gentleman of horror himself, Peter Cushing, it makes you want to search out the offending feature if only to confirm his misgivings. Watching the twisted offering that is *Corruption*, you can understand his concerns, as it is one of the most bizarre, brutal and surprisingly unpleasant films he ever made. Not that the premise is bad—think French director Georges Franju's cult chiller *Eyes Without a Face* (1960) transposed to London's Chelsea in the Swinging '60s—or the acting under par—Cushing is supported by hip names of 1960s British cinema such as Sue Lloyd, Kate O'Mara, An-

Stark horror: One of the few films its star, Peter Cushing, claimed to have regretted making, *Corruption* (1968).

5. The Kitchen 73

thony Booth and Valerie Van Ost. Its cinematography is stunning, particularly the scenes filmed at Hope Gap Beach and Cuckmere in East Sussex. Nor is it, for the most part, overtly violent. In fact, large segments of it might be considered even pedestrian by today's standards.

There are key scenes, however—tamer versions of which were filmed for the U.K. and American markets—that have given the film its notorious reputation. Without dwelling on gruesome details—which have to be seen first hand to be fully appreciated—suffice to say that to restore the damaged beauty of his model girlfriend Lynn (Lloyd), eminent surgeon Sir John Rowan (Cushing) requires a constant supply of fresh pituitary glands, obtained by beheading a string of innocent girls whom he picks up and murders along the way. Then, with the pituitary glans and the help of pioneering laser surgery, he manages to fix Lynn's face, temporarily. With each operation, the surgery's restorative effects become less effective, meaning that, with Lynn's constant cajoling, Sir John must turn to ever more desperate methods to obtain an increasing number of life-saving body parts.

Such a far-fetched storyline allows for a veritable orgy of carnage, including a particularly nasty scene in a sleazy prostitute's London flat, and a frenzied attack aboard a train in rural Sussex. Watching these, it is understandable why Cushing had second thoughts about the film, though one can't help but think that he must have realized what he was doing when, scalpel in hand and covered in blood, he sat astride a semi-naked woman, whom he proceeded to carve up with feverish relish.

These scenes might denote the film's more questionable qualities. One scene, however, towards the end of the film, rivals any of the preceding nastiness by its sheer ability to build tension and suspense to a genuinely disturbing level.

Sir John and Lynn's Sussex bolt hole, on England's south coast, which plays host to the film's second half, highlights the overall unpleasantness of the production by juxtaposing the hedonism of cosmopolitan London life, with a setting of deceptively tranquil and bucolic beauty. Though the clifftop cottage is not exactly furnished as one would except of the weekend retreat of a well-to-do metropolitan couple, a place to escape the pressures of the city and let Sir John focus on restoring Lynn's beauty, it nevertheless retains a sense of threadbare grandeur in keeping with the grimy undertones of the rest of the film. The main rooms—bedrooms and lounge, all of which feature intermittently—are not without shabby appeal. However, the somewhat threadbare appearance of the kitchen—where the most gruesome scene of the film's latter half takes place—looks decidedly cardboard, leading the viewer to deduce that the house's down-at-heel appearance was due more to budgetary constraints than any attempt on the part of the filmmakers to recreate rustic charm.

The wonderfully deranged kitchen scene stands out by achieving an interlude of unexpected tension and suspense amongst the rest of the butchery. Having been besieged in the cottage by a thuggish gang (akin to the infamous break-in scene from *A Clockwork Orange*) whose intention is to rob the rich couple—the tables are turned on the thieves in the most unexpected manner. The crazed surgeon has hidden the head of his latest victim in the icebox so, when Sandy (Alexandra Dane), the gang's female member, decides to make a sandwich, the scene is clearly set for some toe-curling culinary delights. The conclusion may be obvious but, in a sequence which builds palpable suspense, director Robert Hartford-Davis has Sandy return to the fridge several times to obtain various ingredients for her snack, before she eventually opens the icebox and removes the severed head, wrapped in plastic. Even then it is some moments before she unwraps it, to be confronted with the face of actress Valerie Van Ost, obscured by clotted blood and matted hair. The hysterical screams of the unfortunate Sandy, who is not seen onscreen again, are enough to wake the dead, as well as goading her friends in the next room into a course of action which can only end in a orgy of violence from which few escape unscathed.

Dane was apparently so disturbed by the realism of the frozen head that she had great difficulty in completing the sandwich scene, as highlighted by David Hanks in his analysis of the film on the *Encyclopaedia of Fantastic Film and Television* website:

> The film's four-week schedule commenced on 10th July 1967, and most scenes were completed quickly. One exception was the discovery of the head in the fridge.... Actress Alexandra Dane was so shocked by the sight of an apparently decapitated head that she became quite distressed on the first take. The crewmen who had the job of stuffing the head with various offals referred to it as "the laughing Japanese shot." Far East audiences enjoyed a lot of gore, apparently.[1]

As Hanks pointed out, the film had limited box office success. "Over a year after its completion, the film premiered at London's Metropole on 21 November 1968, but was replaced after a week by *Carry On Up the Khyber* (1968). On general release from 8 December, *Corruption* was paired with an Alex Cord spaghetti western, *Un minuto per pregare, un instante per morire* [Dead or Alive] (1968)."[2] All the same, watching this forgotten gem of sleazy British horror, one can't deny the power of its uncomfortable and seedy charm.

Images (1972)

> *Who shot off the goddamn gun? Who shot off the goddamn shotgun in the goddamn house?*

5. The Kitchen

Director: Robert Altman
Written by: Robert Altman, Susannah York (book, *In Search of Unicorns*)
Starring: Susannah York, Rene Auberjonois, Marcel Bozzuffi, Hugh Millais, Cathryn Harrison, John Morley, Barbara Bailey (voice on telephone, uncredited)

Cathryn (Susannah York), a young writer on the verge of a breakdown, is convinced that her husband Hugh (Rene Auberjonois) is having an affair, and haunted by visions from her own past relationships. She insists Hugh takes her to their country house to escape the suffocating confines of the city. Once ensconced in their remote retreat and isolated from the world, Cathryn's fragile mental state continues to crumble with catastrophic results.

Images is the perfect example of the psychological horrors popular during the 1960s and early 1970s, often focusing on confused and vulnerable women, as in Hammer's chiller *Taste of Fear* (1961) and Roman Polanski's shocker *Repulsion* (1965). *Images*' magic comes from the way it forces viewers to question not just Cathryn's tenuous grip on reality, but also their own. As various characters, husbands, lovers, even children(!),

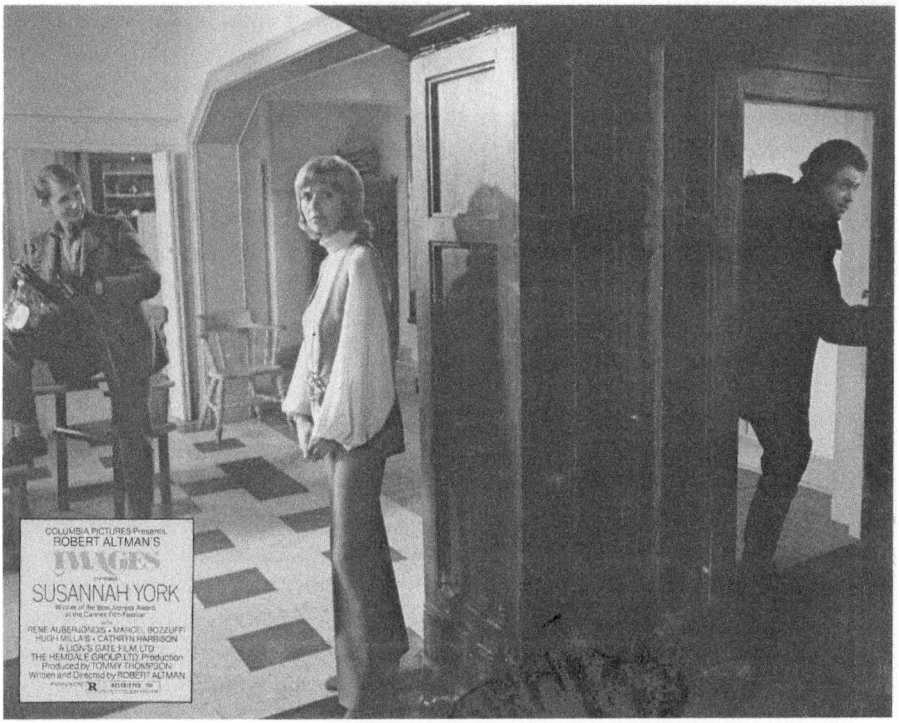

Trouble brewing: (From left) Hugh (Rene Auberjonois), Cathryn (Susannah York) and Marcel (Hugh Millais) play cat and mouse in *Images* (1972).

both past and present, flit through her daily experience, you yourself are forced to query whether who or what you see on the screen is real or imaginary. By the end, you are as bemused—and shocked—as Cathryn herself.

These factors aside, it is undoubtedly the film's visuals which stun viewers. From Cathryn and Hugh's shabby chic, modernistic city mews—think the Lars family's Tatooine farmhouse from *Star Wars: Episode IV—A New Hope* (1977) transposed to some nameless urban jungle—to their country retreat amidst moorland tinted with the wild romanticism of rural Ireland, the film's lack of clarity in relation to specific locations simply adds to its enigmatic feeling, as well as to Cathryn's sense of disjointedness. Many of the interiors where the drama plays out are shot through with varying degrees of calming, sanatorium blandness, and designer shades of rustic off-white, which simply highlight Cathryn's brittle mental state.

Blood forms the main physical embodiment of horror in *Images*. Like the violence, there may not be a lot of it but when it comes—randomly, and when least expected—it does so in great throbbing, ruby red floods, oozing stickily across the surface of a dark leather sofa, or playing at the edges and seeping into a light-colored shag-pile carpet. At another point, after Hugh inadvertently injures his hand with his shotgun while hunting, he races into the house to douse it beneath the kitchen's cold water tap. The white tiled walls above the sink and the cool paleness of the surrounding work surfaces form the perfect backdrop to emphasize the richness of the blood which spurts freely from his butchered appendage. Later, when Cathryn is cleaning the blood-smeared walls, her efforts are emphasized by a lone bottle of tomato sauce on a bench, its redness in stark contrast to the cool, whitewashed beauty of a room which stands at the center of the proceedings.

Like the kitchen of many homes, the one in Cathryn and Hugh's rustic idyll is the room where life happens. The lounge-cum-dining room may be where they welcome and entertain their guests, including their amorous neighbor Marcel (Hugh Millais) and his daughter Susannah (Cathryn Harrison), but the kitchen is where they quarrel and laugh, and where Cathryn fends off the unwanted advances of both Marcel and Rene (Marcel Bozzuffi), her late first husband, who periodically materializes to question her sanity and morals. Separated from it by a bleached wood serving hatch, the kitchen sits apart from the lounge, framed like a stage waiting for the next grisly event from Cathryn's life—both imaginary and real—to play out in full-blooded glory.

Hugh is a photographer who likes to bring his work into the house. Severed deer heads sit majestically on the scrubbed dining table, amongst crisp autumn leaves which scurry across the kitchen floor in the slightest breeze through an open door. An array of sharpened knives hangs on the wall above the sink, focused on at one point as if to suggest some twisted use later in the film. Pantries, staircases and secret alcoves lead from this horror nerve center, all playing host at various intervals to Cathryn's unfolding marital melodrama.

The movie was shot on location in County Wicklow; the wildness of the rugged Irish landscape was well captured by Hungarian cinematographer Vilmos Zsigmond, its bleakness mirroring perfectly Cathryn's feelings of isolation. The script by Altman, along with the book *In Search of Unicorns* which Cathryn writes throughout the film—and which York herself penned in real life—reinforces this, carrying her through a multitude of feelings and emotions towards her eventual mental disintegration.

Images was heaped with praise by the film industry; York won the Best Actress award at the 25th Cannes Film Festival. Altman was nominated for the prestigious Golden Palm at the same event, while composer John Williams received an Oscar nomination for the minimalistic score. However, it got mixed reactions from the press and public. Despite a positive assessment and a three-star review from critic Roger Ebert, who described it as an "intelligently constructed and spectacularly well-photographed film" and something that "Altman admirers should make a point of seeing,"[3] *Images* received a limited theatrical release in both America and the U.K. before virtually disappearing from sight. Which is a shame as both general film lovers, and more specifically those with a palate for subtle horror, have been deprived of a delightfully unhinged and broody gem of tasteful terror.

Poltergeist (1982)

They're here.

Director: Tobe Hooper
Written by: Steven Spielberg, Michael Grais and Mark Victor (screenplay), Steven Spielberg (story), James Khan (novel, uncredited)
Starring: Craig T. Nelson, JoBeth Williams, Beatrice Straight, Dominique Dunne, Oliver Robins, Heather O'Rourke, Zelda Rubinstein, James Karen, Martin Casella, Richard Lawson

The Freelings are like any other American suburban family: Steven (Craig T. Nelson), Diane (JoBeth Williams) and their kids Dana (Dominique Dunne), Robbie (Oliver Robins) and Carol Anne (Heather O'Rourke) live in just another rambling, nondescript California housing estate.

At least until they discover that their home has been built on the site of an ancient Indian burial site, and the spirits of those interred there aren't happy at being disturbed. It's then that the fun starts.

So many stories grow up around some films that it becomes hard to separate fact from fiction. Take, for instance, those concerning the cult horror *Poltergeist*, where the debate about who really directed it has raged for years. Tobe Hooper may be listed on the credits as the man in charge, but there is thought to be more than a grain of truth to suggestions that Steven Spielberg was more heavily involved than as producer and writer on the production. In *Film Review*, Charles Bacon raved that having Hooper as director should alert audiences to "the awesome thrills in store" as "Hooper, you will recall, scared the skin off your flesh with *The Texas Chain Saw Massacre*."[4] Watching the film, however, the chills are clearly more akin to Spielberg's sanitized take on horror *à la Jaws (1975)*, than the Southern boiled, gut-wrenching terror for which Hooper was better known.

Then there are the tragic deaths of two of the film's stars: Dominique Dunne and Heather O'Rourke both died when they were little more than children, and their deaths gave rise to endless theories about the film's "curse." When O'Rourke died of cardiopulmonary arrest and intestinal stenosis in 1988 at age 12, the three films for which she was best known comprised the *Poltergeist* trilogy.

Such things aside, there is no denying the original film in the series is an iconic encapsulation of 1980s Hollywood cinema as well as contemporary American pop culture, from the sprawling estate where the Freeling family lives—each home with its own quirky individualism, yet strangely identical to all the others in the housing development—to the endless array of toys littering Robbie and Carol Anne's bedroom, which are merchandising spinoffs for every major movie franchise from the late 1970s and early 1980s.

The film's first main scene is kitchen-based, seeing the Freelings partaking in the strange modern ceremony of a family breakfast on the go—a bowl piled high with additive-loaded cereal, a gulp of reheated coffee and a slice of toast grabbed as you head out the door. Following this—as she and the young Carol Anne are left behind—Diane admonishes her daughter for staring at the static screen on the television, telling her not to sit and watch it as it will ruin her eyes, before changing the channel to an infinitely more damaging vision of soldiers blowing each other to pieces in a war film. That evening, Diane—desperate to show her husband the tricks of the mischievous spirits which she and Carol Anne have discovered that day—tries to placate her bored child's pleas of hunger, with the promise of a visit to that mecca of fast-food consumerism, Pizza Hut.

Happy families: (Clockwise from lower left) Oliver Robins, Dominique Dunne, Craig T. Nelson, JoBeth Williams and Heather O'Rourke with Rip (the dog), are all smiles in a publicity still for *Poltergeist* (1982).

Most of the film's major set-piece spectaculars—such as Robbie being digested by a possessed garden tree, and Carol Anne's subsequent abduction by the rabid spirits which haunt their home—lose much of their unpleasantness thanks to their sheer magnitude and special effects polish. The scenes in the kitchen, most of which happen near the beginning of the manifestations, are, on the other hand, shocking by their apparent harmlessness, emphasized by the simplicity of the setting. At first the spirits seem friendly, their presence only made obvious by their apparently innocent pranks, which take place against a background of pale pine cupboards and work surfaces in the Freelings' up-to-the-minute kitchen. Once the spirits begin to perform, the room seems to magically expand in height and length, to allow for a spectacular balancing act where the kitchen chairs are stacked precariously on the table, reaching towards the ceiling. Later Carol Anne—sitting cross-legged and complete with American football helmet—is propelled at speed by the spirits along the length of the kitchen floor, much to Diane's delight and Steve's shock.

It is also in the kitchen's reassuring surroundings where members of the family—after Carol Anne's abduction—break down and reveal everything about their ordeal to the group of initially skeptical, then terrified, college psychics, led by Dr. Lesh (Beatrice Straight), investigating the case. Watching the film, it seems appropriate that these moments of almost introspective calm before the storm, should take place within a room generally accepted as the heart of the home. Only later—after the arrival of the feisty spiritualist Tangina Barrons (Zelda Rubinstein), called upon to get things under control—does the action really move into the main house. Its cluttered appearance is more suitable for the fire-and-brimstone finale which eventually engulfs the Freelings' home.

The early kitchen scenes, which highlight the beginning of the spirits' invasion of the Freeling family and their home, also emphasize some different though no less damaging horrors that were becoming pre-eminent in everyday culture and life at the time, namely the power of television, commercialism and the increasing disintegration of the central family unit. *Poltergeist* may now be considered as marking the high point of the public's love affair with the horror blockbuster—films with well-crafted, high-octane shocks, but little else—that started in the 1970s with the likes of *Jaws* (1975) and *Halloween* (1978) before culminating in Wes Craven's *Scream* franchise two decades later. What set it apart from its contemporaries were its subtler and frequently more menacing messages of the factors which threatened all those watching, and which continue to do so to this day.

Psycho II (1983)

It's 22 years later, and Norman Bates is coming home.

Director: Richard Franklin
Written by: Tom Holland, Robert Bloch (characters)
Starring: Anthony Perkins, Vera Miles, Meg Tilly, Robert Loggia, Dennis Franz, Hugh Gillin, Claudia Bryar, Robert Alan Browne, Ben Hartigan, Lee Garlington, Tim Maier, Jill Carroll, Chris Hendrie, Tom Holland, Virginia Gregg (Norma Bates' voice, uncredited)

5. The Kitchen

Over 20 years have passed since Norman Bates (Anthony Perkins) was put away for the deaths of several people, whom he killed while under the influence of his dead mother Norma. Deemed safe by the authorities, Norman is released and returns home to the mansion overlooking the isolated Bates Motel, to resume management of the business. However, once again under the spell of the house, Norman's fragile mental state begins to deteriorate. Then the murders start.

How do you make a sequel to a film as iconic as Alfred Hitchcock's *Psycho* (1960)? The answer is, with difficulty. Which is perhaps part of the reason why it took 23 years before Universal brought Anthony Perkins home to the house which had made him a star and which, to a greater or lesser degree, overshadowed his career.

It is debatable as to whether revisiting the house was wise. Becoming increasingly inferior with each successive outing—there have been at least four to date, as well as a questionable remake of the original and, surprisingly, an effective television spin-off—the first sequel is the best, though even it isn't a patch on Hitchcock's masterpiece. In an interview with *Film Review* magazine in October 1983, Anthony Perkins, probably the only person, other than Hitchcock, in a position to comment with any

Kitchen sink drama: Mary Loomis (Meg Tilly) is suspicious when Norman Bates (Anthony Perkins) claims to be a reformed character in *Psycho II* (1983).

authority, believed that *Psycho II* was a worthy successor. "Hitchcock was brilliant. But I do feel we haven't let him down. I think the people who liked *Psycho* are going to enjoy this one also. It has all the ingredients. It has a fine, original story and it is discreet and fair."[5]

Though the film contains its fair share of unpleasantness—a particularly gruesome scene towards the climax is enough to rival anything seen in the original—the lasting horror here is, like in its predecessor, psychological. Cutting, stabbing and slicing your way through a line of unfortunate victims, may be disturbing when you're in the moment, but it's Norman's inner neurosis which really plays mind games with the viewer.

The best of these scenes take place in the kitchen of the Bates family home—that great icon of American pop culture which, according to Hitchcock, was based on the house from Edward Hopper's 1925 painting "The House by the Railroad."[6] Wisely, the filmmakers changed little about the original house and motel. *Psycho*'s gothic Victorian monstrosity became as much part of the *Psycho* mythology as Perkins' portrayal of the unhinged Norman Bates, as instantly recognizable to film lovers as the Vandamm House from *North by Northwest* (1959) and the Freeling home from *Poltergeist* (1982). Indeed, the style and feel of the film, captured by director Richard Franklin and cinematographer Dean Cundey, perfectly evokes that of its predecessor, to the extent that the sequel feels like a straight continuation of the story. In his review, critic Simon Button went as far as to suggest that Hitchcock would have approved of the duo's work. "Together with a Louma Crane they have turned out a movie of breathtaking style and bravura camerawork which the master would have been well-proud of."[7]

As in *Psycho*, the Bates mansion is a truly ominous house of horrors. Set high on a hill, like some great brooding bird of prey, the house has an unsettling appearance, echoed throughout the rooms inside, except perhaps the kitchen. Barely seen in *Psycho*—where the real horrors lay hidden in the cellar—the kitchen this time round truly becomes the center of the house. Many of the main characters—Lila and Mary Loomis (Vera Miles and Meg Tilly), Dr. Bill Raymond (Robert Loggia), Sheriff Hunt (Hugh Gillin) and his deputy and Emma Spool (Claudia Bryar)—either pass through the room briefly, or stay longer to confront Norman on his home turf. Despite being sparsely furnished and stocked only with the bare essentials (the house remained unoccupied for most of Norman's incarceration), the room nonetheless retains a comfortable and welcoming air, in contrast to the heavy wood and Victorian reserve of the other rooms.

Other rooms in the house offer settings for several more gruesome moments: The cellar, hall and main staircase, as in the original film, are locations for some particularly nasty scenes. However, the kitchen is where the viewer discovers the real Norman and where, in more informal surroundings, he comes closest to letting his guard down. As in many homes, visitors often pay a call at the kitchen door of the Bates house, as opposed to the formal front entrance, while the room itself offers a relaxed environment where guests can unwind. The kitchen is where Norman's psychiatrist, Dr. Raymond, leaves Norman, having accompanied him to the house, reassured that the fragile man is happy to be back home. Here it is, after taking up Norman's invitation to stay, that Mary—Norman's colleague from the local diner where he finds employment—unwittingly confronts him with a kitchen knife that Norman has conveniently hidden at the back of a drawer. This dramatic encounter allows for plenty of facial distortion and mental anguish on Norman's part, as the knife awakens memories of his traumatic past.

The film contains twists and shocks aplenty, enough to keep horror hounds happy, including interesting developments on the mother-child relationship from the first film, mirrored here in that between Mary and her mother—who turns out to be Lila Loomis from *Psycho*. Aptly the film ends—in the kitchen—with Norman discovering the identity of his real mother, before putting an end to her once and for all—in graphically hard-hitting fashion—then placing her body in the chair by her bedroom window, so she can keep a watchful eye on her devoted son and beloved motel.

Scream (1996)

> *No*, you *listen to me, you little bitch! You hang up on me again and I'll cut you like a fish!*

Director: Wes Craven
Written by: Kevin Williamson
Starring: Drew Barrymore, Roger Jackson, Kevin Patrick Walls, David Booth, Carla Hatley, Neve Campbell, Courteney Cox, David Arquette, Skeet Ulrich, Rose McGowan, Liev Schreiber, Linda Blair, Henry Winkler, Wes Craven

Alfred Hitchcock was to blame. Before his genre-defining chiller *Psycho*, it was virtually unheard of to kill off your main star at all, let alone only a third of the way into the action. Even more so when the star in question was female, and of the caliber of Janet Leigh. But that, of course, is just what he did, an audacious move that catapulted Leigh to movie immortality.

Jump forward several decades and another director took a leaf from Hitchcock's script, but upped the ante. Like cinema's master of menace, filmmaker Wes Craven had made a successful career out of keeping audiences on the edge of their seats for over 20 years with terror classics like *The Last House on the Left* (1972) and *The Hills Have Eyes* (1977). Then in 1984 he dreamed up (literally) *A Nightmare on Elm Street* and its archetypal anti-hero character, Freddy Krueger, and the rest, as they say, is history.

Even the best of Hollywood's filmmakers—as Hitchcock would have testified—are only as good as their last hit, and by the mid–1990s Craven's star was losing its box office luster. Always the king of re-invention, he took the directorial reins of a new shocker, which rejuvenated the horror genre and spawned a slew of sequels, as well as a seemingly endless wave of copycat teens-in-peril slasher films for a whole new generation of teenage fright fans.

If imitation *is* the sincerest form of flattery, then Craven and writer Kevin Williamson's razor-sharp homage to the golden age of the late 1970s, early '80s teenage slasher film was a veritable love fest for all Jason, Michael and Freddy fans. It also worked so wonderfully because, like all the best horror, it had a comic undertone, retaining the sense that it never took itself too seriously, as critic Jeff Gordinier pointed out:

> Poised on the knife edge between parody and homage, Wes Craven's thriller is an ingeniously unsettling tribute to the splatterific teen horror films of the '80s. The characters have been raised on endless VCR replays of those same films. And so the appearance of a psycho in their midst becomes a case of life imitating schlock. The killer's mask suggests a plastic version of Edvard Munch's "The Scream," and it has the eerie effect of reflecting the audience's—as well as the victim's—fear right back at it.[8]

Scream initially launched to little hype. But soon the film, with its slick mix of sick murders and referential darker-than-dark black humor, grabbed the imagination of cinema-goers and became the sleeper hit of 1997. Another aspect, which quickly became a highlight of the continuing series, was the use of Hitchcock's shock tactic of killing off one of the film's biggest stars early on, though Craven and Williamson went one better and did away with them even before the opening credits. Top billing may have gone to David Arquette, Neve Campbell and Courteney Cox as the poor unfortunates who have to deal with the murderous onslaught which takes over their town, but it was the prolonged and graphic attack on Drew Barrymore in the kitchen of her family's isolated, sprawling home, and her subsequent murder in the garden within only a few feet of her unwitting parents, which kept everyone talking.

Though Casey is eventually finished off in the garden—with a clever twist resulting in her mother (who has just returned from a night out) hearing the last gasps of life from her daughter over the phone—it is in the kitchen where the main action originates and plays out. It's here where we first meet Casey, preparing popcorn as she settles down for a night in front of the TV, as well as where she first speaks to her killer on the telephone and finds a knife with which to protect herself.

Barrymore's death scene utilized elements which had been seen in countless horror films—alone in a big house, crank phone calls, a masked killer—but combined them in a punchy manner and at such breakneck pace, that they appeared fresh, clever and above all scary. What's worse than being terrorized by an unseen assailant, seeing a loved one murdered before your eyes, as happens with Casey's boyfriend Steve (Kevin Patrick Walls), and then being killed yourself only a breath away from possible safety? As with the most effective chillers, the real horror in the opening sequence of *Scream* comes from the fact that it plays out in familiar surroundings and an environment that you, the viewer, can relate to. We may not all live in the luxurious surroundings of the Beckers' family home, but their house is sufficiently recognizable that the viewer feels safe: a sprawling country house, standing amongst corn fields, far enough removed from the main road to provide privacy, yet not so far that the inhabitants feel cut off from civilization. The open plan design of the house—rooms lead into others without the restriction of walls, while floor-to-ceiling windows reveal everything to the outside world—provides Casey with few places to hide from her would-be killer, as well as providing a virtually obstacle-free interior for the ensuing chase.

Sorry, wrong number: Casey Becker (Drew Barrymore) and a prank caller making small talk in *Scream* (1996).

Barrymore comes from a long line of horror thespians—her grandfather was Hollywood idol John Barrymore and her great-uncle Lionel Barrymore was the star of such sinister classics as *Mark of the Vampire* (1935) and *The Devil-Doll* (1936). However, the Tinseltown princess, probably best known as the cute little Gertie from *E.T.* (1982), who has starred in dozens of films during a long and storied career—including several cult horror movies—looked destined to end up like so many other troubled Hollywood kids, washed up and burned out before she even hit her twenties. Her speedy dispatch at the beginning of *Scream* rescued her, bringing her to public attention again and reaffirming her as a major adult star for decades to come. Casey's murder within the film's first ten minutes not only ensured Barrymore's status as a horror legend, but also set the pattern for subsequent films in the series, with a major guest star being killed during the pre-credits sequence, among them Jada Pinkett Smith in *Scream 2* (1997), Liev Schreiber and Kelly Rutherford in *Scream 3* (2000) and Aimee Teegarden and Britt Robertson in *Scream 4* (2011).

6

The Cellar

He forced his legs to carry him down the steps, and when he had cleared the roof overhang he shone his light across the visible cellar, which took an L-turn thirty feet further up and went off God knew where.

—*'Salem's Lot*, Stephen King (1975)

What is it about the cellar of a house that elicits such strong feelings of discomfort amongst otherwise rational, levelheaded people? Most of us—like Hank, the odd-job man who visits the room at the bottom of the disreputable Marsten House in Stephen King's *'Salem's Lot*—want to get any business we have there over and done with so we can leave as quickly as possible.

Perhaps it's the sense of removal from the real world that unsettles us. For, whether used to store mundane things like coal or wine, or something more menacing such as the mysterious contents of the spanking new freezer in Amicus' terror anthology *Asylum* (1972), the room at the bottom of the house always harbors an air of abandonment. Most times, of course, the hidden horrors are mere figments of our over-fertile imaginations. Occasionally however—like the unfortunate Jessica Van Helsing, played by Joanna Lumley in Hammer's *The Satanic Rites of Dracula* (1973)—what we discover there is worse than we feared, simply reinforcing the cellar's forbidding reputation.

Psycho (1960)

A boy's best friend is his mother.

Director: Alfred Hitchcock
Written by: Joseph Stefano (screenplay), Robert Bloch (based on the novel by)
Starring: Anthony Perkins, Vera Miles, John Gavin, Janet Leigh, Martin Balsam, John McIntire, Simon Oakland, Frank Albertson, Patricia Hitchcock, Vaughn Taylor, Lurene Tuttle, John Anderson, Mort Mills

It's difficult if not impossible to make a new comment on one of the most iconic films in cinema history. Whatever new nugget of information you think you've uncovered about *Psycho* has probably been discussed before. As a result, when focusing on the rooms of one of the world's most instantly recognizable dwellings, it would be easy to fall for the obvious. However, though the bathroom of Room 1 of the Bates Motel—which, technically speaking, isn't part of the house—usually springs to mind, the rooms in the house itself are equally disturbing.

As with much of Hitchcock's work, *Psycho* is a feast for the senses. Shot in black and white, the film utilizes odd angles and snappy editing to creative effect, an approach which played in the film's favor upon its release, as critic Jack Harrison highlighted in his *Hollywood Reporter* review (June 17, 1960):

> The film opens with a typical Hitchcock touch, a long slow pan shot, over the town of Phoenix, Arizona, swinging down to a hotel window to reveal a torrid love scene typical of the French "new wave" school. The main story is laid against the background of an isolated motel and an adjoining eerie mansion. As in all Hitchcock films, the camera effects and explorations here are a vital and exciting element, establishing a weird realistic quality, sharpening the terror, building the suspense.[1]

Like a portal to a lost era, *Psycho*'s gothic mansion which sits, brooding, on the hilltop, drips with heavy Victoriana: any inch not housing some antique knick-knack is covered in musty velvet or brocade. The second-floor bedroom of Mrs. Bates, in all its regal splendor, is glimpsed momentarily as Lila Crane (Vera Miles) searches for the old lady in the hope of finding some clues to the whereabouts of her own missing sister Marion (Janet Leigh). In the sequels, other areas of the house—the kitchen, bathroom, attic—are revealed, each playing a significant role in the unfolding saga of Norman Bates (Anthony Perkins) and his troubled family history.

In the original film, though, one other room stands out from the rest, creating a climax second only to the infamous shower scene in its ability to startle the unsuspecting viewer. Though the cellar scene, where Lila eventually discovers the grisly secret of the Bates mansion, relies heavily on viewers not guessing what is really sitting in the armchair in the center of the room, the power of the eventual revelation retains its power to shock even in successive viewings.

Just as earlier the bathroom seemed tailor-made for the murder of a vulnerable woman caught with her guard down, so the cellar is the perfect setting to house the rotting corpse of Mrs. Bates. Presumably it has spent most of its time ensconced in the dead woman's bedroom; when her loving son hides his mother's body in the cellar, its new abode seems much more appropriate. Dry and tidy—it's referred to at one point as a fruit cellar—the room's dusty appearance, lit with a single, bare light bulb, is more tomb-like than the warm, comfortable rooms above. Approached by a broad flight of stairs directly beneath the house's main staircase, the cellar's stark appearance, with bare walls and stone floor, clearly used as little more than a place to store fuel and bric-a-brac, sits in stark contrast to the living rooms above.

Until Lila enters the cellar—more from necessity than choice—the viewer is as in the dark as Lila about what lies hidden there. Lila goes to the house to speak with Mrs. Bates, while Marion's boyfriend Sam (John Gavin), who's accompanied her to the motel, distracts Norman. Realizing something's wrong, Norman overpowers Sam before returning to the house where, in a panic, Lila hides in the one place she thinks is safe, the cellar. This culminates a scene which ratchets the tension to the limit. The viewers know something is waiting down there. They also know that Norman is fully aware Lila has gone there: He hesitates on the way up the main stairs, sensing Lila on the flight below, before going to his mother's room to dress in her clothes. Even so, the double whammy (Lila swiveling the chair in the center of the cellar to discover Mrs. Bates' mummified body, followed immediately by Norman's appearance in the doorway in full mother mode, knife poised for the kill) is enough to scare anyone. Despite Sam arriving just in time to save Lila from the same fate as her sister, there is a split second, in the dimly lit room, where viewers share the defenseless woman's surprise and alarm.

The cellar features prominently in the film's sequel, *Psycho II* (1983). Though Lila manages to survive the terrors of *Psycho*, in a strange twist of fate the cellar from which she barely escapes is the very same room where she meets her own end over 20 years later. It also allows for a moment of poetic justice in *Psycho II*, when Norman becomes accidentally trapped in the attic of the house, mirroring his placing of his mother's body in the cellar at the opposite end of the house in the original film.

It never ceases to surprise when, with the benefit of time, you read a critic's thoughts on a film's original release. In his review of *Psycho* for the September 1960 issue of *films and filming* magazine, commentator Peter Baker was, let's say, a little less than complimentary about the film now considered by many as a classic: "The British Censor has improved on the film by cutting drastically a nauseating bathroom murder. Because these violent, twisted trappings are not the stuff that Hitch is blessed with the talent to give us."[2]

Perhaps one should be grateful. As a result, the authorities likely didn't touch the subtler cellar scene, which remains one of horror cinema's most effective surprise endings.

The Pit and the Pendulum (1961)

> *And now, my dear Nicholas, I have you exactly as I want you—helpless.*

Director: Roger Corman
Written by: Richard Matheson (screenplay), Edgar Allan Poe (based on the story by)
Starring: Vincent Price, John Kerr, Barbara Steele, Luana Anders, Antony Carbone, Patrick Westwood, Lynette Bernay, Larry Turner, Mary Menzies, Charles Victor, Randee Lynne Jensen

The Pit and the Pendulum, the second of director Roger Corman's Poe film adaptations for American International Pictures, based loosely on the horror stories of Edgar Allan Poe, is considered by many the best in the series. Watching this exercise in over-the-top, gothic melodrama, one can understand why: The filmmaker and Vincent Price, his bad boy of choice, hold nothing back in a tale of murder and madness set in a castle on the Spanish coast. As writer John Stanley highlighted in his 1994 book *Crea-*

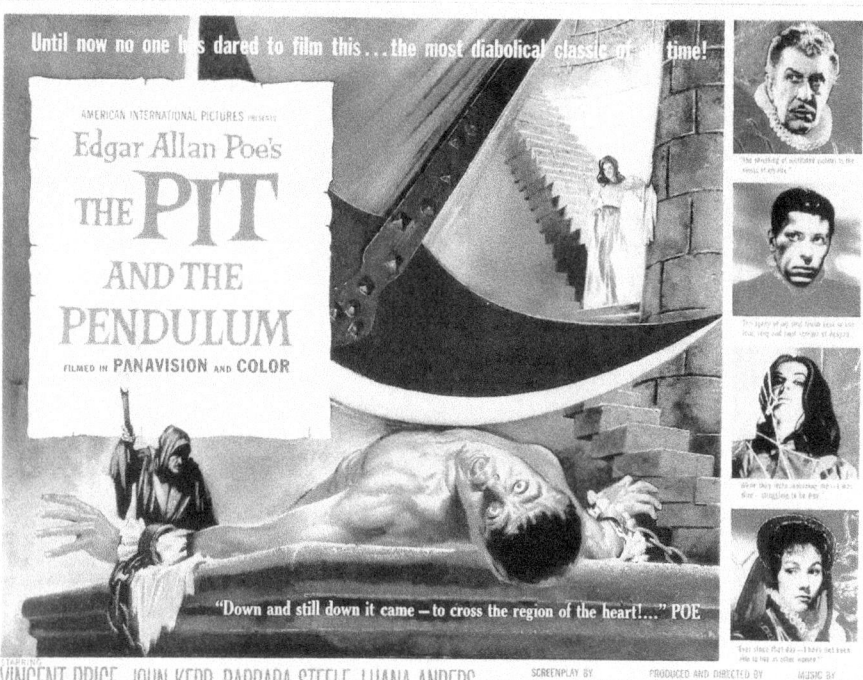

Depths of despair: cutting-edge horror in a nightmarish poster for director Roger Corman's 1961 version of Edgar Allan Poe's *The Pit and the Pendulum*.

6. The Cellar

ture Features Movie Guide Strikes Again, everything came together in a mad confection of on-screen grisliness.

> Excellent adaptation of Edgar Allan Poe's tale starring Vincent Price, but Poe's narrow storyline about a prisoner tortured by a razor-edged pendulum swinging closer and closer to his restrained body has been expanded by Richard Matheson into a Gothic masterpiece of horror.... Producer-director Roger Corman was at his inspired height making this AIP masterwork.[3]

Many of Poe's short stories, such as the one from which Corman took his inspiration for *The Pit and the Pendulum*, dealt with real psychological horrors as opposed to the make-believe. As a result, the terrors of Corman's on-screen visualizations—here put into words by prolific scripter of horror, Richard Matheson—appear much more realistic. Based around the mental disintegration of Spanish nobleman Nicholas Medina (Price), driven to the point of madness by his supposedly dead wife Elizabeth (Barbara Steele) and her lover Dr. Leon (Antony Carbone), *The Pit and the Pendulum* drowns in half-seen suggestions which may or may not be real.

Francis Barnard (John Kerr) arrives at the castle of Nicholas, the husband of his late sister Elizabeth, to investigate her suspicious death. A series of mysterious events culminates in a chilling battle between the two men, ending in tragedy in the catacombs deep beneath the ancient home of the Medina family.

Much of the film, taken up with melodramatic, domestic repartee between the central characters, takes place in a few rooms of the main castle. However, although the cellars beneath, which expand into a fathomless subterranean torture chamber, feature mostly towards the end of the film, when the action is transported below, the warmer, more hospitable air of upstairs soon dissipates and a chilled and foreboding atmosphere takes hold.

What self-respecting medieval fortress—especially one owned by a chief perpetrator of the Spanish Inquisition, as Nicholas' father Sebastian Medina was—would be complete without a fully equipped torture chamber? Approached by way of great, studded wooden doors and steep flights of stone steps, the cellars of Castle Medina are in reality a series of interconnecting rooms, each home to increasingly disturbing nightmares. Every conceivable medieval torture device, from the rack to the Iron Maiden, as well as ever-ready braziers of hot coals and wall-mounted manacles, await the visitor to this underground warren of despair. Bare stone walls and flagged floors as well as jail-like rooms with iron doors have, one imagines, played host to numerous unfortunate apostates over the years.

Down here, behind a stone wall, Nicholas entombed the body of his wife whom he believed—on the advice of Charles—to be dead. She's not; in fact, with the help of Charles, she's the perpetrator of a series of bizarre events designed to send Nicholas mad. But suspense arising from a game of detection is not the aim of the film. Instead, this is a platform designed to showcase Price's skills as a solo artist stealing, as he does, virtually every scene he's in with facial contortions that reveal the torment of the guilt-ridden man within.

Neither is it a film which relies on gory delights, instead using suspense to ratchet up the tension during an effective edge-of-the-seat climax. Nicholas, completely deranged after having killed Charles, has chained his brother-in-law Francis beneath a swinging pendulum with a razor sharp blade which edges ever closer to the torso of the prostrate man. It is a close shave (literally) for Francis: Lying on an altar-like island in the middle of a chamber, his imminent demise is watched by murals of hooded inquisition priests, the whole presided over by a raving Nicholas, who swings on the rope which brings the pendulum of death ever nearer to Francis' shuddering body.

Needless to say, Francis survives by a hair's breadth, saved by Nicholas' sister Catherine (Luana Anders) and his servant Bartolome (Charles Victor)—though not before Francis, and the viewer, is exposed to a fantastical environment enough to send even the most grounded individual mad. In a similar way to what Hammer was doing at the same time, Corman and his regular collaborator, art director Daniel Haller, made what were in fact very basic sets, appear larger than life on the screen. As film historian Carlos Clarens pointed out, clever camera angles and a lot of imagination went a long way in Corman's fantasy world:

> Constrained by larger but still limited budgets, the director has extracted the last ounce of effect from Daniel Haller's eye-deceivingly vast but far from spacious sets by his use of free camera movements. And with [cinematographer Floyd Crosby's] assistance, he has exploited to their limit the possibilities of Pathécolor, obtaining sensuously sepulchral tones of blue, puce, green and mauve.[4]

Asylum (1972)

Rest in pieces.

Director: Roy Ward Baker
Written by: Robert Bloch
Starring: Richard Todd, Sylvia Syms, Barbara Parkins, Robert Powell, Patrick Magee, Herbert Lom, Geoffrey Bayldon, Sylvia Marriott, Peter Cushing, Britt Ekland, Megs Jenkins

"To the maker of horror films, humor can be a useful tool. By including a few intentional 'jokes,' he can relax the audience so that when the climactic shock comes, the desired effect is improved."[5]

6. The Cellar

I have a surprise for you: Walter (Richard Todd) gives Ruth (Sylvia Syms) the chop in *Asylum* (1972).

Humor is difficult to get right, especially in the field of horror. Added unnecessarily (as was often the case with the addition of slapstick in genre films from the 1930s and 1940s), it slows the pace, reducing proceedings to farce. But used sparingly and in its darkest form, it can work, as critic Alex Stuart's account of Amicus' *Asylum* highlights. Sharp, cleverly spicing a situation with sophisticated savoir-faire, it releases tension, leaving the viewer off-guard with regard to the horrors to come.

The perfect use of dry, black humor comes in the story "Frozen Fear" from *Asylum*, the film which marked the apotheosis of Amicus' horror anthologies, written by Robert Bloch, author of *Psycho*, and master of the short, sharp shock. Its chilling opening tale revolves around the nefarious plans of cheating husband Walter (Richard Todd) and his young lover Bonnie (Barbara Parkins) to get rid of his rich wife Ruth (Sylvia Syms). The initial confrontation between the warring spouses (when Ruth returns in the late afternoon, to find Walter already home and apparently well-oiled) and the ensuing irrevocable breakdown of their marriage condensed into five minutes of screen time, is bliss to behold.

> **RUTH:** Walter. You're home early.
> **WALTER:** I didn't get into town today.
> **RUTH:** But you did get into the brandy.
> **WALTER:** This happens to be my first drink.
> **RUTH:** Not your last, I'm sure.

As months of frustration and pent-up emotions pour out in a tirade of accusations and caustic putdowns, the scene is set for the chilling denouement to the couple's unhappy union, as the action spills from the lounge to the cellar of their house.

Clever asides peppering the dialogue lifted many of Amicus' films above the ordinary. In "Frozen Fear," Walter's sardonic concern when warning Ruth to "mind the steps" as she unwittingly descends into the cellar to her approaching death is pure paronomasial magic.

In many ways "Frozen Fear" shouldn't work, either as a story or in its onscreen execution. Amongst the main components of good horror, especially in the medium of film, is the element of surprise. Eliminate that and you've lost one of its most appealing qualities. From the outset here, we are aware of exactly what is about to happen (at least, in theory). The fact you know something nasty awaits Ruth on her return home adds an extra frisson of excitement to the viewing experience.

It opens with a phone conversation between Walter and Bonnie, and you immediately know they're planning to kill Ruth and that it's going to be gruesome. Despite—or maybe in spite of—this, the segment remains one of the film's best. Watching the scenario unfold, you can't help but hold your breath. Will Walter have a (highly unlikely) change of heart at the last minute? Can Ruth turn the tables on her husband and his scheming paramour? Mmm, well … we'll see. When the remarkable shock sequence occurs—Walter cuts Ruth down to size in the cellar, then packs her remains into a newly installed fridge-freezer, before falling victim to her reanimated corpse—it creates a genuinely unexpected climax to the couple's tense relationship.

Bonnie's subsequent discovery of the horrors in the cellar—at the cost of her beauty—is given a cartoon quality which dilutes the sharpness of what's gone before. Though heavy with subtle irony, the sight of Ruth's various body parts encased in brown paper and string lumbering towards the hysterical Bonnie, who ineffectually brandishes the same axe Walter used to dispatch Ruth, appears risible in the light of the earlier sharp humor.

The secret to the success of Amicus' compendium horror films was the environments in which they took place. Playing out in everyday settings to which the viewer could relate, made the horrific situations all the more believable. It is in "Frozen Fear"'s on-screen depiction however that another apparent anomaly is felt, particularly where the cellar is concerned. An air of orderliness fits perfectly, of course, with the main body of Walter and Ruth's house. This is the comfortable home of an affluent couple—Walter clearly doesn't have to work; as Ruth snidely reminds him, he is "happy to live off my money." Art director Tony Curtis—responsible in the 1970s for the look of an endless parade of British shockers including *I Monster* (1971) and *Madhouse* (1974)—went to town on the look of "Frozen Fear," with a colorful mix of kitschy glass, plastic and chrome statement pieces so typical of the era.

The real difficulty occurs when the action transfers to the cellar, where what should potentially be the film's most gruesome scene plays out. With ample space for a sink, tools, disused garden implements and, of course, the gleaming new freezer, the expansive underground room looks like the cellar of any modern suburban home—the room where everyone hides their junk. You can't help feeling, though, that it should suffer some disruption when Walter murders his wife. If you do a hatchet job on someone—quite literally in Walter and Ruth's case—surely you or the room, or both, will show some signs of blood, if only as smears on your pristine Savile Row shirt. But no. After a quick run round with the mop, both the cellar and Walter appear no worse for wear than if he'd simply been putting up a new shelf. Clearly—this being Amicus and the 1970s—huge geysers of blood covering every available surface was never in the cards. However, the odd spattering of ruby-red gore might have brought an additional touch of realism to the proceedings.

"Frozen Fear" manages to capture the essence of the cellar, a room frequently dismissed as the poor relation to the rest of a home.

The Satanic Rites of Dracula (1973)

My revenge has spread over centuries and has just begun!

Director: Alan Gibson
Written by: Don Houghton (screenplay)
Starring: Christopher Lee, Peter Cushing, Michael Coles, William Franklyn, Freddie Jones, Joanna Lumley, Richard Vernon, Barbara Yu Ling, Patrick Barr, Richard Matthews, Lockwood West, Valerie Van Ost, Maurice O'Connell, Peter Adair, Maggie Fitzgerald, Pauline Peart, Finnuala O'Shannon, Mia Martin, John Harvey, Marc Zuber, Paul Weston, Ian Dewar, Graham Rees

There's something odd going on at an isolated mansion on the outskirts of London, something wicked involving influential members of the British establishment. Sent to investigate, Secret Service agent Peter Torrence (William Franklyn) and Scotland Yard Inspector Murray (Michael Coles), along with Jessica Van Helsing (Joanna Lumley), granddaughter of occult specialist Lorrimer Van Helsing (Peter Cushing), get more than they bargained for. The building houses the headquarters of a Satanic sect, led by a shadowy character with links to the Van Helsing family, who plans to use Jessica to wreak his ultimate revenge upon humanity.

The Satanic Rites of Dracula—or *Count Dracula and His Vampire Bride* as it's known in America—has over the years been almost universally dismissed by Hammer fans and critics alike. Which is a shame, considering the film's significance in several respects. Made during the company's waning years, when attempts to update the Dracula theme by placing him in contemporary settings met with mixed reactions, *The Satanic Rites of Dracula* was different. It marked the last time Hammer was to pair Lee and Cushing in the same production. Cushing would tackle vampires for them once more in 1974's *Legend of the 7 Golden Vampires*, but Lee felt that enough was enough, refusing to resuscitate the count again, at least for Hammer.

Equally important was that *Satanic Rites* was one of the few where Hammer allowed a female character (Jessica Van Helsing) to hold her own against her male counterparts. Joanna Lumley had a life before *Absolutely Fabulous*, the British television sitcom which put her indelibly on the map through her iconic role as the permanently inebriated fashion editor, Patsy Stone. To some, however, she will always be Purdey, the high-kicking companion to Patrick Macnee's government operative Steed, in the '70s re-

Cellar dweller: Jessica Van Helsing (Joanna Lumley) gets the measure of one of Count Dracula's victims (Pauline Peart) in *The Satanic Rites of Dracula* **(1973).**

6. The Cellar

vival of the cult TV series *The Avengers*. Though she blazed a feminist trail in the show, an equal with Steed and fellow agent Gambit (played by the suave Gareth Hunt), she was no newcomer to playing feisty females on the screen. In fact, the character of Jessica Van Helsing could have been seen as a prototype for the blonde-bobbed action girl she was to become a few years later.

From her first appearance in the film, you know that Jessica's no air-headed young woman, happy only to serve coffee to guests visiting her grandfather's home. Like Jerry Evans, the feisty lab assistant with a mind of her own in *Murders in the Zoo* (1933), Jessica, as her grandfather readily points out, knows as much about his work as he does. When Torrence and Murray go to investigate Pelham House—the country pile where sinister occurrences have been taking place—Jessica tags along, proving she's equally keen to be involved in the action. Though her presence is never fully explained, her inclusion at this stage could be dismissed as a mere excuse to up Hammer's obligatory bare flesh quota at the segment's climax. But on closer inspection, there's more to it. Left in the car by her male companions, Jessica sneaks onto the grounds of the house, before finding her way into the building's cellar, with graphically hellish consequences. Though featuring in the film only briefly, the cellar of Pelham House is a thoroughly unpleasant place. The remaining building is, for the most part, welcoming. Here though is a room in the bowels of the house, where Dracula's female victims are kept in crate-like coffins or chained to the walls, in readiness for whatever horrific plans he has for them. The upstairs rooms of the house may feature some of the film's more dubious "occult" references, but it's undoubtedly the cellar that looks and feels just plain nasty.

Dry and well-lit, with low, vaulted ceilings, the room nonetheless has an air of claustrophobia. When Jessica makes her way in, though initially unperturbed by the room's seemingly innocent appearance, she is soon shocked by the hapless victims of Dracula she finds chained to its walls, including a missing secretary from Torrence's office. When she is attacked by the vampires, as they stealthily creep from their boxes, the scene soon degenerates into a grimy-toned orgy of flailing arms, hands and ripped clothing. Of course, Torrence and Murray, who are upstairs, race to her assistance once alerted by Jessica's screams, but not before you're confronted with an effectively disturbing scene of sexually tinged horror. The appearance of Torrence and Murray at this point also provides ample opportunity for Murray to protect Jessica, reinforcing the close relationship between them which builds throughout the film.

Murray returns to the house, putting an end once and for all to the unfortunate inhabitants of the cellar. As everyone knows, vampires live in mortal fear of running water, and here they are reduced to a writhing mass of agony and pain after Murray turns on a conveniently placed water sprinkler with catastrophic results. This mass destruction of the female vampires, filmed in slow motion, plays out in grainy sepia tones, which one can only imagine was an attempt on the part of the filmmakers to imbue the proceedings with an air of '70s psychedelia.

Amongst the various titles under which the film is known is the amusing if somewhat convoluted *Dracula Is Dead...and Well and Living in London*. Which, upon reflection, might be more succinct than the name the company eventually went with. Though it does have its fair share of devilish mumbo-jumbo, there is not really any more here than in many of Hammer's other horrors, most of which were influenced to some degree by the occult. On the other hand, the film has a dreamlike quality, common to many productions filmed in Britain's capital during the 1970s. This makes *Satanic Rites* one of the most unjustly derided offerings from Hammer's later years.

Salem's Lot (1979)

> *Jason, do you believe a thing can be inherently evil? A house. The Marsten house, for instance. Can it be evil in its stone foundations, in its wooden beams, in the glass of its windows, in the plaster of its ceilings ... evil?*

Director: Tobe Hooper
Written by: Paul Monash (screenplay), Stephen King (based on the novel by)
Starring: David Soul, James Mason, Lance Kerwin, Bonnie Bedelia, Lew Ayres, Julie Cobb, Elisha Cook, Jr., George Dzundza, Ed Flanders, Geoffrey Lewis, Clarissa Kaye-Mason, Barney McFadden, Kenneth McMillan, Fred Willard, Marie Windsor, Barbara Babcock, Bonnie Bartlett, Joshua Bryant, James Gallery, Robert Lussier, Brad Savage, Ronnie Scribner, Ned Wilson, Reggie Nalder, Ernest Phillips

For a building—like any character in a film, television show or book—to be truly memorable, it has to have its own identity. No one remembers the mirror-image houses on the council estate, or the flat which is a blueprint for all the others in the high-rise block. But place a dilapidated mansion on the edge of town, or on a quiet road just off the main highway, and you're guaranteed to create a building as foreboding as any flesh-and-blood person. Norman Bates' home, which he shared with his batty alter ego, is obvious but there are others equally unsettling.

Take the old Marsten house from *Salem's Lot*, directed by master of the macabre Tobe Hooper and based on Stephen King's bestselling novel of small-town American terror. Here's a building truly deserving its ominous reputation. Like a brooding eagle sitting on a hill overlooking Salem's

6. The Cellar

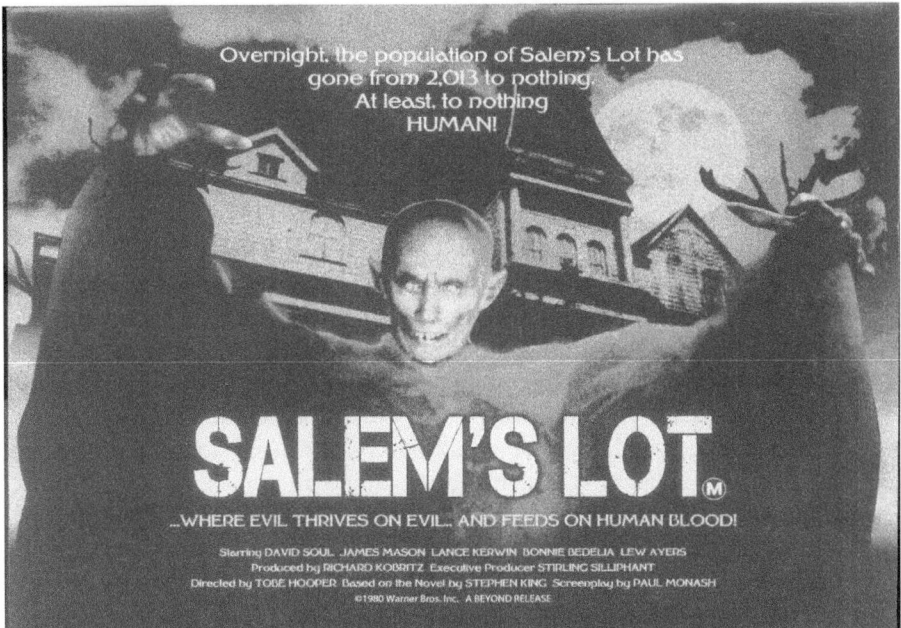

Brooding menace: Reggie Nalder and the Marsten House loom large in a promotional poster for the 1979 Warner Bros. Television production of Stephen King's classic chiller *'Salem's Lot*.

Lot, the house has been the scene of countless murders, suicides and inexplicable occurrences during its long and storied history. Now it has taken on an even more disturbing air. The new owners—antique dealers Richard K. Straker (James Mason) and Kurt Barlow (Reggie Nalder)—are seldom seen, mysterious crates are delivered in the dead of night and stored in the cellar, and the place has a general ambience of death and decay.

Climactically, when the truth about the mansion is finally revealed, it becomes a house of carnage as novelist Ben Mears (David Soul)—visiting the town to research the building as the basis for his next book—and his friends are caught in a bloody battle with the ultimate incarnation of evil.

If anyone could bring to life King's vision of the archetypal haunted house (empty rooms, cobweb-strewn attics and dim, dusty corridors), it was Hooper. The genial Texan had created a milestone in horror cinema several years earlier, with his take on a freaky farmhouse from his home state in the notorious *The Texas Chain Saw Massacre* (1974). In *Salem's Lot*, Hooper gives viewers a new house whose presence is every bit as menacing as Leatherface's isolated homestead, and appears to saturate the story's proceedings, spreading its malignant influence over everything and everyone who has the misfortune to pass through its shadow.

In the film, the house appears almost as an extension of Barlow the vampire, which was clearly intentional as production designer Mort Rabinowitz explained in *Cinefantastique* magazine: "We wanted a rotting, sick appearance, almost as if—in discussions with the director and producer—we were looking into the body, the heart of the vampire. It reflects his whole being more so than just a decayed house. So we decided to go for an abstract image."[6]

The main part of the house seen in the film—other than its front facade which is frequently looming somewhere in the background, as someone walks down the town's main street or looks out of their bedroom window—is the cellar. Though the hallway, landing and a couple of upstairs rooms feature in the final showdown between the forces of good and evil, it is really the room downstairs in which the pivotal confrontations take place. Accessed by way of a bulkhead door on one side of the house, the cellar here is like that in many large American homes, removed from public view and entered from the outside by a steep flight of stone steps. Most of the characters who find themselves in the house get in by this means, except for Straker who alone seems to use the front door.

The room itself, though clearly a storage and work space, is nonetheless tidy and brightly lit, even if a little unwelcoming in atmosphere. Though sparsely furnished—there's little in it save a few packing boxes—the bareness forms the perfect backdrop to emphasize what plays out there. Everything it's used for in the film has a purpose of evil. It's first seen when two local truck drivers are hired by Straker to deliver a crate to the house and leave it in the cellar. Convinced there's something live in the crate and then hearing noises upstairs, they flee from the room and drive off without locking the door behind them.

Next up, Straker himself visits the room, with a living sacrifice—in the form of a local kid—for his vampire master, who he knows is now loose in the house or surrounding area. Unwrapping the child from a black polythene bag, Straker lays him on a wooden trestle table in the center of the room, before turning the light out and closing the door. What happens to the boy is anyone's guess but as he reappears later in vampiric form, it's a safe bet that it's something unpleasant. The final time the cellar makes an appearance is when Ben, his girlfriend's father Dr. Bill Norton (Ed Flanders) and a schoolboy, Mark Petrie (Lance Kerwin), are trapped in it with a horde of vampires, before breaking into the main house for what proves, quite literally, to be one hell of a showdown.

The film was made as a miniseries for American television, though alternate versions were filmed for release in European cinemas. As a result, there were concerns over Hooper's style: Being a director so intrinsically linked with the big screen through *The Texas Chain Saw Massacre* and

Deathtrap (1976), how would his work translate to the small screen? In the end, as the filmmaker explained in the *Cinefantastique* article, this was not an issue which overly concerned him, resulting in what remains one of film's most disturbing and atmospheric interpretations of vampire lore:

> For one thing, my style is ingrained in me. It does not change. It improves, perhaps, but it does not change. Also, *Salem's Lot* does rely on the same kind of dynamics as *Chainsaw*. It is scary, it is atmospheric, but in a different way; I do not have to cheat the audience to bring it to television.[7]

7

The Bedroom

The room itself was covered by tapestries and family portraits and contained other "dark" and "old fashioned" furniture including some bizarre carved wooden figures. In short it had a gloomy and ominous atmosphere and people were wary of sleeping there.—The Haunted Bedroom (known as the "ghost room"), Corby Castle, Cumberland, England.
—*The Haunted Realm,* Simon Marsden (1987)

The bedroom is the room in the house which reveals most about its owner. It is here that we are at our most private and intimate as, if we do share it with anyone, it is generally only our chosen partner or someone we have invited in. When people or things invade this room, we can feel violated.

It should hardly be surprising that those behind countless horror films have used the bedroom as the focal point for some dastardly goings-on. Unfortunately, as seen in everything from Arthur Lowe's gruesome decapitation in *Theatre of Blood* (1973) to Johnny Depp's "wet dream" screen debut in *Nightmare on Elm Street* (1984), the bedroom in horror seems seldom to be the place to get a good night's sleep. Still, when the bogeyman does manage to track you down to your private lair, the room we call our own also provides plenty of secret nooks and crannies in which the victim can hide, as Jamie Lee Curtis discovered with a closet during the climax of *Halloween* (1978). So turn out the light and pull up the bedclothes, for, as we'll see from our selection here, you never know who or what might be hiding under the bed.

Frankenstein (1931)

"Something is going to happen. I feel it! I can't get it out of my mind."

7. The Bedroom 103

Director: James Whale
Written by: Francis Edward Faragoh, Garrett Fort (screenplay), Robert Florey (screenplay—uncredited), John L. Balderston (adapted story), Mary Shelley (original novel), Peggy Webling (play)
Starring: Colin Clive, Mae Clarke, John Boles, Boris Karloff, Edward Van Sloan, Frederick Kerr, Dwight Frye, Lionel Belmore, Marilyn Harris, Michael Mark

James Whale's seminal *Frankenstein* was not the first big-screen adaptation of Mary Shelley's infamous tale of body horror—that accolade belongs to director J. Searle Dawley's 1910, 16-minute short made for the Edison Studios in New York. However, it took Whale's version to put the mad scientist and his monstrous creation on the cinematic map, in a film which influenced horror cinema and the career of its leading star—Boris Karloff—forever. The film is so chock full of influential visions—Frankenstein's electrically powered laboratory literally crackling with life, the death of a little girl at the hands of the creature which caused endless censorial debate—it's almost impossible to cast new light on something which has been so thoroughly dissected over the years. However, although most writing on the film focuses—understandably—on the relationship between Henry Frankenstein (Colin Clive) and his creation, one other

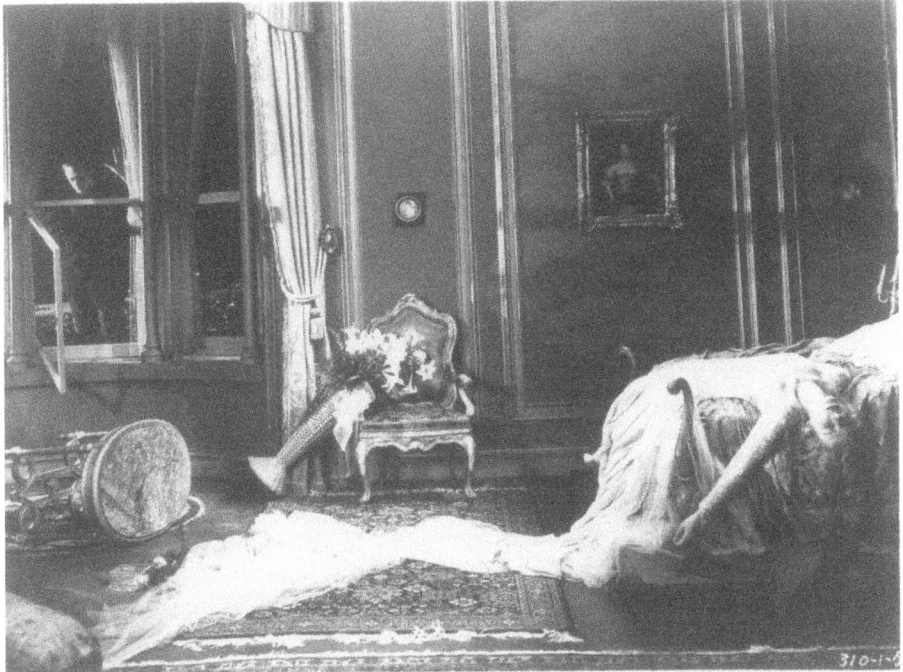

Swoon effect: The Monster (Boris Karloff) startles Elizabeth (Mae Clarke) in *Frankenstein* (1931).

person's confrontation with the Monster and its effect on her life is often overlooked.

Henry's future wife Elizabeth—infused with a melodramatic intensity by American actress Mae Clarke—is a character as critical to her future husband's existence as his creature. Her eventual bedroom encounter with the beast is one of horror cinema's most dramatic yet neglected scenes. Proclaiming Clarke—in her portrayal of Elizabeth—to have made "a perfunctory ingénue role charming,"[1] Alfred Rushford Greason in his review for *Variety* magazine (December 7, 1931) was somewhat damning with faint praise. Though typically over-excitable, in the fashion of the time, Elizabeth is nonetheless unafraid to confront possible dangers as seen when, in the midst of a thunderstorm, she insists on accompanying Henry's friends—Victor Moritz (John Boles) and Dr. Waldman (Edward Van Sloan)—to the isolated watchtower where Henry conducts his experiments.

Despite the scenes in Henry's laboratory being best known in terms of cinema history, those set in his father's house on his wedding morning—and particularly the ones featuring Elizabeth in her bedroom—remain the most atmospheric. All women have jitters before they get married, and Elizabeth is no exception. Who could blame her when her future husband has all but ignored her in the build-up to their wedding? Here, as she confronts Henry in her bedroom at the Frankenstein mansion, all her fears and frustration, accumulating over the previous months, come to a head. Though everyone believes the Monster to have been disposed of, Elizabeth can't help but feel a sense of foreboding, that something dreadful is about to happen. And how right she is.

The encounters between Elizabeth and Henry are, on the whole, stiff and staid, restricted by the conformities of the age. The film was both produced in and set in a time when passion was played out with a decorum and reserve which allowed nothing but the most chaste displays of emotion, even between those in relationships. This doesn't stop the suggestion of risqué subject matter—such as why Elizabeth appears to live at the home of her future husband before their marriage—which although clear, is never expanded upon. The unspoken sexual chemistry between Elizabeth and Henry, however, simply heightens the intensity and physicality when she eventually comes face to face with the creature.

The bedroom in which Henry shuts Elizabeth for her own safety while he and others go in search of the creature, is decorated in a sumptuous Edwardian–faux baroque fusion, with more than a hint of bohemian decadence. Amongst copious arrangements of bridal flowers, the room's furniture, though limited, is intensely dramatic. Richly woven rugs cover a polished wooden floor while the walls are dominated by suggestive portraits of classically semi-clad women.

The appointment of the room is clearly designed to heighten the dramatic effect of the eventual confrontation between Elizabeth and the creature: the moments before he attacks her, spying her through an open window as she, unaware of the approaching danger, anxiously paces, is a master class in tension-building. Will she turn in time to see him, or succumb to the attack without realizing what hit her? The suggestion that the ensuing encounter results in more than her mere traumatization hovers tantalizingly in the background. Did the creature do more than simply startle the vulnerable woman? Who knows. However, the way in which Elizabeth's prostrate body is discovered after Henry and the household race to the bedroom on hearing her screams, suggests this is so. She has been thrown across the end of her ornate bed, surrounded by upended tables and overturned vases of flowers. The suspicion that the creature has had his way with Elizabeth is clear. And of course a bedroom, as seen here, is the perfect setting for such an encounter. This is your sanctuary, the one place in the house where you should feel safest and most relaxed. Yet it is also the room where you are frequently at your most vulnerable. It is the perfect setting to allude to any number of perplexing—and chilling—sexual possibilities.

It's hard to analyze a film so iconic not just within the horror genre, but also the complete lexicon of classic cinema. The films from the studio most famous for its canon of creature features, and whose name became a byword for early horror cinema, nonetheless varied in quality. However, as pointed out by writer Kim Newman, *Frankenstein* is the exception, enduring as their most mesmerizing production of the period: "The Universal horror cycle runs the gamut from perfection through pastiche and pulp to parody, but *Frankenstein* remains chilly and invigorating, the cornerstone of its entire genre."[2]

The Devil-Doll (1936)

> *"... a grotesque movie about revenge and miniaturisation."*[3]

Director: Tod Browning
Written by: Garrett Fort, Guy Endore, Erich von Stroheim (screenplay), Richard Schayer (dialogue contribution—uncredited), Tod Browning (story), Abraham Merritt (novel)
Starring: Lionel Barrymore, Maureen O'Sullivan, Frank Lawton, Rafaela Ottiano, Robert Greig, Lucy Beaumont, Henry B. Walthall, Grace Ford, Pedro de Cordoba, Arthur Hohl, Rollo Lloyd, E. Alyn Warren, Claire Du Brey, Juanita Quigley

Is it possible that South African–born film writer Alan Frank missed the point, with his abrupt dismissal of the classic thriller *The Devil-Doll*?

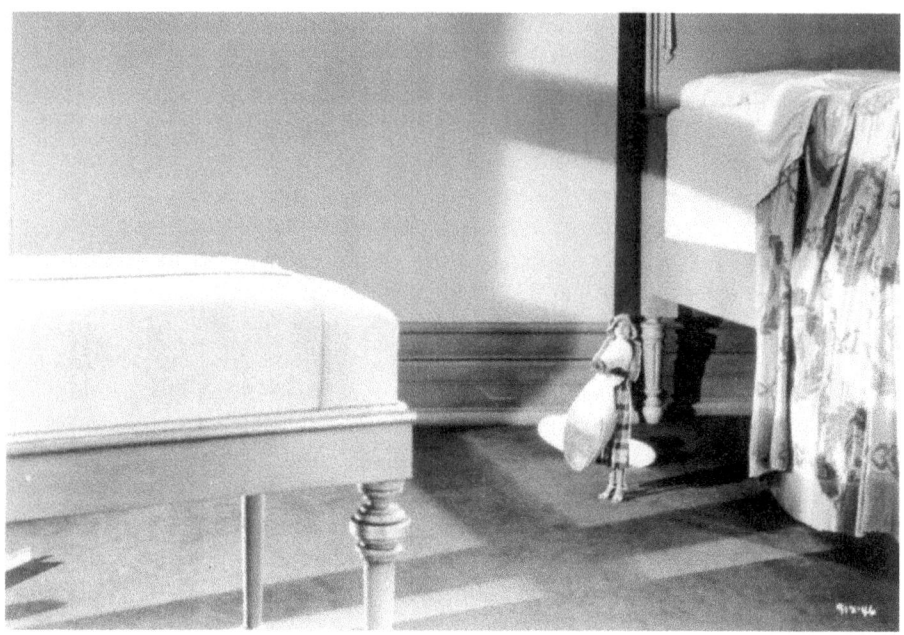

A step up: Lachna (Grace Ford) scales new heights in *The Devil-Doll* (1936).

Watching the film, considered a minor masterpiece from cult director Tod Browning, you can't help but question whether Frank's description concerned a completely different film. In the light of modern genre cinema, Browning's production is more gothic "melodrama" than horror. It never reaches the unpleasant heights of contemporary "mad scientist" chillers such as director Robert Florey's *Murders in the Rue Morgue* (1932), while the film's "family" and romantic undercurrents threaten at times to dilute much of its menace. There may be no denying the film's dark and broody atmosphere. But "grotesque"?

The Devil-Doll's storyline (by Browning) was based loosely on the pulp horror novel *Burn, Witch, Burn!* by Abraham Merritt, published in 1932 and adapted for the screen by Garrett Fort, Guy Endore and Erich von Stroheim. It revolves around former banker Paul Lavond (Lionel Barrymore) who, after escaping from prison, takes revenge on former colleagues responsible for his incarceration, by means of a collection of miniaturized human "dolls." In reality the film bears marginal similarities to Merritt's book, the main one being they both feature characters who become paralyzed and, though still alive and conscious, can no longer react to the world around them.

Erich von Stroheim was better known as an actor and director. His name on the writing credits undoubtedly added novelty factor to the film's script but it was Endore and Fort's involvement that gave it darkness, shot through with an understated black humor. Endore and Fort were well versed in the horror genre. In a writing career spanning over 30 years, Endore, amongst numerous screenplays, co-wrote with Bernard Schubert a previous Browning chiller, *Mark of the Vampire* (1935). He had also penned, in 1933, the gothic novel *The Werewolf of Paris*, on which Hammer's only foray into lycanthropy, *The Curse of the Werewolf* (1961), was based. Fort, though dying comparatively young at 45, accumulated over 60 screen writing credits. He was responsible for bringing not only two horror classics—*Dracula* and *Frankenstein*—to the big screen in 1931, he also put words into the mouth of *Dracula's Daughter* (1936). In *The Devil-Doll*, the three writers imbued the various characters—both good and bad—with an urgency which in turn colored the pace of the film, seldom letting its 78 minutes of running time drag.

Rhetorical shine aside, what makes *The Devil-Doll* work so well is its juxtaposition of the various environments in which its story unfolds. From the opening scenes, where Paul and his friend Marcel are pursued through murky swamps after their escape from prison, to Paul's climactic confrontation with his daughter's fiancé Toto (Frank Lawton) atop the Eiffel Tower, the settings serve to emphasize the storyline and characters, making all appear larger than life. It is also these individuals' abodes, set within these locales, which serve to bind the film's different story threads, and in the process become almost character-like themselves. From the isolated hovel where Paul and Marcel hide out while developing the reduction process discovered by Marcel and his unhinged wife Malita (Rafaela Ottiano) to the decadently appointed Parisian townhouse of Paul's ex-colleague, the arrogant banker Emil Coulvet (Robert Greig), the houses take on lives of their own. This is seen perhaps most vividly in the pivotal bedroom scene—in Coulvet's house—which stands out as one of the film's most memorable for several reasons, not simply as the best example of its method of portraying the miniaturization of the "dolls."

The Devil-Doll was made in the days before CGI and other modern miracles. The main method used here to give the impression of the miniaturized characters is supersized props. A mix of split screen and glass shot processes were used when Paul's shrunken "dolls" are seen in relation to normal-sized humans. Appearing alone however, as when Paul sends his favorite "miniature" Lachna (Grace Ford) to wreak revenge on Coulvet, the use of supersized everyday objects—beds, chairs and doors—takes on a surreal air as they tower over the shrunken human, while still lending the proceedings a believable familiarity. Outsized props as seen here have featured frequently in horror cinema, from the sinister (*Dr. Cyclops*, 1940), to the terrifying (*The Incredible Shrinking Man*, 1957) and surreal (*The

Company of Wolves, 1984). In the bedrooms of Coulvet's family, however, they bring added dimension (literally) to proceedings: children's building blocks at the door to his daughter's bedroom loom like 5th Avenue skyscrapers while the eiderdown covering his wife's bed appears as an undulating ocean of gray satin.

It's also here that several of the film's key elements culminate in a symphony of suspense and disbelief. Though Paul and the miniaturized Lachna are up to no good, the viewer's sympathies are clearly meant to lie with them. Since Paul is simply taking revenge on a man, not only unpleasant but also clearly less than scrupulous in his affairs, the viewer never feels less than sympathetic towards Paul and his plight. Lachna's life is in danger—from the monstrous obstacles in her path as she traverses the deadly bedroom environment—at the same time that there is a possibility that Paul—waiting for Lachna in the street below—might be discovered at any moment. The result is genuine, edge-of-the-seat tension.

Though *The Devil-Doll* is largely a stylistically shocking thriller, with horrific and romantic overtones, it remains a captivating example of effectively advanced (for its time) visual effects, as emphasized in the bedroom scenes. As critic Frank S. Nugent aptly summed up, "[T]he picture relies mainly, and with understandable assurance, upon such ingenious bits as Miss Ford's demonstration of Alpine skill in climbing (via a slipper, footstool, bench and drawer handles) to the top of a dressing table…,"[4] heights which few filmmakers have scaled since with such finesse.

The Brides of Dracula (1960)

> *Ha ha ha haaaa, look. You needn't be afraid, she's dead. She's dead and he's alive!*

Director: Terence Fisher
Written by Jimmy Sangster, Peter Bryan, Edward Percy (screenplay)
Starring: Peter Cushing, Martita Hunt, Yvonne Monlaur, Freda Jackson, David Peel, Miles Malleson, Henry Oscar, Mona Washbourne, Andree Melly, Victor Brooks, Fred Johnson, Michael Ripper, Norman Pierce, Vera Cook, Marie Devereux

Marianne Danielle (Yvonne Monlaur) is traveling alone in Transylvania, on her way to take a post at an exclusive school for young ladies. Stranded one night, she accepts the hospitality of the mysterious Baroness Meinster (Martita Hunt), who invites the young woman to stay at her castle. Only when Marianne arrives at the castle does she discover that the baroness doesn't live alone, and that her son, the baron (David Peel)—whom she keeps chained—is a follower of the late vampire Count Dracula. After Marianne unwittingly sets him free, the baron wreaks his

7. The Bedroom

Now see what you've done: Baroness Meinster (Martita Hunt, seated) breathes her last, as Marianne Danielle (Yvonne Monlaur) and Greta (Freda Jackson, pointing) look on in *The Brides of Dracula* (1960).

revenge upon his mother, then sets out to make Marianne a bride of the undead.

Following the success of *Horror of Dracula* (1958), it was inevitable that Hammer would make another vampire film, but one which would have much to live up to. *The Brides of Dracula* could have failed in numerous ways. How would a follow-up work without Christopher Lee reprising the role of Dracula? Lee was not only involved with prior engagements but had also shown little interest in returning to the role so quickly for fear of being typecast. Would another film work if all mention of Dracula was removed, except for alluding to him with the title and an opening monologue?

Watching the film, however, such fears are soon put to rest, as the tone is quickly set: A narrator's voiceover intones a few words which create the sinister and uneasy ambience that envelops the film. "Transylvania. Land of dark forests, dread mountains and black, unfathomed lakes. Still the home of magic and devilry as the nineteenth century draws to its close." The result is widely considered one of the company's best films, vampire or otherwise. Not only is David Peel's younger and sexually alluring Baron Meinster a wonderfully worthy successor to Lee's more mature nobleman, but the jettisoning of Dracula in all but name gave *Brides* the opportunity to establish itself as a film with an identity of its own. In the documentary *The Making of* The Brides of Dracula, which accompanied *Brides*' 2013 Blu-ray release, it was revealed that the film was originally intended to be entitled *Disciple of Dracula*, which would have removed even further the shadow of the vampire count from the story.

For a film so highly charged sexually, there is perhaps another aspect worth highlighting, namely its homoerotic overtones, a thematic undercurrent which hovers at the edges of many vampiric based works though it is seldom developed further. In his book on Terence Fisher, film academic Peter Hutchings draws attention to certain scenes which, in the 1960s, may have been seen as perfectly innocent, but which today could be read very differently: "Of all Hammer's Dracula films, *The Brides of Dracula* is the one that most clearly poses the possibility of homoerotic desire."[5] Any conflicts, however, over portraying such unacceptable acts onscreen—as when Baron Meinster gets his fangs into Van Helsing (Peter Cushing)— were, as Hutchings points out, easily covered up. "The act of biting is concealed from us by Meinster's cloak, but given that the vampire's bite or 'kiss' is generally presented as an erotic act, the raised cloak might be conceivably seen as a censoring device, covering something unrepresentable."

Overall, the film may be the perfect example of Hammer's expertise in making something from nothing: Its visual appearance, courtesy of production designer Bernard Robinson and cinematographer Jack Asher, results in one of the company's most believable and engrossing recreations of a haunted land of gothic evil. However, it must surely be the young baron's opulent sitting room-cum-bedroom—the ultimate bachelor pad— which creates the most impact. Haunting the mind long after the film's end, the room stands out not simply because of its appointment, or the evil which plays out within it, but also because of what it represents within the film.

Surprisingly little is shown of the room, but what you do see gives scale and depth to Castle Meinster and the baron's position within it. When Marianne initially spies him from her bedroom balcony, the baron is standing on a terrace to one side of the castle, far below. Only accessible through a small door in the corner of the castle's great hall—which you have to bend to get through—and then along a corridor, it is clear the baron is meant to be seen as having been "cut off" from the main household. The room, although beautifully finished with rich tapestries, heavy wooden furniture and silk and velvet coverings, is remarkable Spartan in its contents: Apart from a refectory table and bench, a few armchairs and a couch, there is little else. The apparent lack of any bed—this is, after all, where the baron spends all his time—is later explained when, during Van Helsing's exploration of the room, he draws back some heavy curtains to reveal an alcove housing the vampire nobleman's coffin. Here is a room which, although comfortable, is in actual fact little more than a prison cell, complete with manacles which the baron's mother has used to keep him imprisoned for his (and everyone else's) safety.

The room is also the place where many of the film's pivotal scenes takes place, including Marianne's first meeting with the baron. It is where the baron later takes his revenge on his mother by inducting her into the cult of the undead, and where in turn Marianne discovers the truth about the man she has been seduced by, when she is shown the lifeless body of the baroness by her maid Greta (Freda Jackson).

Critic John Stanley described Fisher's direction of *Brides* as "using heavy Freudian symbolism."[6] As good a way as any of describing the numerous implications lying just beneath the film's surface.

The Abominable Dr. Phibes (1971)

Oh, don't take him out like that. Least cover his face up, what's left of it.

Director: Robert Fuest
Written by: James Whiton, William Goldstein
Starring: Vincent Price, Joseph Cotten, Virginia North, Peter Jeffrey, Norman Jones, James Grout, Hugh Griffiths, Terry-Thomas, John Cater, Aubrey Woods, John Laurie, Caroline Munro, Guy Standeven

Dr. Anton Phibes (Vincent Price) vows revenge on the doctors who operated on his dying wife (Caroline Munro), but couldn't save her, following a car crash. With the help of his beautiful assistant Vulnavia (Virginia North), Phibes dispatches each using one of the plagues of Egypt. With hapless Scotland Yard Inspector Trout (Peter Jeffrey) and his band of bumbling police officers on the case, there's little to stop Phibes carrying out some of the most horrible and ingenious murders in the annals of British crime.

For a film so full of stylish wit, it's difficult—perhaps even wrong— to highlight one particular scene above others. Which is why, with *The Abominable Dr. Phibes*, you get three bedroom scenes for the price of one. In turn ornate, gruesome and serene, the rooms, although each intrinsically different, sum up in their own way what the film is about.

The film opens in one of the bedrooms and the scene features the first on-screen murder, without doubt one of its most unpleasant amongst a veritable cornucopia of unpleasantness. Reflecting the period in which the film is set, the room is incredibly atmospheric. There's nothing more unnerving than the thought of something fluttering in the shadows of your bedroom once you've turned the bedside light out. And in that of Dr. Dunwoody (Edward Burnham), there are plenty of shadows. It's a room paneled in dark wood, complete with fireplace, bookshelves and heavy, ornate furniture; it seems appropriate that the plague with which Phibes dispatches Dunwoody involves him being attacked by bats. Though bats are not strictly speaking one of the ten plagues of Egypt, the fourth one did involve wild animals, which can encompass bats and a number of other creatures later Phibes uses, including rats. Here, though, the bats cause enough mayhem and bloody carnage to frighten the most stout-hearted of men to death, before they even lay teeth to skin.

Though Dunwoody's death may be the only one to take place in an actual bedroom, another two rooms function in the film as sleeping quarters, more than justifying their inclusion here. Towards the film's climax,

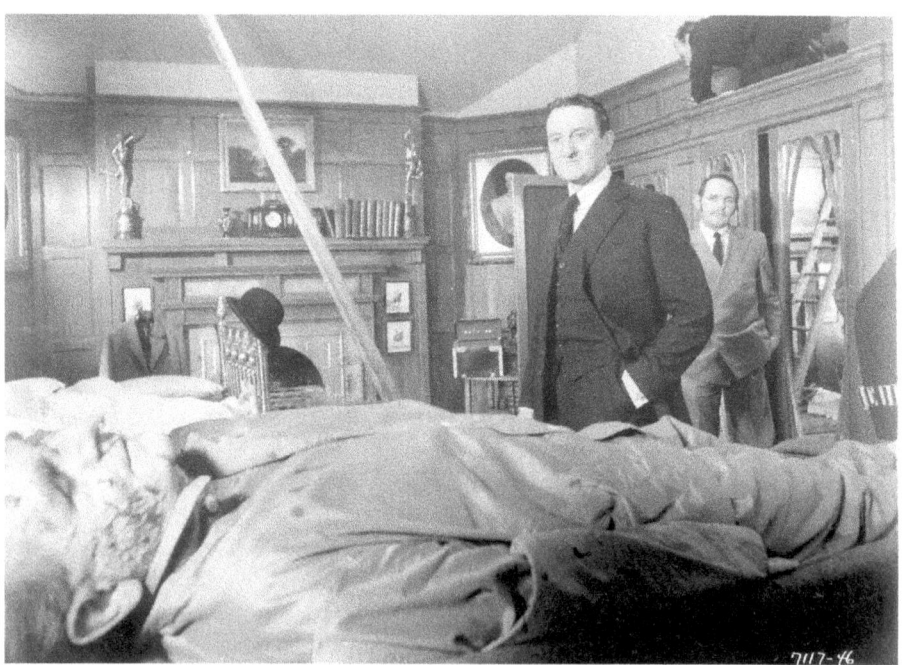

Dead to the world: Dr. Dunwoody (Edward Burnham) sleeps it off, as Inspector Trout (Peter Jeffrey, standing, dark suit), Sgt. Schenley (Norman Jones, standing, light suit) and Morgan (Guy Standeven, crawling up top) investigate his demise, in *The Abominable Dr. Phibes* (1971).

7. The Bedroom 113

after the police have worked out Phibes' dastardly plans, they realize that anyone involved in the wife's failed operation is likely to be murdered, including Nurse Allen (Susan Travers). Forced to sleep at the hospital where she works, under supposed police protection, means she is having to spend the night in a makeshift bedroom, complete with perfunctory hospital furniture of rudimentary iron bedstead and clinical bedside table. The Spartan appearance of the room merely emphasizes what is surely one of the film's most ingenious yet cringe-inducing deaths. After breaking into the room above Nurse Allen's, Phibes proceeds to drill through the floor and cover the sleeping woman in a sticky concoction distilled from boiled Brussels sprouts. He next proceeds to empty a canister of locusts through the opening, which soon make short work of the nutritious syrup and the unfortunate woman beneath. As expected, Inspector Trout and his ineffectual police back-up arrive too late to save her.

Appropriately enough, the film closes the way it opens, in a bedroom, although this time the room in question has more of the air of a waiting room than one of death. Hoping to return later and discover a way of re-

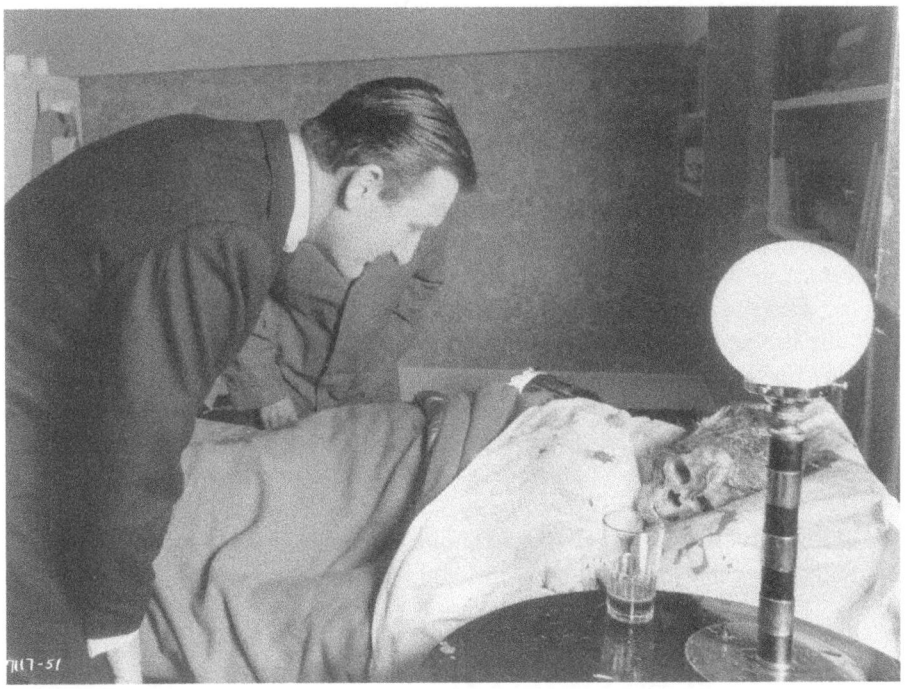

The bare bones: Inspector Trout (Peter Jeffrey, left) and Sgt. Schenley (Norman Jones, behind Jeffrey, his face hidden) examine what remains of Nurse Allen in *The Abominable Dr. Phibes* (1971).

suscitating his dead wife, Phibes, embalming himself by remote control, lays himself to rest alongside the body of his wife, hidden in sumptuously appointed coffins beneath the cellar of his house. The film ends with Inspector Trout walking over the very floor which has covered Phibes and his wife in darkness, the last plague of Egypt.

It's strange, watching the film now, to remember that, although what happens in front of the camera appears intrinsically "British," much of what took place on the other side was American in essence: The film's production company (American International), co-producer (Louis M. Heyward), screenwriters (James Whiton and William Goldstein) and its main stars (Price and Joseph Cotten) were all American.

Both *The Abominable Dr. Phibes* and its follow-up *Dr. Phibes Rises Again* (1972) have an air that permeated many British films and television series made during the 1960s and '70s—an effortless, unspoken "stylishness" captured by the film's English director, Robert Fuest. In *The Horror People*, John Brosnan discussed Fuest's eye for the arresting image: "Until 1962 he was a designer with ABC-TV (London). His interest in visual design has been evident in all the feature films he has directed. First directed TV commercials, then progressed to TV series, including eight episodes of the quirky, and popular, *Avengers*."[7] Watching *The Abominable Dr. Phibes*, you can imagine them as extended—if somewhat gruesome—stories of the surreal television show.

Another interesting fact concerns what—or rather who—you don't, for various reasons, see in the finished production. The British actress Joanna Lumley, who went on to find fame as Purdey on television's *The New Avengers*, had her part as a laboratory assistant cut, while the gentleman of horror, Peter Cushing, who'd originally been cast as Dr. Vesalius, pulled out at the last moment due to his wife's ongoing illness. Marvelously camp and beautifully atmospheric though the final film is, one can only imagine what might have been if Price and Cushing had got the opportunity to face off on screen.

Several other Phibes films were planned, though one sequel was all that saw the light of day: *Dr. Phibes Rises Again*'s less than stellar box-office performance stymied plans for a continuing story franchise. Even so, there's no denying *The Abominable Dr. Phibes* is the most exquisitely bizarre and unsettling piece of horror cinema, guaranteed to cause sleepless nights, and not just for Phibes' ill-fated victims onscreen.

Theatre of Blood (1973)

> *My god, it's him! What'll he think? Let me go. He's insanely jealous. He'll kill me. Arrrrrrrgh ...*

7. The Bedroom 115

Director: Douglas Hickox
Written by: Anthony Greville-Bell (screenplay), Stanley Mann and John Kohn (idea)
Starring: Vincent Price, Diana Rigg, Ian Hendry, Harry Andrews, Coral Browne, Robert Coote, Jack Hawkins, Michael Horden, Arthur Lowe, Robert Morley, Dennis Price, Milo O'Shea, Eric Sykes, Madeline Smith, Diana Dors, Joan Hickson, Renée Asherson, Bunny Reed, Peter Thornton, Charles Sinnickson, Brigid Erin Bates, Tony Calvin (uncredited), Tutte Lemkow, Stanley Bates, Eric Francis, Sally Gilmore, John Gilpin, Joyce Graeme, Jack Maguire, Declan Mulholland), Charles Gray (Solomon Psaltery's voice—uncredited)

Theatre of Blood star Vincent Price considered it one of his personal favorites. It's a clever, sharp and wonderfully caustic take on the eternal feud between the acting fraternity and their sworn enemies, the critics.

Pushed over the edge by the cutting remarks of a group of theater critics who had little good to say about his Shakespeare performances, actor Edward Lionheart (Price) attempts suicide by throwing himself into the Thames. He is saved from a watery grave by a group of down-and-out winos and returns to take revenge on his detractors. With the assistance of his devoted daughter Edwina (Diana Rigg) he gives the performance of

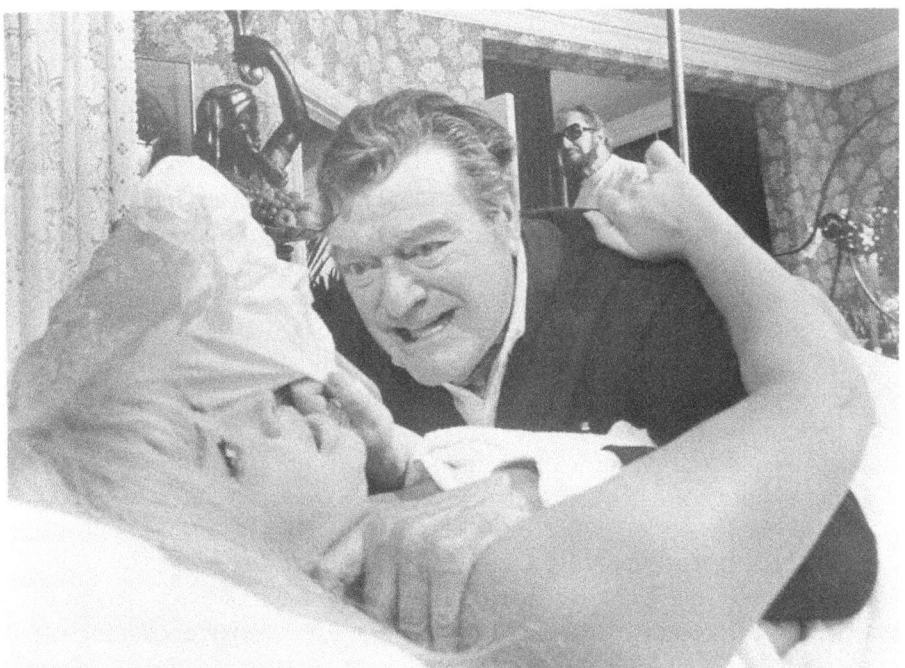

Crime of passion: Maisie Psaltery (Diana Dors) is smothered by husband Solomon's (Jack Hawkins) attentions while Edward Lionheart (Vincent Price in background) beats a hasty retreat in *Theatre of Blood* (1973).

his life as he dispatches each of his tormentors using methods he extracts from his beloved Bard's most famous works.

It's hard to know where to start when trying to sum up *Theatre of Blood*. Words don't do justice to a film featuring near-perfect performances, a sublime plot and countless locations which highlight not just Australian writer Anthony Greville-Bell's script—described as "imaginative"[8] by Danny Peary—but that magical essence of 1970s London which simply can't be put into words, and which the viewer absorbs almost by osmosis. From a chocolate-box cottage in Putney and state-of-the-art penthouse in Vauxhall to a mansion flat in Hammersmith, the houses used for the dwellings of the various critics, epitomize the louche and wealthy lifestyles these type of people would have lived. It is the scenes in Solomon Psaltery's (Jack Hawkins) house, however, which take this opulence to a higher level.

Much of the film's action, including several murders, takes place in a range of rooms within the various houses, including at least two bedroom scenes, making it almost impossible to highlight one. The death scene of Psaltery's wife Maisie (Diana Dors) is by no means the most gruesome featured—her post-massage strangulation can hardly compete with such delights as drowning in a vat of wine or being fried alive under a beauty salon hairdryer hood. Her comeuppance is nonetheless significant, as its location—the bedroom of the South West London house she shares with her husband—represents the essence of the film as a whole. Here is the home of a couple for whom the bohemian decadence of the cosmopolitan literati is all par for the course. Overlooking the Thames on the Chelsea Embankment, their period terrace is the last word in opulence, providing plenty of opportunity for some classical Shakespearian imagery, such as when, from a high window, Maisie beckons her visiting masseur (who, unknown to her, is a heavily disguised Lionheart) to visit her in her bedroom above. The room where Maisie's life is cut short—with its massive brass bedstead and confection of white furnishings—is the epitome of the boudoir of a lady of leisure.

In a film dripping with innuendo (subtle and otherwise), it is clear that, although more mature, Psaltery and his wife aren't inhibited in the bedroom. Potted ferns and lace trimmings abound in a room with the sumptuous air of belonging to a couple (and, in particular, to Maisie) who like to laze around and who are in no rush to leave its relaxing environs. Great play is made as Maisie draws out her words when explaining her and her husband's "hectic sssssocial life" to her masseur. Her terrified description of her spouse, when she realizes he's arrived home early and is smashing down the bedroom door, paints a picture of a man who is clearly madly—nay, obsessively—in love with his wife. Which, of course, leads to his downfall. Inspired by Shakespeare's *Othello*—where, believing his wife Desdemona to have been unfaithful, her husband strangles the innocent woman in a fit of rage—Solomon breaks into the bedroom and, ignoring Lionheart as he watches gleefully from the sidelines, proceeds to suffocate Maisie with a pillow. Dors, no stranger to horror films or to taking on the role of a vamp, was perfectly cast as the innocent, misunderstood Maisie, while Hawkins combined the right mix of buttoned-up Britishness and suppressed passion. Hawkins had lost his voice some years previously due to throat cancer, and his lines were dubbed by the actor Charles Gray. This brings an added touch of the macabre to the proceedings. One of the few deaths in the film not to directly involve a critic as the victim, Psaltery ends up as good as dead when he is arrested for Maisie's murder. Though other characters may suffer more elaborate demises, that of Maisie—and as a result Psaltery—provides a brief moment of pathos amongst the otherwise grisly goings-on.

Utilizing the rooms of a house within its wider story, the result is one of horror cinema's best examples of where the spaces in question become true characters in themselves.

8

The Nursery and Schoolroom

And then, those memories of childhood began to be stirred again and I dwelt nostalgically upon all those nights when I had lain in the warm and snug safety of my bed in the nursery at the top of our family house in Sussex, hearing the wind rage round me like a lion, howling at the doors and beating upon the windows but powerless to reach me. I lay back and slipped into that pleasant, trance-like state somewhere between sleeping and waking, recalling the past and all its emotions and impressions vividly, until I was a small boy again.
—*The Woman in Black*, Susan Hill (1983)

We might not all have been fortunate enough to have our own nursery or schoolroom at home, though they were likely much more common a hundred years ago than now in the early twenty-first century. Many of us do know, however, what it was like as a child to have a bedroom of one's own, where we slept, played and did our schoolwork, which is tantamount to much the same thing. And, not unlike the real one which Arthur Kipps remembered from his childhood in Susan Hill's ghostly tale *The Woman in Black*, our pseudo-nurseries were usually places of warmth and security from the storms of the outside world.

Which is not necessarily the case when such rooms appear in horror films. Whether in some grand Victorian mansion such as in director Jack Clayton's exquisite *The Innocents* (1961), or a nondescript terrace flat in present-day London like that in the twisted drama *The Ones Below* (2015), these rooms are often places where evil festers and sick schemes unravel. And, as you will see, few of the scenarios unfolding here, uphold the strict Victorian belief that children should be seen and not heard.

Dead of Night (1945)

"The Christmas Party"
I didn't know. So that ... that little boy. It was .... I'm not frightened. I'm not frightened. Oh, please hold me tight, oh, hold me tight.

8. The Nursery and Schoolroom   119

Directors: Alberto Cavalcanti
Written by: Angus MacPhail
Starring: Michael Allan, Sally Ann Howes, Barbara Leake

Regarded by horror-film aficionados as one of the finest examples of its kind, Ealing's *Dead of Night* is remarkable for several reasons. Exquisite to watch, infused with life by members of the cream of the British acting fraternity, and with a storyline blending humor, drama and the macabre in equal measure, the film was one of the first to be told in compendium form, an approach which has become a genre staple in the years since.

An overarching story, in the traditional form of the anthology film, connects the various tales. Architect Walter Craig (Mervyn Johns) is invited to the country for the weekend by Eliot Foley (Roland Culver) and his mother (Mary Merrall) to discuss some work which they would like done to their house. On his arrival, Craig is alarmed to discover that he recognizes the Foleys' house from a recurring dream, although he has never visited it. Intrigued by his story, several other weekend guests recount a supernatural experience they have had, culminating in an ambiguous conclusion to the weekend gathering.

As with the best ghost collections, not all the stories told hit the mark. In fact it wouldn't have gone amiss if some of them had been dropped altogether. A couple were when the film was released in America including, rather bafflingly, our chosen example set in a haunted nursery, as well as a tiresome story concerning a ghostly golfing duo.

All the tales, except the golfing story, are marvelously unsettling, as Bosley Crowther noted in his *New York Times* review:

> Such folks as like to drag their friends into the parlor, turn out the lights and swap tales of the weird and supernatural will certainly enjoy the new film at the Winter Garden, the British-made *Dead of Night*. For this is precisely a package of those curious and uncanny yarns designed to raise secret goose pimples and cause the mind to make a fast check on itself.[1]

The story set in the nursery, which presumably Crowther missed, turns out to provide the best example of what he discusses. Expertly combining the period and modern to subtly disturbing effect, the supernatural experience of the Foleys' youngest guest, Sally O'Hara (Sally Ann Howes), stands apart as the most atmospheric. Several years previously, Sally was spending Christmas with family friends at their rambling country house, where they were holding a party for the local children. Being the eldest, Sally felt out of things but agreed to join in a game of Sardines. Searching for a place to hide, she discovered a distressed young boy called Francis in a nursery room high up in the attics of the house. Calming the child and putting him to bed, Sally raced downstairs where she told those assembled about her encounter. She was understandably shocked when told that there was no one of that description staying at the house. But it sounded very like a child who was murdered in the attic nursery by his jealous half-sister many years before.

So what makes Sally's story, the second of the five, so effective?

In truth, it's the perfect haunted house yarn. Set at Christmas (as all the best ghost stories are), it takes place in a large, sprawling house, complete with long, lonely corridors, narrow, twisting staircases and empty, forgotten rooms. It also features children—Sally and Francis—as its main characters, an element that always adds an extra frisson of vulnerability to horror, as in films like *The Innocents* (1961) and *The Others* (2001) where children play lead roles.

The nursery is accessed through a dusty old junk room where Sally attempts, after being discovered, to fight off the unwanted advances of Jimmy Watson (Michael Allan), the son of the house's owners. This room's state of disarray highlights the coziness of the nursery where she subsequently finds herself. The nursery—which is as important, if not more so, than the human characters—is marvelously atmospheric. Like something from *Mary Poppins* (1964), it's removed just far enough from the main house so as not to disturb the adults, or in a potential case of fratricide as with Francis and his sister, to hear a child's cry for help. Like all children's nurseries in Victorian times, the one in *Dead of Night* feels like it belongs to a different world. Separated from reality here is a room, complete with beds, chairs, tables to eat at and, of course, desks at which to have lessons, meaning children need never leave its confines until they're old enough to enter adult society or—as in the case of Francis—never.

Like all the best ghostly tales, a chill remains even after Sally has returned to the security of the real world. She knows she's safe—the first thing she does when the truth of her encounter dawns on her, is to beg Jimmy's mother to "hold me tight." The chance that what she's just experienced could be true is enough to freeze the blood.

A story such as the nursery tale requires actors who can lend the characters just the right degree of vulnerability, which both Howes and the little boy who plays Francis capture perfectly on screen. Howes went on most famously to become the feisty heiress Truly Scrumptious in the cult fantasy *Chitty Chitty Bang Bang* (1968). But what of the child who was Francis? The part was most likely performed by Barry Ford, mentioned merely as playing a minor uncredited role in the cast. A shame though this is, considering his character is one of the saddest and most haunting in the film, the mystery surrounding who actually played the character of Francis adds an extra degree of mystery to the story.

Whether Bosley Crowther eventually got to share the experiences of

Sally O'Hara in the nursery at the top of the house is not recorded. One can only imagine, however, that if he did, it would only have reinforced his opinion of this deliciously unsettling celluloid example of the haunted house.

The Innocents (1961)

It was only the wind, my dear.

Director: Jack Clayton
Written by: William Archibald and Truman Capote (screenplay), John Mortimer (additional scenes and dialogue), Henry James (based on the story "The Turn of the Screw")
Starring: Deborah Kerr, Peter Wyngarde, Megs Jenkins, Michael Redgrave, Martin Stephens, Pamela Franklin, Clytie Jessop, Isla Cameron, Eric Woodburn

Listed by Martin Scorsese as amongst his top ten horror films, *The Innocents* (based on American author Henry James' *The Turn of the Screw*) is probably as near perfect an example of the classic ghost story

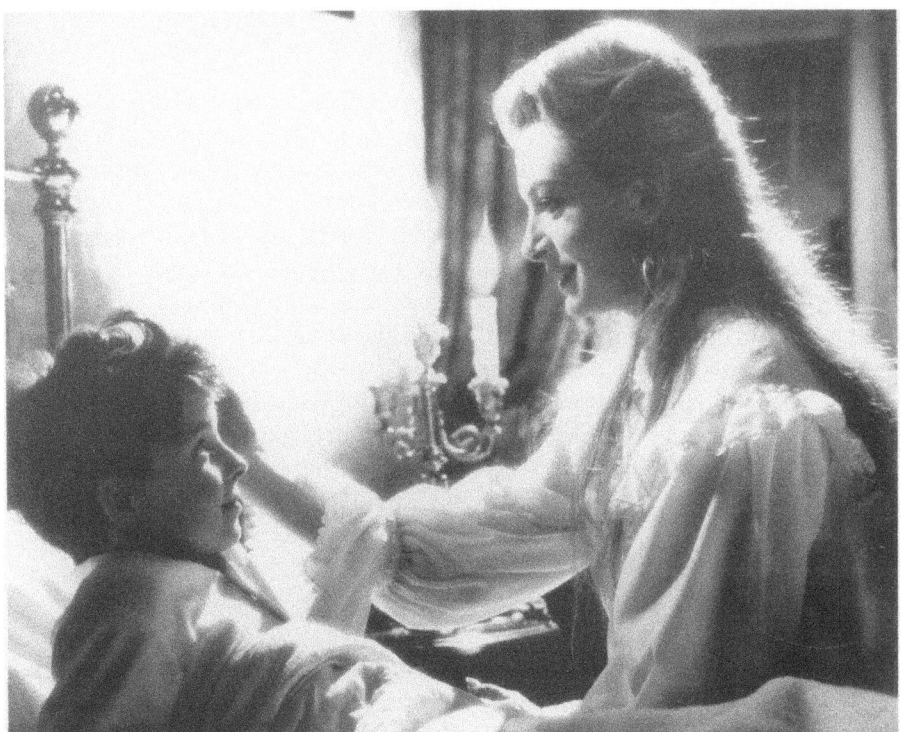

There, there: Miles (Martin Stephens) is comforted by Miss Giddens (Deborah Kerr) in *The Innocents* (1961).

on screen as you could wish to find. It concerns Miss Giddens (Deborah Kerr), a Victorian governess sent to look after two children, Miles (Martin Stephens) and Flora (Pamela Franklin) at Bly, a rambling mansion deep in the English countryside. The film uses atmosphere rather than visceral imagery to create lasting unease. Its success lies in its combination of a brilliant story with exquisite production values and a superlative cast. Bosley Crowther noted in the *New York Times* that the film uses these elements to perfection:

> Folks who have never seen a movie set in a scary old house, where the doors creak, the wind howls around corners, ghosts pace the long, dark halls and hideous, spectral faces appear in the windows at night, should find themselves beautifully frightened and even intellectually aroused by Jack Clayton's new picture, *The Innocents*....[2]

Although the film's action unfolds throughout the house and grounds, it is the scenes set within the children's schoolroom which remain the most chilling. Here is a room, isolated from the main house, which feels as though it forms a connection between this world and the next. If the other rooms in the house—such as the drawing room, where Miss Giddens appears to spend much of her time with the children—are warm and inviting in an overstuffed Victorian manner, the schoolroom is the complete antithesis of this.

Wonderfully lit by a large bay window overlooking the rooftops of Bly and down to the gardens below, the room itself, set within the attic of the house, is austere functionality. Miss Giddens' desk sits against the window on a raised platform while the main floor and walls are taken up with the children's desks and an assortment of globes, bookshelves, maps and charts. Finished with bare wooden floors and a heavy door, it has the restrictive air typically associated with a Victorian schoolroom where the teacher (or governess) commands from the front, and their charges are seen and only speak when questioned.

One scene in the room stands out, its unexpectedness making it all the more disturbing. Worried when Miles and Flora begin to behave peculiarly, Miss Giddens decides to go to London to voice her concerns to their uncle (played by Michael Redgrave). While waiting for the carriage to arrive, Miss Giddens hurries to the schoolroom to collect some things for the journey. Searching a bookshelf in a dim corner, she, and the viewer, suddenly become aware that she is no longer alone though the room was empty moments earlier. Turning, she is greeted by the apparition of a woman in black sitting mournfully at the desk by the window; the woman neither speaks nor acknowledges Miss Giddens. This is the ghost of Miss Jessel (Clytie Jessop), the children's previous governess, who had had an affair with Peter Quint (Peter Wyngarde), their uncle's valet, and committed suicide when Quint died in an accident. Despite appearing only briefly in the room, gone as quickly and silently as she came, Miss Jessel emanates malevolence and malice as she sits in what was once her domain framed by the gathering dusk beyond the window, her presence remaining in the room like a lingering odor long after she's gone. When the housekeeper comes to tell Miss Giddens that her carriage is waiting, she finds the young woman at the desk refusing to go to London as planned. The appearance of Miss Jessel in the schoolroom, coupled with the sinister aura of the rest of the house, has been enough to force Miss Giddens over the edge, into a madness from which she does not recover, culminating in the film's tragic yet ambiguous outcome.

The film had major American involvement in the form of backing from 20th Century–Fox, while one of its screenwriters was Truman Capote of *Breakfast at Tiffany's* fame, the other being English author John Mortimer, well known as the creator of the humorous character Rumpole, in *Rumpole of the Bailey*. Otherwise, it was a very British affair. The depth of vision which gives the film its brooding appeal in the house's candlelit corridors, contrasted by an intense, almost artificial light when the story moves into the sprawling grounds outside, was created by cinematographer Freddie Francis, director of classics like Hammer's *Paranoiac* (1963) and Amicus' *Dr. Terror's House of Horrors* (1965). Art director Wilfred Shingleton, who worked on David Lean's masterpiece *Great Expectations* (1946), created wonderfully over-the-top, yet intimate Victorian interiors, complemented perfectly by costume designer Sophie Devine's exquisite reproductions of period clothing.

Deborah Kerr, in the role she is said to have considered her personal favorite, gave a performance which chills, just like the ghosts that haunt the empty corridors of the lonely house and gardens. She received stellar support from Peter Wyngarde (later famous as television's dandy sleuth *Jason King* in the 1970s) as Quint, and character actress Megs Jenkins as the housekeeper Mrs. Grose (a role she repeated in a 1974 television adaptation of *The Turn of the Screw*).

As Cath Clarke noted in a 2013 *Time Out* review, multiple viewings fail to diminish its chilling impact. As a result, it remains what is widely consider the definitive interpretation of James' vision.

> You can watch *The Innocents* twice and walk away with different conclusions. Psychological horrors have imitated its ambiguous ending ever since. Few have pulled it off half as creepily.[3]

The Changeling (1980)

> *That house is not fit to live in. No one's been able to live in it. It doesn't want people.*

Don't Go Upstairs!

Director: Peter Medak
Written by: William Gray, Diana Maddox (screenplay), Russell Hunter (story)
Starring: George C. Scott, Trish Van Devere, Melvyn Douglas, Jean Marsh, John Colicos, Barry Morse, Madeleine Sherwood, Helen Burns, Francis Hyland, Ruth Springford, Eric Christmas, Roberta Maxwell, Bernard Behrens, James B. Douglas, J. Kenneth Campbell, Chris Gample, Voldi Way, Michelle Martin, Janne Mortil, Paul Rothery, Sammy Smith, Antonia Rey, Randolph Blankinship, Travis Major

Attempting to rebuild his life following the death of his wife and daughter in a freak car accident, composer and university professor John Russell (George C. Scott), leases a disused Victorian mansion, in the hope that its solitude will restore his creative juices. But malevolent supernatural forces, dormant in the empty house for decades, are reawakened with far-reaching consequences for Russell and those who cross his path.

> Most horror films these days are not for the squeamish. *The Changeling* is old-fashioned in that respect: it's not for the nervous.[4]

There are generally two elements which make horror films memorable: atmosphere and the visceral. Seldom, though, do they combine in one production and, as often as not, it is the visceral which wins out at the cost of atmosphere. However, as David Castell points out, when ambience is handled properly, the need for over-the-top viscerals is greatly reduced. In fact, as Castell adds, the strength of director Peter Medak's film lay, more often than not, in the power of suggestion: "Here it is George C. Scott among the spirits in a very superior example of the species whose horrors are never (well, only in a flashback) seen."[5]

Unfortunately, the film occasionally succumbs to the weakness befalling many similar exercises of the period, such as *The Sentinel* (1977) and *Ghost Story* (1981), in that it veers towards being too clever for its own good. Here, a storyline that concerns a changeling child from somewhere in a powerful family's past returning to haunt those in the present, although inventive, loses some of its impact by becoming convoluted.

There is some unpleasantness in the mix; the particularly nasty aftermath of a car crash stands out. Fortunately, these moments are few and far between, offering just enough abrupt surprises to splice together the action. A slow, methodical building of tension on several occasions, shattered by sudden jolts of the unexpected—breaking windows, slamming doors, inexplicable noises stopping as abruptly as they start—ensures the viewer's attention doesn't waver. And all unfolding in the most spectacularly gothic setting.

What a marvelous old building Russell's house is. Story upon story of endless empty rooms such as a library stocked with classic titles, and a music room large enough to accommodate a hundred-piece orchestra. The filmmakers surpassed themselves in creating an atmospheric environment, perfect for all sorts of supernatural nastiness: endless stretches of emptiness and melancholia, with areas connected by forgotten passageways and disused staircases.

> The ghost lurks in narrow, confined spaces and age-old cobwebbed rooms, and director Peter Medak's camera tracks relentlessly through these claustrophobic environs like an invader in some old and murky painting stirred to life.[6]

The sense of otherworldliness starts as Russell is driven through the grounds of the property by Claire Norman (Trish Van Devere) of the local historical society, who owns the house, and it intensifies as he explores the house itself, climaxing with his discovery of the hidden nursery at the top of the building. Approached by a narrow staircase, the entrance to which has been inexplicably boarded up, this is clearly a room the owner of the house would rather had been forgotten. The reason why soon becomes apparent.

Filled with artifacts from a turn-of-the-century childhood—leather-bound books, tin soldiers and a little music box—the room, coated in a thick layer of dust, is dominated by a dilapidated wheelchair designed for a child. Small and cluttered—it is at points during the film seen in flashback, complete with roaring fire and cozy lighting—this was a space created for a child in the era when they were seldom acknowledged in public. Even so, it still has an air of warmth and safety, as is so often felt in the nurseries of Victorian and Edwardian children. All of which reinforces the horrors of the event which unfolded in the room all those years before, the results of which form the core of the paranormal activities which haunt Russell soon after he moves in.

The state of the room as it was—rich, comfortable, lived in—juxtaposes with its condition when Russell discovers it. Dirty, ramshackle and forgotten, this is the kind of space where time stands still; when you enter, you feel like you've been cut off from the rest of the world. Its position, tucked from sight at the top of a steep staircase, as often the case in the large houses of the rich, is also appropriate. How the wheelchair inexplicably finds its way from this inaccessible aerie, into the main house, provides not only one of the film's most shocking moments, but also adds to the enigmatic air which overshadows the proceedings.

Like the nursery at the top of the house which Russell rents, *The Changeling* has largely been overlooked in the years since its release. Perhaps it is a little too stately, even pedestrian, for modern horror tastes. However, the film has stood the test of time, remaining as stylishly sinister as the house at the center of its ghostly happenings.

The Woman in Black (2012)

I believe even the most rational mind can play tricks in the dark.

Director: James Watkins
Written by: Jane Goldman (screenplay), Susan Hill (from the novel by)
Starring: Daniel Radcliffe, Misha Handley, Sophie Stuckey, Jessica Raine, Roger Allam, Lucy May Barker, Ciarán Hinds, Shaun Dooley, Mary Stockley, Alexia Osborne, Alfie Field, William Tobin, Victor McGuire, Cathy Sara, Tim McMullan, Daniel Cerqueira, Liz White, Alisa Khazanova, Ashley Foster, David Burke, Janet McTeer, Aoife Doherty, Sidney Johnston, Emma Shorey, Molly Harmon, Ellisa Walker-Reid

Much fanfare heralded the big-screen adaptation of English author Susan Hill's best-selling ghost story *The Woman in Black*. Not only was it adapted for the screen by Jane Goldman, the screenwriter with a Midas touch, but it marked the latest offering from the rejuvenated Hammer Films, whose previous efforts at re-entering the horror fray had met with mixed success. Most significantly, it featured actor Daniel Radcliffe in his first post–Harry Potter lead role, and as a result had much riding on it for the young actor.

In many ways the film works, though it's never quite the terrifying experience that reading Hill's original 1983 classic proved to be, nor indeed its subsequent 1989 TV movie adaptation or stage version which still plays to packed houses in London's West End (a run of almost 30 years). The result however is wonderfully atmospheric. Like the theatrical version, it relies heavily on inference over an onslaught of gory visuals, as Claudia Puig highlights: "As opposed to modern horror flicks like the *Saw* movies, where gruesome violence can almost blunt fears, *The Woman in Black* is a tasteful, old-school frightener, emphasizing suspense and foreboding over blood and guts."[7]

The film differs from the book with the addition of new characters, an expanded plotline and a reworking of the conclusion. However, the lonely house, on an island in the marshes, reached by a causeway accessed only when the tide is out, is still there, a disturbing presence overshadowing much of the film. Large parts of the story play out beyond the confines of the house, many of which feel slow and without the unsettling effect of those which unfold within the gloomy mansion and its grounds.

Solicitor Arthur Kipps (Radcliffe) is sent to Eel Marsh House, a decaying mansion sitting off England's northeast coast, to conduct business on behalf of his London firm. Going through the papers of its late owner Mrs. Drablow (Alisa Khazanova), Kipps discovers the death certificate of her sister Jennet Humfrye (Liz White), whose spirit haunts the house. Jennet hanged herself in its nursery after her son Nathaniel (Ashley Foster)—whom she had given up to Mrs. Drablow and her husband for adop-

8. The Nursery and Schoolroom

tion—drowned when the car in which he and Mrs. Drablow were traveling sank in the marshes. In the succeeding years, the spirit of the vengeful Jennet—the "Woman in Black"—has returned to haunt the area, her appearance generally being regarded as a harbinger of doom.

Eel Marsh House as a whole is startling enough, the last place on Earth you would want to be left alone in after dark. A gothic monstrosity, complete with mullioned windows, grand oak staircases and a gallery festooned with faded tapestries, its walls hide a myriad of forgotten rooms. The surrounding estate—complete with family graveyard—has been abandoned to the vagaries of time and nature. All this pales beside the seeping unpleasantness and evil emanating from the vicinity of the house's nursery, leaving the viewer in little doubt that this is where the fun will take place.

Here is a room, locked upon Kipps' initial visit, then unexpectedly open when he returns to further investigate the mystery surrounding the house. Clockwork toys, musical carousels, dolls and schoolbooks sleep in a layer of dust, untouched since the fateful day that little Nathaniel left the house for the last time. A rocking chair that belonged to the child's governess sits silently by the window, until Kipps is alone in the house. Now any sane person hearing noises coming from a supposedly locked room, in an isolated house in which they are meant to be alone, would vacate the premises forthwith. But where would the fun bein that?

Kipps makes his way to the room—now conveniently open—only to be subjected to the true horrors of Eel Marsh House. Here he is haunted by visions—real or not, the viewer is never sure—of the dead Jennet, returned to take revenge upon the living for what she saw as the death of her son due to neglect by her uncaring sister. Evil, like a black slick, spreads across the bed and encroaches upon Kipps, while the rocking chair, with a life of its own, dances madly forward and back, only to stop as abruptly as it started. These horrors culminate in an appearance of Jennet, which is enough to make Kipps flee the house in fear of his life.

The nursery makes one final appearance. Determined to lay Jennet's spirit to rest, Kipps and Sam Daily (Ciarán Hinds), a local landowner, retrieve Nathaniel's body from the marshes and return it to the nursery. With Jennet appearing placated by his attempts to reunite her with her beloved son, Kipps leaves Eel Marsh House. That her dreaded apparition makes one final, grisly appearance hardly comes as a surprise; this *is* gothic horror. But of the house and its haunted nursery, no more is seen, the lonely pile left to its sad existence amongst the wilds of the marshlands.

The Woman in Black is atmospheric and, in places, chilling. The film's look is faultless, as you'd expect with a top-notch production team involved, including Emmy-winning art director Paul Ghirardani, renowned for his realistic period reproductions. It is in this area that the film comes closest to recapturing Hammer's old magic and their ability to create atmosphere through settings. Whether it is enough to reinvent the company for a new generation, or whether, like the inhabitants of the lonely Eel Marsh house, they should be left in peace, is another matter altogether.

The Ones Below (2015)

I know what I want. And I focus on getting it.

Director: David Farr
Written by: David Farr
Starring: Stephen Campbell Moore, Clémence Poésy, David Morrissey, Laura Birn, Deborah Findlay, Sarah Malin, Anna Madeley, Jonathan Harden, Sam Pamphilon, Franc Ashman, Christos Lawton, Laila Alj, Joseph Mills, Elliot Mills, Stephanie Jacob, Tuyen Do, Alex Avery, Natasha Alderslade, Grace Calder, Robert Roman Ratajczak, Blaise Simmons-Johnson

Justin (Stephen Campbell Moore) and Kate (Clémence Poésy) live a seemingly idyllic life. With a beautiful London flat, rewarding high-powered jobs and a baby on the way, everything appears wonderful. But when the "perfect" couple, Jon (David Morrissey) and his pregnant wife Theresa (Laura Birn), move into the flat below, things begin to unravel, with tragic and unimaginable consequences which none of them could have foreseen.

A psychological "chiller" from BBC Films, writer-director David Farr's *The Ones Below* is so simple, so gorgeous to watch yet downright disturbing in its possibilities, that the viewer is hooked from the opening credits until its unexpectedly twisted denouement.

Had this film been produced by a larger production company, a way would have been found to provide it with a cop-out "happy" conclusion. One of the best things about works from independent filmmakers like BBC Films, however, is the lack of obligation to play to every whim of fickle mass audiences.

Which is just the case with *The Ones Below*. Here is a film which finds unease in everyday surroundings and a situation which, though you keep telling yourself it can't happen, you realize can and is. Normality here is what is truly unsettling. Justin and Kate's frequently humdrum existence of juggling jobs and home life, is counterbalanced with the happiness experienced by bringing a new baby into the world. All of which juxtaposes jarringly with the rigidity of their new neighbors Jon and Theresa. Their *Stepford Wives* world of perfection—clipped box hedges in the garden, His and Hers bathroom towels and membership of the most exclusive clubs in town—couldn't be more contrasting.

8. The Nursery and Schoolroom

As with the anally retentive Jon and Theresa, look here is everything. But, as Allan Hunter highlighted in his analysis of the film, cinematographer Ed Rutherford's less-is-more approach brings unease as well as depth to the outwardly idyllic settings:

> Ed Rutherford's lush cinematography adds to the polish of the production with his exploration of minimalist apartments and framing of seductive swimming pools adding to our sense of the characters lives and inner emotions.[8]

The room in the film which personifies this best is the nursery Jon and Theresa create for Peter, the child they longed for, but lose through a tragic accident in Justin and Kate's apartment. It was not directly Justin and Kate's fault, the heartbroken couple nonetheless blame them for their loss. When Theresa starts obsessing over their new son Billy (Joseph and Elliot Mills), offering to look after him at every opportunity, Kate becomes suspicious. Suspicion is confirmed when she surreptitiously lets herself into Jon and Theresa's apartment, only to discover with horror their secret nursery—a shrine to Billy who has, in the warped imagination of their neighbors, taken the place of their dead son Peter. A room which is a continuation of the clinical perfection of Jon and Theresa's beautiful world. On a lower floor, at the end of a corridor, here is a room, hidden away, which sits in perpetual readiness for the arrival of a baby who will never come. Where every detail is exquisite, from the furnishings and toys in co-ordinating shades of pastel blue and white to the wooden letters sitting on the chest of drawers, spelling out the name PETER. Welcoming, soothing and comforting, everything in the room has the sole aim of imbuing anyone who enters with a sense of calm. Except for the sinister photo hanging behind the cot, of a happy couple with their imaginary son, a photo of Jon and Theresa with Billy.

The sudden shock of seeing the photo—taken during one of Theresa's covert babysitting operations—provides the perfect double whammy to a scene which ratchets up the tension marvelously. Its appearance, shocking subject matter and clear message, are merely emphasized by the almost ecclesiastical purity of its surroundings.

The nursery, compared to the other rooms seen in the film, appears relatively briefly, in only a couple of scenes. Following her initial discovery of the incriminating photograph, Kate persuades Justin to accompany her when she returns to confront Jon and Theresa about what she found in their apartment. That the photograph has been removed simply reveals to Kate, and the viewer, that her neighbors are on to her. However, with no evidence, the ensuing situation simply makes Justin believe his increasingly neurotic wife has eventually lost the plot, a conclusion which ultimately ends with devastating results.

In keeping with the overall feel of the film, there's no heartwarming conclusion, though it sustains a sense of disbelief until the closing scenes. It's hard to believe the perpetrators could, and do, get away with such an ingenious crime, its simplicity merely adding to the seeping sense of disturbing horror, and leaving the victims of the story broken, damaged and destroyed.

The Ones Below's depiction of a seemingly familiar London, tinged with an unobtainable otherworldliness, isn't real. Its leafy suburban streets—somewhere north of Regents Park—lined with narrow, multi-story townhouses, reached by flights of faded stone steps, rarely exist except in the imagination of writers and filmmakers. Outwardly blessed lives of people like Kate—who works from home, her timetable punctuated only occasionally with visits to her studio at the V&A—are the stuff of fantasy. However, considering the truth which, like here, often simmers beneath the surface of these dream worlds, perhaps that's for the better.

9

The Bathroom

"Children should never have baths," my grandmother said. *"It's a dangerous habit."*
—*The Witches*, Roald Dahl (1983)

Few children would disagree with Grandmother's sage counsel in *The Witches*, the perennial favorite about a boy and his grandmother who do battle with a coven of malevolent witches. What kid, after all, would admit to liking a bath? It's not just children, however, who should be wary of bathtubs, and showers, and bathrooms generally.

Forget the shower and bathroom which could be said to have started it all off: The choice of the tiled chamber of horrors from *Psycho* (1960) is so obvious, it's almost as painful as Norman Bates' kitchen knife. There are 101 other, equally disturbing depictions of the room where the occupant is often naked and laid bare, literally. And, as films like the deliciously creepy *Squirm* (1976) and haunting *What Lies Beneath* (2000) prove, you don't need something sharp to cut short your relaxing soak, though razor-fingered Freddy Krueger might have something to say about that.

Hands of the Ripper (1971)

You just wait till you see yourself in this. Oh, Miss Anna, you're going to look lovely tonight. Everyone's going to be looking at you. You're going to be the belle of the ball, you just wait and see.

Director: Peter Sasdy
Written by: Lewis Davidson (screenplay), Edward Spencer Shew (original story)
Starring: Eric Porter, Angharad Rees, Jane Merrow, Keith Bell, Derek Godfrey, Dora Bryan, Marjorie Rhodes, Lynda Baron, Marjie Lawrence, Norman Bird, Margaret Rawlings, Elizabeth MacLennan, Barry Lowe, A.J. Brown, April Wilding, Anne Clune, Vicki Woolf, Katya Wyeth, Beulah Hughes, Tallulah Miller, Peter Munt, Philip Ryan, Molly Weir, Charles Lamb, Lewis Alexander, Maxwell Craig, Josie Grant, Dido Plumb, Nadine Stapleton, Ann Way

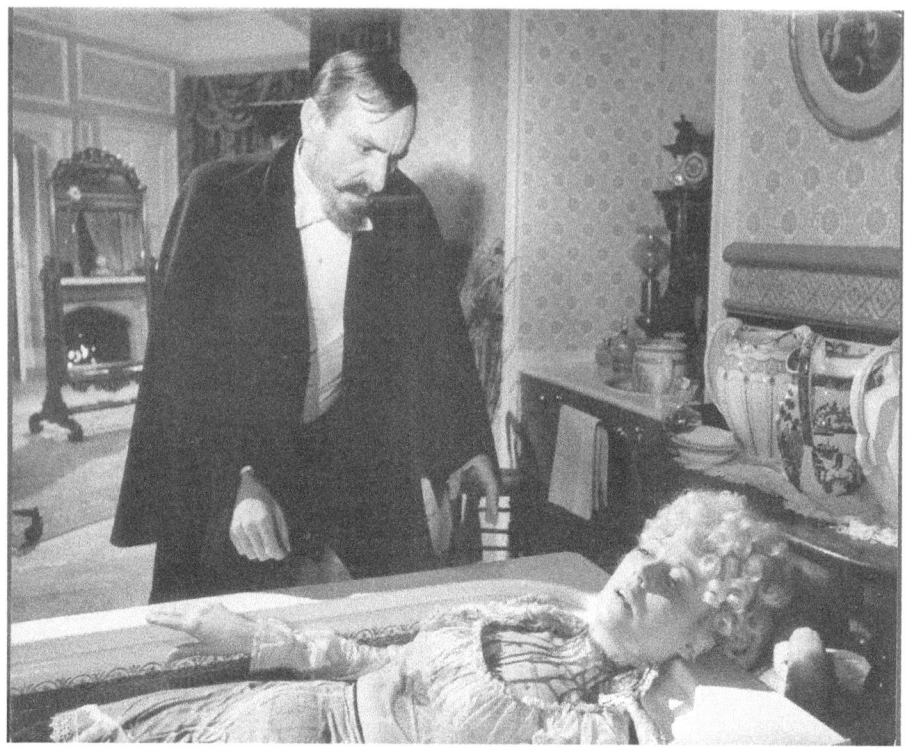

Blood bath: Dr. Pritchard (Eric Porter) is shocked to find Dolly (Marjie Lawrence) in the bath in *Hands of the Ripper* **(1971).**

Hands of the Ripper is surprisingly fresh for one of Hammer's later productions. An attempt to combine atmospheric period horror with graphic gore and vague undertones of Freudian psychobabble, it managed to pull off the unusual combination with considerably more success than their similar outing from the same period, *Dr. Jekyll & Sister Hyde* (1971). Generally preferring to leave deep delving into the human psychosis to their contemporary, psychological dramas such as *Paranoiac* (1963), Hammer here tried to spice things up by making one of the two central characters—Eric Porter's Dr. John Pritchard—a student of the (at the time) fledgling psychiatrist Freud. However, as *New York Times* reviewer A.H. Weiler pointed out, even the great shrink himself might have had his work cut out understanding the characters here:

> Eric Porter, as a dour, dedicated pioneer "follower of that man Freud," is decidedly anxious to cure her beyond the call of duty and the Hippocratic Oath. But Miss Rees keeps hearing those voices and stabbing people until she and the good doctor wind up dead in St. Paul's Cathedral. All things considered, Freud himself might have had a hard time with Miss Rees and company.[1]

9. The Bathroom

Indeed, it is when the film enters the twilight world of psychoanalysis, as Pritchard tries to get to the bottom of a spate of bizarre murders terrifying Victorian London, that the film loses its punch: Lengthy segments involving the psychiatrist's couch could easily have been shortened with no ill effect. The film is saved by several set-piece murders, reflecting the growing fondness for visceral violence in horror cinema during the 1970s. Given the obvious relationship between the film and Jack the Ripper, it's clear the filmmakers would have a field day where the killings were concerned. But even they managed to outdo themselves with the viciousness with which various characters are stabbed and slashed, with everything from a handful of elaborate hatpins to a lady's lorgnette. These untamed and largely unheralded explosions of violence come to a head in a scene about a third of the way into the action, startling both for its complete unexpectedness and the fact the victim is innocent, kind and totally undeserving of a grisly fate. That it unfolds in the intimate surroundings of a Victorian lady's boudoir, adds to its brutality.

Unaware of her troubled background, Pritchard saves young orphan Anna (Angharad Rees) from a life of exploitation and possible prostitution, taking her home to live with himself and his son Michael (Keith Bell) in their grand London townhouse. Setting aside his late wife's bedroom for Anna's use, he leaves her in the capable hands of his parlor maid Dolly (Marjie Lawrence) with orders to get Anna ready to join the family, plus Michael's fiancée Laura (Jane Merrow), for supper. Dolly, overcome with Anna's transformation once she has bathed and dressed, kisses her on the cheek to wish her luck. Conveniently, it is a kiss along with anything sparkly (in this case, a necklace) that sets of the murderous streak within Anna, and there are gruesome consequences for poor Dolly.

If the term "Freudian" had been in use at the time of the story, it would have captured perfectly the grotesqueries befalling anyone unfortunate enough to show kindness to Anna, usually in the form of an innocent kiss. There is no better example of this than the death of Dolly. Emphasizing the brutality of the death, Dolly places great store by the fact that Anna is now a "lady" and she a mere maid, her low-cut servant's dress revealing ample amounts of neck for Anna to slash and stab at with a shattered hand mirror. The sight of poor Dolly staggering backwards into the bathtub concealed in a partitioned corner of the bedroom, blood flowing from a huge gash in her neck where the jagged remains of the mirror are now embedded, would be enough to send even the most hardened killer gaga.

It is as much the opulence of the bedroom-cum-bathroom—complete with gilt mirrors, brocade curtains and heavy wooden furniture, combined with the self-indulgence of its layout—which makes Dolly's murder one of the most spectacular in any Hammer horror. Long before en-suite bathrooms became commonplace, the positioning of a roll-topped tub in a tiled room, curtained off from an adjoining bedroom, was solely the domain of the aristocracy. One can imagine a lady's maid running a bath as her mistress peruses the mail over breakfast in bed or, as we see here, preparing her gown and jewels as madam bathes before leaving for dinner or the opera.

It isn't only the richness of the room which makes it significant in the film. Michael is offended when he discovers his father has given his mother's room to Anna (a complete stranger) instead of to Laura, who has come to stay in the run-up to their wedding. It is also—apart from the hallway and Pritchard's study–consulting room—the only room in the house to be seen in the film, focusing the viewer's attention even more on the grisly murder which plays out within it.

As David McGillivray highlighted in his review, director Peter Sasdy could not be faulted for the contemporary style and topics with which he colored *Hands of the Ripper*:

> Sasdy's intention throughout was evidently to present an interesting, "realistic" impression of London in the [1890s]: urchins, prostitutes and muffin-sellers throng the alleyways while behind locked doors a forward-thinking doctor (Eric Porter, adapting well) takes Anna in for psychoanalysis, a revolutionary new treatment described by his contemporary Freud.[2]

All of which surely makes the film, though not without its shortcomings, one of the more imaginative entries from Hammer's later canon.

Squirm (1976)

> *Hope you have better luck than I did. There wasn't any water at all before.*

Director: Jeff Lieberman
Written by: Jeff Lieberman
Starring: Don Scardino, Patricia Pearcy, R.A. Dow, Jean Sullivan, Peter MacLean, Fran Higgins, William Newman, Barbara Quinn, Carl Dagenhart, Angel Sande, Carol Jean Owens, Kim Iocouvozzi, Walter Dimmick, Leslie Thorsen, Julia Klopp, Ralph Flanders, Albert Smith, Jim Shirah, Harold Mumm, W.A. Lindblatt

The House of Hammer, the British pulp horror magazine published during the late 1970s, positively wallowed in showing the most graphic stills from the seemingly never-ending run of gruesome films then saturating the market. Though eagerly lapped up by kids not old enough to see the films themselves, photos from titles like *The Crazies* (1973) and *Satan's Slave* (1976) often promised something more disturbing than the films served up in reality. The magazine went to town on promoting one film, offering tickets to an exclusive London screening in December 1976, as well as allotting it two full pages in its June 1977 issue: *Squirm*, which for once surpassed the disturbing delights hinted at by its promotional material.

New Yorker Mick (Don Scardino) is visiting his girlfriend Geri Sanders (Patricia Pearcy), who lives with her sister Naomi (Jean Sullivan) and widowed mother Alma (Fran Higgins) in the sleepy town of Fly Creek, Georgia. He has picked the wrong time to come south: Fly Creek has just been hit by one of the biggest storms in living memory. The freak weather has had a devastating effect on the local worm population, used as fishing bait by visitors to the area. With power lines down and broken electric cables feeding live current into the wet soil, the previously docile invertebrates have now become a flesh-munching army, with Fly Creek, and its unfortunate inhabitants, lying directly in their path.

Let's be honest: *Squirm* was never going to win awards, with its dubious acting and rickety, makeshift sets. However, whatever finesse was lacking in these departments was more than made up for with some genuinely disturbing imagery. As Julian Fox noted, writer-director Jeff Lieberman played the visual possibilities of several thousand pulsating, flesh-eating worms to the max:

> I must confess to finding the film almost too hard to take, though, on the grounds that it is certainly the most horribly graphic exercise in sustained terror that I can remember seeing. It is obscene in its emphasis on visual shock and quite riveting in spite of it.[3]

Numerous shock sequences are scattered throughout the film, but it is those which take place in the bathroom of the Sanders' home which truly make the skin crawl. Given the bathroom is the first place seen in the film, the viewer can be assured that it's going to play a major part in the proceedings.

The bath itself—with wall-attached shower head—is hardly state-of-the-art. Indeed, like much of the Sanders farmhouse, everything to do with the bathroom is basic. However, as you see little of the room other than the bath itself, it serves its purpose as a backdrop for some key sequences. Geri takes a shower in the opening scene, which establishes her character's vulnerability as well as her fragile relationship with her young neighbor Roger (R.A. Dow), who fantasizes about her when spying on her through the bathroom window, as he works up a sweat in the garden below.

Later, filthy after a boating accident in the river, Geri heads again to the bathroom to take a shower. Now naked, she reaches over the bathtub and manipulates the taps, and a host of writhing, plump, juicy worms emerge from the shower head, dangling ever nearer to her bare back.

When no water comes out of the tap, a frustrated Geri turns it off, and the worms retreat just before they can do any damage. Geri misses all this, as she never once looks at the potentially death-dealing shower head the whole time she stands beneath it. But what schlock filmmaker lets common sense get in the way of building suspense?

The bathroom appears once more, playing a pivotal role in the finale. Geri's sister Naomi, deciding to have a bath, this time actually gets as far as filling the tub with hundreds of squirming annelids. Her eventual confrontation with a heaving wall of worms provides a clever twist at the end, but not before offering up some marvelously creepy imagery as dusk falls in the candlelit house.

There are other, much worse scenes, in the graphic sense. The demise of town loser Roger, which is drawn out over the final third of the film, is particularly toe-curling, providing some wonderfully icky opportunities to showcase the early work of makeup wizard Rick Baker. However, it's the scenes of Geri and Naomi in the bathroom which are the edgiest, and genuinely unsettling. Lieberman wasn't afraid to pay homage to one of cinema's greatest suspense practitioners, Alfred Hitchcock, and one of Hitch's best shock moments, the shower scene from *Psycho*. What plays out in the bathroom here is just as discomfiting and equally unlikely to encourage people into the shower.

Geri's close call is, of course, a wildly silly scenario. Worms are unlikely ever to emerge from a shower head, no matter how dodgy your plumbing is, or be sucked back up just on the point of dropping from the fixture when you turn it off again. Then again, innocent worms are unlikely to be turned into carnivorous, flesh-eating life forms just because electricity leaks into the ground. The whole premise of the film is preposterous, and as a result requires viewers, as with many horror films, to suspend their rationality. If, however, you manage to do this, watching *Squirm* can be an effectively skin-crawling experience.

A Nightmare on Elm Street (1984)

> *Maybe we're going to have a big earthquake. They say things get really weird just before.*

Director: Wes Craven
Written by: Wes Craven
Starring: Heather Langenkamp, Johnny Depp, Robert Englund, John Saxon, Ronee Blakley, Amanda Wyss, Jus Garcia, Charles Fleischer, Joseph Whipp, Lin Shaye, Joe Unger, Mimi Craven, Jack Shea, Ed Call, Sandy Lipton, Jeff Levine, David Andrews, Donna Woodrum, Shashawnee Hall, Carol Pritikin, Brian Reise, Ash Adams, Don Hannah, Leslie Hoffman, Paul Grenier, Charles Belardinelli

9. The Bathroom 137

The house in the poster which accompanied the release of writer-director Wes Craven's genre-changing *A Nightmare on Elm Street*—a 1960s bungalow in a suburban cul-de-sac—bears little resemblance to the one shared by the film's heroine Nancy (Heather Langenkamp) and her divorced mother Marge Thompson (Ronee Blakley). It does, though, perfectly capture the film's emphasis on community and the bond between the young people who live on Elm Street. As in that other community horror *Halloween* (1978), the inhabitants live close enough to call upon their neighbors in times of need, yet are removed enough to maintain a sense of isolation: the perfect example of the remoteness which adds an edge of horror to modern living.

Many years ago, child-killer Freddy Krueger (Robert Englund) was captured by a group of Elm Street parents and burned to death in retaliation. Now Freddy has returned and is haunting the dreams of Nancy (Langenkamp)—the daughter of Marge (Blakley), one of the vigilante parents—in a waking nightmare which leaves people feeling more than a little cut-up.

Most of 1428 Elm Street appears to be a picture of suburban tranquility: manicured lawn, picture-perfect facade, and slightly cluttered yet

Sleep it off: Heather Langenkamp's image dominates the poster for writer-director Wes Craven's genre-defining classic *A Nightmare on Elm Street* (1984).

lived-in interior, leaving only its cellar, housing an antiquated boiler system, with any real sense of the sinister. Not only was it a boiler room—at a school—where Freddy met his end years before, at the hands of Marge and the other local parents, but the one in her own home is where she hides a gruesome memento of that fateful night.

The cellar may be the most visually disturbing room in the Thompson house but it's the bathroom which plays host to one of the film's most unexpected and shocking sequences. As Janet Leigh discovered in *Psycho*, though the bathroom may be where you feel you should be at your most relaxed, it is also, as a result, where you're frequently at your most vulnerable, as is the case for Nancy.

The bathroom is a continuation of Marge and Nancy's house as a whole, comfortable, not ostentatious. No gold-encrusted marble bath of Egyptian proportions here. Instead, the room is slightly cramped, with a peg on the door for your robe and a bathroom suite in soporific toned plastic, with a bath just big enough for Nancy, an inflatable bath pillow, some bottles of something smelly. And, of course, Freddy.

Combining vulnerability with sexuality, this scene is all the more unpleasant because what happens here has, or could—to a degree—have been experienced by us all at some stage. Who hasn't fallen asleep in the bath, only to splutter back to consciousness as the warm water rises. Endeavoring to relax after yet another day of near fatal, sleep-induced incidents, Nancy finds comfort in a bathtub of hot, soapy water. But, as the steam ascends, so does Freddy's razor-fingered glove, between her legs. We see the discomfiting sight of Nancy, eyes closed, as the gauntlet's metal talons slice their way towards her through the suds, only to be frightened back beneath the water when Marge knocks on the door to inquire whether her daughter is okay. The scenes when Nancy is pulled by Freddy into a seemingly endless void beneath the water, are perhaps the film's tensest and most frantic. It's hardly spoiling the surprise to reveal that Nancy escapes Freddy's sodden clutches at this stage, as it does after all happen only halfway through the action. Nonetheless, the bath scene remains one of the film's most realistic and disturbing because, of all the scenarios which play out, falling asleep in the tub is one of the few which could actually happen.

The real house—bar a few cosmetic changes—is still recognizable as the place where Nancy confronted Freddy. The address is 1428 North Genesee Avenue, Hollywood—Craven kept the number for the Thompson's house in the film. It's now a state-of-the-art home, though it has kept the recognizable red front door from the 1985 sequel *A Nightmare on Elm Street 2: Freddy's Revenge* and copious follow-ups, a stark reminder of its dark past.

Typically for an example of the teenage slasher genre (which *A Night-

mare on Elm Street could be said to have kick-started), the movie did not receive over-zealous praise from mainstream critics. *Variety*, in a review for its 1996 *Movie Guide*, considered it something of a missed opportunity, particularly on the part of Craven: "[He] tantalizingly merges dreams with the ensuing wakeup reality but fails to tie up his thematic threads satisfyingly at the conclusion."[4]

On the other hand, Craven was a filmmaker who was tuned into the teenage zeitgeist whatever the period, as he'd proved with *The Last House on the Left* (1972) and would again with the smash hit *Scream* (1996). What his target audience wanted were characters they could relate to, not issues of depth, as young Nancy proves when she looks in the mirror after several nights of sleep deprivation and exclaims, "God, I look 20 years old!" This, coupled with gross-out escapism which still leaves you smiling, is just what his masterpiece delivered, and still does to this day.

Final Destination (2000)

> "In death there are no accidents, no coincidences, no mishaps, and no escapes."

Director: James Wong
Written by: James Wong, Glen Morgan and Jeffrey Reddick (screenplay), Jeffrey Reddick (story)
Starring: Devon Sawa, Ali Larter, Kerr Smith, Kristen Cloke, Daniel Roebuck, Roger Guenveur Smith, Chad Donella, Saenn William Scott, Tony Todd, Amanda Detmer, Brendan Fehr, Forbes Angus, Lisa Marie Caruk, Christine Chatelain, Barbara Tyson, Robert Wisden, P. Lynn Johnson, Larry Gilman, Guy Fauchon, Randy Stone, Mark Holden, Marrett Green, Fred Keating, John Hainsworth, Pete Atherton, Nicole Robert, Kristina Matisic

Following a premonition that the plane he and his high school class mates are on will explode on take-off, Alex (Devon Sawa) gets himself and several of his friends evicted from the plane, hence cheating death when his fears come to pass. Now regarded as a freak by the survivors because of his apparent second sight, he must save them from Fate, which seems to have it in for those who managed to cheat it the first time around.

Critic Walter Addiego damned the film with faint praise:

> Amid all the picture's rote gotcha stuff, several of the creepy killings show a thimbleful of imagination. (And, yes, it *is* a crummy subject for creative effort.) These scenes involve household objects rigged up, with morbid wit, into convoluted Rube Goldberg death machines.[5]

While perhaps being harsh about the deaths which pepper the plot, most of which are nonetheless skillfully executed, Addiego had a point about the means used to achieve them. Like the machines created by American cartoonist Rube Goldberg and his British counterpart Heath Robinson, designed to tackle simple tasks in over-complex ways, the death machines in *Final Destination* transfix the viewer. We have all seen stabbings, decapitation and garroting play out before, but how about when these occur not at the hands of a human enemy, but through Fate itself? When it manipulates, for instance, a crash between a car and a train that sends a metal shard spinning through the air to slice through a guy's head as though it were butter. Or, in the case of the film's *pièce de résistance*, a genuinely harrowing bathtub strangulation, the build-up to which is as disturbing as the death itself.

Much of the film's appeal lies in the familiarity of its situations. Horror arising from everyday occurrences (even if contrived) is all the more effective because the viewer can, to a degree, relate to it. Dying in a plane accident or being hit by a truck is, in truth, more frightening than being cut to bits by some fictional bogeyman.

As with many successful films, good horror can also sink or swim depending on the environment where it is set. Where this is concerned, it helps if the location is real, and somewhere that you can recognize. So it's ideal that the bathroom where Alex's friend Tod (Chad Donella) meets his end—the first of the bizarre "accidental" deaths to follow in the path of the opening set-piece killing—is instantly recognizable as the one from your own home. Here, there are none of the state-of-the-art fixtures and fittings found in the en-suite of some showpiece mansion. Instead, you have the cluttered, shared washroom of a family house, where underwear dries on a retractable line over the bath, and razors share space with the toothpaste in the wall-mounted vanity cabinet. The bathroom is also the ultimate private room, the one place in the house where people hesitate to enter if it's "engaged," even if the occupant is screaming for help.

Forget that there appears to be some form of paranormal entity—or Fate as it's called here—instigating each of the character's deaths. The resultant methods of killing are genuinely unnerving, particularly in the case of the drawn-out bathroom scene. The tension here is ratcheted up thanks to several skin-crawling false starts, as Tod first cuts himself shaving, then proceeds to clip his nose hair with a pair of nail scissors, before reaching across to plug his ghetto-blaster into an open electrical socket. All this done as a mysterious pool of water from a leak behind the toilet edges ever closer to where he stands, making inevitable the slip which leads to his death. When it at last happens, and Tod falls into the bath, to be garroted by the clothesline, the sight of him struggling to find a footing on the bath's slippery ceramic surface as his life ebbs away is intensely disturbing.

You could, of course, claim that the elements preceding the various deaths in the film are too contrived or downright stupid to be in any way believable. Who, for instance, is going to take a portable music box with an AC adaptor into a bathroom? In a clever twist, the obvious culprits here are seldom the ones which ought to result in death. Where Tod's end is concerned, being strangled over the bath by the clothesline was the last and least obvious of a host of options. However, it's the fact these hazards are so clear which makes them all the more shocking. People die every day as the result of accidents caused by common objects and situations found in the home.

There are only so many manufactured deaths you can employ before you lose what little credibility you have; the franchise ended with its fifth installment in 2011. However, there was no escaping the originality of the killings and the disconcerting familiarity of the tools which instigated them in the original episode.

What Lies Beneath (2000)

> *There's a ghost in my house. I saw her in the water, beside me, in the bathtub.*

Director: Robert Zemeckis
Written by: Clark Gregg (screenplay), Sarah Kernochan and Clark Gregg (story)
Starring: Michelle Pfeiffer, Katherine Towne, Miranda Otto, James Remar, Harrison Ford, Victoria Bidewell, Diana Scarwid, Dennison Samaroo, Jennifer Tung, Eliott Goretsky, Rachel Singer, Daniel Zelman, Ray Baker, Wendy Crewson, Amber Valletta, Joe Morton, Sloane Shelton, Tom Dahlgren, Micole Mercurio, Donald Taylor, Jayson Argento, J.C. Brandy, Mark Patrick Costello, Steven Dell, Linda Li, Fabio May, Julian Roca-Chow, Carolyn Wendell

With her teenage daughter gone to college, and husband Norman (Harrison Ford) engrossed in his research at a local university, Claire Spencer (Michelle Pfeiffer) is left with nothing but silence for company in their isolated lakeside home. She encounters an manifestation one night; Norman dismisses it as her mind playing tricks. Claire starts questioning whether she's as alone as she first believed. It is a question which leads to a devastating discovery.

Have you ever noticed how horror films set in people's homes often feature houses to die for—quite literally, in many cases. There are exceptions to the rule: No one in their right mind would live in that hovel in the woods which harbors something nasty in the basement, or the dilapidated farmhouse at the end of the lane where the family from Hell has eked out a solitary existence for generations. On the other hand, most of us would

Bad hair day: Claire Spencer (Michelle Pfeiffer) feels washed out in *What Lies Beneath* (2000).

give our back teeth to own that dreamy country mansion or breathtaking city apartment where the successful young couple live, at least until their malevolent sitting tenants come knocking.

Which brings us to the house in director Robert Zemeckis' paranormal thriller *What Lies Beneath*. In his review of the film's 2001 video release, Ed Gonzalez captured perfectly the essence of an abode which, on the face of it, would be the furthest thing you could imagine from a house of horror:

> New England life always looks good in the movies (spacious homes near sparkling lakes; boats bopping on the horizon; strategically placed wharves), and Zemeckis so painstakingly evokes the normalcy of this hot-apple-pie milieu that the only thing missing is the accompanying Odorama scratch-n-sniff card. Nothing wrong could ever happen here, especially if you're a genetic engineer named Norman Spencer (Harrison Ford) with a wife as voluptuous as the lonely Claire (Michelle Pfeiffer).[6]

Forget that the owners are both, in their own way, psychologically troubled. That there's something fishy about the new couple who move into the house next door. Or that a dark secret lies at the bottom of the lake. Who cares about such things when the residence in question is 15 Willoughby Lane. A house which wouldn't look out of place in *Architectural Digest*. Horrors aplenty happen throughout the house and the surrounding area, including the climax which provides a typically crowd-pleasing conclusion to events. But none of these though raise the same chills as the events which play out in the bathroom.

Of course, clues that this room will be the focus of any disturbing activities in the film are clearly signposted from the outset: The marvelously sinister poster which accompanied its release featured a bath with nothing but a claw-like hand emerging over the edge. The paranormal atmosphere is established early on when Claire's relaxing soak in the room's statement bathtub is interrupted by an unwelcome guest. And we won't even start on the electrical socket, hairdryer and gothic, jagged framed vanity mirror, all of which are omens of trouble if ever there were any.

The room is the setting for several ghostly manifestations, and some of the film's most disturbing scenes, including a particularly tense nail-biter just prior to the climax. These are, of course, all the more unsettling because what happens here could happen to anyone: The normality of the scenarios and the bathroom itself make everything all the more unnerving. From the opening moments when we first meet Claire soaking in the steam-shrouded tub, until the finale which reveals whether the preceding horrors have been a figment of her imagination, the depiction of a comforting—albeit luxurious—bathroom, a safe haven from the rigors of the day, is familiar to us all. Terry bathrobes and thick pile towels are heaped beside a roll-top bath, while creamy scented candles offset the dove gray paintwork and white tiles.

The beauty and romance of the room make the horrors all the worse when they unexpectedly hit from nowhere. Featuring several shock sequences, originating both naturally and otherwise, it spends most of the time atmospherically—if a little unbelievably—shrouded in a virtual pea-souper of mist: you can't help thinking that such an otherwise beautifully appointed bathroom would have a better ventilation system. This dense fog hides a profusion of horrors—both imaginary and real—as well as the ornate tub itself, the focal point for a suicide, a murder and an attempted murder. Though this cursed bath may look like the ultimate place to chill out, in reality it reinforces the fact that the bathroom can be amongst the most lethal in the house.

By its very nature, there are unavoidable comparisons between *What Lies Beneath*, combining paranormal, horror and psychological uncertainties (are Claire's supernatural encounters real or imaginary?), and the work of Hitchcock. Overlooking the obvious bathroom/*Psycho* (1960) analogies, its clever ambiguity results in a film that has similarities to such mind-game classics as *Suspicion* (1941) and *Spellbound* (1945). As Bob

Graham wrote, such parallels worked in the favor of *What Lies Beneath*, resulting in a modern classic of understated, subtle disquiet:

> Is *What Lies Beneath* a supernatural thriller? Or is it all in the mind? They might even come to the same thing, which is one of the reasons this latest Zemeckis production keeps percolating in the memory long after all the Hitchcockeyed referencing—and the screams—have died down.[7]

10

The Attic

> "C'mon. We can turn it into a fun game: 'What's Scarier, the Basement or the Attic?'"
> —*The Haunting of Blackwood House*,
> Darcy Coates (2015)

Darcy Coates raised an interesting conundrum in her novel *The Haunting of Blackwood House*: Though the main part of a house is generally welcoming and friendly, the rooms at either end have always been enveloped with an air of mystery.

In the days of grand stately homes and gentrified townhouses, the basement was usually where the staff worked, while the attics housed their sleeping quarters or those of the family's children. In modern homes, the attic—though still occasionally used as a bedroom as seen in *The Amityville Horror* (1979)—is now generally kept for storing things you want hidden from sight. Which makes it an ideal environment for the horror film. Whether being used to keep objects, people or practices locked safely away, attics have served a multitude of purposes for horror practitioners.

The position of the attic—at the top of the house, often reached by a steep, narrow staircase—makes it arduous to approach, and frequently difficult to swiftly escape from. It also makes an ideal vantage point from which to watch the outside world—as Norman Bates discovers in *Psycho II* (1983). And it can be difficult to attract people's attention from an attic in times of danger. All of which simply adds to the overall sense of the attic as a room with a feeling of removal from the rest of the house, or even the world.

The Picture of Dorian Gray (1945)

Perfection of the outside. Murderous corruption within.

Director: Albert Lewin
Written by: Albert Lewin (screenplay, based on the novel by Oscar Wilde)
Starring: George Sanders, Hurd Hatfield, Donna Reed, Angela Lansbury, Peter Lawford

In an obscure corner of the Art Institute of Chicago hangs the original portrait by American artist Ivan Albright, painted for use in MGM's sumptuous filmization of *The Picture of Dorian Gray*, Oscar Wilde's famous novel of secrets and depravity set in Victorian London. The portrait shows Gray in a state of decay, after he claimed, early in the story, that he'd give his soul if he could remain young, while his portrait grows old. Still

Uncanny likeness: Dorian Gray (Hurd Hatfield) reveals his dark secret in *The Picture of Dorian Gray* **(1945).**

retaining its ability to shock 70 years after the film's release, the painting remains an arresting image in the film for two reasons. The hideous portrait springs from the screen when it appears in glorious Technicolor, after the remainder of the film has played out in black and white. It is, however, thrown into stark relief, as the old attic schoolroom in which it is stored is surprisingly Spartan by comparison to the rest of the house, emphasizing the shock of the painting when it's climactically revealed.

The movie's mysterious and haunting tone is established early on, when a friend of Gray asks, concerning his locked attic, "What rare things have you stored away there, Dorian?" The decadent young man-about-town's cryptic reply, "Skeletons of inquisitive guests," surely says more than any verbose description ever could about the locked room at the top of his London townhouse. This old attic schoolroom—into which the viewer is allowed to peer at various points throughout the film—holds the secret of Gray's life force, and hence the essence of the film as a whole.

Perhaps more than any other of Wilde's novels, *The Picture of Dorian Gray* (published in the July 1890 issue of Lippincott's literary magazine) best sums up the prolific writer and his work. Mirror-imaging Wilde, who lived in an age when he had to suppress his homosexual tendencies, Gray leads a double life of sorts, the secret of which he keeps hidden within the upstairs room.

Like the attic rooms in many films, and indeed in real life, the one here is surprisingly devoid of life. The sense of separation from the main house often felt in an attic room emphasizes its use, whether that be for something good or bad. When the viewer is initially introduced to the room—after Gray decides to use it to lock his portrait away from prying eyes—there is little in it to repel: It appears remarkably neat and orderly for a room which Gray confesses to seldom used. As the film progresses towards its dramatic conclusion, the room remains clean and tidy, like a reflection of the eternally young Gray. The only object in it which appears to decay is the hidden portrait.

The man behind the look of this Hollywood production, partly responsible for its rich atmosphere, was art director Cedric Gibbons, who received an Oscar nomination for *Dorian Gray*. Gibbons, who had previously brought the world of the Emerald City and Munchkinland to big-screen life in *The Wizard of Oz* (1939), went to town when visualizing the main rooms of Gray's house: a characteristically over-the-top Victorian confection of marble, statues, potted ferns and lush drapes. These contrast—as they do in so many films which feature attic rooms—with the austere, schoolroom severity of the place where Grey keeps his portrait under wraps.

The film is famous for featuring a young Angela Lansbury in her third screen outing (she received her second Oscar nomination for her performance). Its attic also holds a special place in film history, for hiding one of the most shocking secrets ever revealed in horror cinema.

The Devil Rides Out (1968)

The beauty of woman ... the demon of darkness ... the unholy union of "The Devil's Bride."

Director: Terence Fisher
Written by: Richard Matheson (screenplay, based on the novel by Dennis Wheatley)
Starring: Christopher Lee, Charles Gray, Nike Arrighi, Leon Greene, Patrick Mower, Sarah Lawson, Paul Eddington, Rosalyn Landor, Russell Waters, Yemi Goodman Ajibade

Focusing on the efforts of the Duc de Richleau (Christopher Lee) and Rex Van Ryn (Leon Greene) to save their young friend Simon Aron (Patrick Mower) from the grip of an occult society led by the sinister Mocata (Charles Gray), Hammer's *The Devil Rides Out*, is in reality little more than several long chase sequences interspersed with the occasional Satanic set-piece. It is these set-pieces, however, and in particular the one which takes place in the attic of Simon's country house, which create the dark and brooding air which shrouds the film. The pivotal scene, taking place in the converted attic space, sees the initially skeptical Van Ryn finally convinced about the existence of evil by de Richleau, as he uncovers the true purpose of the outwardly innocent and innocuous room.

The occult chiller, based on the novel by Dennis Wheatley, the arch purveyor of all things devilish in twentieth-century English literature, was a classic example of what Hammer had become adept at producing during the late 1960s: horrific situations taking place within the safety of the everyday world. With their fingers on the pulse of popular taste, the company had moved towards psychologically edged horror in order to appeal to a younger demographic. Though *The Devil Rides Out* plays out in an earlier era—the 1920s—the monsters here, for the most part, are human, and the evil situations at its core could take place at any time if you believe in that sort of thing. Gone are Hammer stalwarts Dracula and Frankenstein, replaced by two opposing groups of people fighting on behalf of the forces of good and evil.

The attic is where it all happens. Though it features in the film for a relatively short time, what takes place in the room at the top of Simon Aron's house is integral to the plot and how the story later unfolds. Here the viewer, along with de Richleau and Van Ryn, discover exactly what the naive Aron has got himself involved in.

10. The Attic

The devil is in the detail: Director Terence Fisher and cult star Christopher Lee (right) discuss the finer points of Satanism on the set of *The Devil Rides Out* (1968).

Hammer was accomplished in the art of putting across their message with such conviction that the viewer believed it too, no matter how preposterous. The realism and authenticity of *The Devil Rides Out* settings serve to emphasize this. As with many attics depicted in horror films, Aron's seems innocuous when initially encountered. To the casual observer, the room appears to be an observatory in which the rich young owner can indulge in his astronomical endeavors. Though the obscure symbols inlaid on its floor may alarm someone more learned in the ways of the Devil (for instance, de Richleau), to a layman like Van Ryn, they seem innocent enough, a mere extension of the astronomical paraphernalia which takes up much of the room.

In the design of the room, there is the unmistakable touch of Bernard Robinson, the art director and production designer responsible for Hammer's distinctive look since its earliest forays into horror with *The Curse of Frankenstein* (1957) and *Horror of Dracula* (1958). A master at making something from nothing, Robinson created many broodingly atmospheric sets over the years on minuscule budgets, a skill which was used to great effect when bringing to life the attic in Aron's house. Here, apart from some pictures and charts on the walls, the intricate design on the floor, and a few mechanical instruments sitting on top of cabinets, the room is dominated by a large telescope sitting on a raised platform, beneath a glass-domed roof.

After de Richleau and Van Ryn confront Aron in the attic and coax from him the true purpose for the room, the starkness of its decor begins to make sense. The room is intended for use by Mocata and his followers (Aron is soon to become a member); its almost monastic simplicity makes an appropriate setting in which the religious cult can conduct their blasphemous rituals. Its simplicity also heightens the impact of a scene a short time later, when de Richleau and Van Ryn return to the house after Aron escapes from them, having now come under the full influence of Mocata. At this point, the two friends come face to face with a devil in human form, whose appearance is all the more alarming and unexpected when seen within the environs of an outwardly innocent country house.

Much of the remainder of the film—apart from an over-the-top Satanic orgy held in the middle of a remote forest clearing—plays out in the homes of several well-to-do characters, each more richly decadent than the last. But none of these houses or their rooms manages to leave its mark on the film—both visually and mentally—the way that Aron's attic lair does.

Frightmare (1974)

You won't tell anyone, will you, Eddie? It'll be our secret, won't it? These people, they've no friends, no relations. No one will miss them. Let's go back, Eddie. It's not right that you should be here. In future I'll come here by myself.

Director: Pete Walker
Written by: David McGillivray (screenplay), Pete Walker (original story)
Starring: Rupert Davies, Sheila Keith, Deborah Fairfax, Paul Greenwood, Kim Butcher, Fiona Curzon, John Yule, Trisha Mortimer, Victoria Fairbrother, Edward Kalinski, Victor Winding, Anthony Hennessey, Noel Johnson, Michael Sharvell-Martin, Tommy Wright, Andrew Sachs, Nicholas John, Jack Dagmar, Leo Genn, Gerald Flood

Dorothy Yates (Sheila Keith) was a sick woman. With the help of her devoted husband Edmund (Rupert Davies), she committed atrocities too sickening to describe. As a result, they were both locked away for decades.

10. The Attic

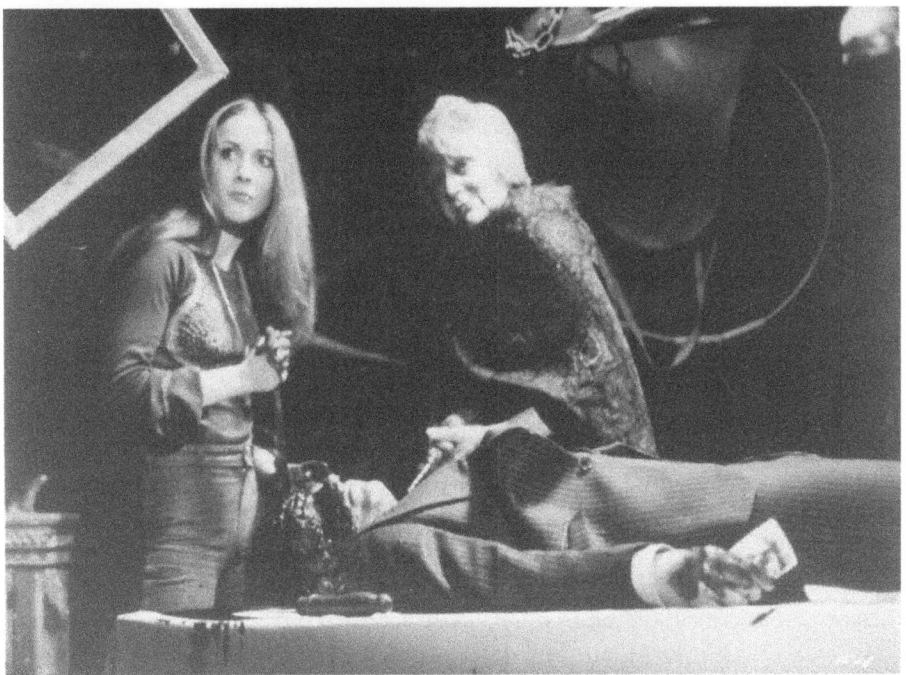

My head's splitting: Debbie (Kim Butcher) and her mother Dorothy (Sheila Keith) perform cranial DIY on the unfortunate Graham (Paul Greenwood) in *Frightmare* (1974).

Now they're cured and are living in rural obscurity on the outskirts of London. Jackie (Deborah Fairfax), Edmund's daughter from a previous marriage, discovers that her stepmother might not be as fully cured as she's led everyone to believe, and may have reverted to her old habits. At the insistence of her father, Jackie has agreed to a little "harmless subterfuge" in order to stop her stepmother going too far. Unfortunately for everyone involved, their intervention may have come too late.

British filmmaker Pete Walker, the genius behind such unsavory offerings as *Die Screaming, Marianne* (1971) and *The Flesh and Blood Show* (1972), would probably be the first to admit that few if any of his films were ever going to win awards. Despite being competently made and, considering their budgets and subject matters, remarkably polished productions, the essence of Home Counties terror—and some would say gratuitousness—which haunted many of his films was unlikely to win him fans amongst the film industry intelligentsia.

This seems to have been of little concern to a director who has been quoted as saying that one of his principal aims was to have fun with his work. Watching *Frightmare* (considered by many to be his masterpiece), it's impossible to escape the underlying feeling that, dark, seedy and remarkably downbeat though the film is, all those involved had a whale of a time making it. All of which is emphasized by David McGillivray's dark and witty script. Unlike many screenwriters who think verbosity can cover any number of sins, McGillivray—Walker's writer of choice—knew how to make his characters convey volumes with a mere word or a curl of the lip—for example, when Keith as the unhinged Dorothy is manipulating the weak-willed Edmund or the suspicious Jackie.

The film's settings serve to accentuate the grotesqueness of the situation. In London, much of the action is restricted to cheerful yet utilitarian flats of twentysomethings, soulless inner-city shopping precincts and sterile hospital offices. Not until the proceedings move to the remote Sussex farmhouse inhabited by Dorothy and Edmund does the film develop the disturbing and foreboding air which gives real life to it. Dorothy's victims—who all arrive at her house by means of a taxi, believing they're going to have their fortunes told—must be a desperate collection of lost souls if they're not put off by their first sight of the house. One look at its weather-beaten exterior, overgrown, mud-caked yard and forlorn location, chilled by a constantly moaning wind, should be enough to spook these unfortunates into hightailing it back to civilization. Instead, they enter the house of horrors, welcomed by the deceptively hospitable Dorothy, only to meet their ends in the most ferocious ways.

Little is seen of the interior of the house save for the sitting room where Dorothy reveals her victims' dead-end futures—normally at the point of a handy, steaming hot poker—and the attic, which is the scene of some truly grisly goings-on. The downstairs room's homely, country-cottage appearance—complete with open fire and comfortable, high-backed armchairs—sits in stark contrast with the room upstairs, its dark, dusty and cluttered condition accentuating the grisly goings-on as the film reaches its horrific climax.

The minute Jackie comes to the house and, despite her father's protestations, climbs the twisting stairs to the top floor—attracted by the whine of an electric drill emanating from behind a door at the end of the gloomy landing—viewers know things won't end happily. The palpable shock as she enters the disorderly room to see her stepmother hovering, power tool in hand, over the lifeless body of Jackie's boyfriend Graham (Paul Greenwood), a student psychiatrist who had come to the house to check on Dorothy and Edmund, has to be seen to be believed. It's one of horror cinema's best shock sequences.

Here, amongst the dressmaker's dummies, packing boxes and old bicycle wheels, is a wooden bench forming the centerpiece of a makeshift abattoir presided over by two characters who'd appear more at home in

The Texas Chain Saw Massacre (1974) than some rural Home Counties backwater. In fact, watching *Frightmare*—with its overriding air of decay and grime—you sense more than a few similarities between it and Tobe Hooper's seminal shocker. Until the closing frames, where Dorothy and Edmund's other daughter—Jackie's half-sister, Debbie (Kim Butcher), who shares her mother's unsavory palate—murderously descend on Jackie, the viewer can't quite believe that Jackie won't escape. But this film, with its cozy depiction of DIY cannibalism in twentieth-century England, is the work of a filmmaker who delighted in bleak and downbeat endings. *Frightmare* is the best example.

In the March 1975 issue of the British magazine *films and filming*, Derek Elley was in the minority amongst mainstream film commentators with his enthusiasm for Walker's blackly humorous, no-holds-barred approach to horror: "The main reason...for my enthusiasm for Walker's horror exercises so far is that he is one of the few directors today who is concerned with shocking, rather than tickling, his audiences,"[1] Something which his films—and in particular *Frightmare*—still manage to do, even in today's world of less than subtle violence.

The Ghoul (1975)

Well, it can't be human, can it? It feeds on human flesh!

Director: Freddie Francis
Written by: Anthony Hinds
Starring: Peter Cushing, Veronica Carlson, Stewart Bevan, Alexandra Bastedo, Ian McCulloch, Gwen Watford, John Hurt, Don Henderson

This obscure and frequently overlooked chiller is often unjustly dismissed as a graphically unpleasant potboiler and Hammer derivative. Produced by Tyburn Films, the poor relation to Hammer and Amicus, *The Ghoul* shares many elements with its more illustrious counterparts: Written by Anthony Hinds and under the guidance of director Freddie Francis, it features British horror favorites Peter Cushing and Veronica Carlson. What the film lacks in subtlety, it makes up for in atmosphere, with the use of the archetypal English country house and bookended with the revelation of something nasty in the attic. Aptly, the film was released in the U.S. under the alternative title *The Thing in the Attic*.

With a 1920s house party in full swing, we see bright young thing Daphne (a frothy performance from Carlson) winning a morbid game which culminates in the discovery of her boyfriend Billy (Stewart Bevan) faking suicide in an attic. Billy and Daphne challenge their friends Geoffrey (Ian

May the gods forgive us: Dr. Lawrence (Peter Cushing) and his housekeeper Ayah (Gwen Watford) contemplate past sins in *The Ghoul* (1975).

McCulloch) and Angela (Alexandra Bastedo) to a car race to Land's End. Several miles into their journey, Billy and Daphne run out of fuel after getting lost in dense fog. Left alone by Billy, who's gone to find petrol, Daphne sets off to explore the area, only to discover they are near a mansion owned by the sinister recluse Dr. Lawrence (Cushing). Lawrence, a defrocked clergyman, lives in isolated grandeur with his unhinged gardener Tom Rawlings (John Hurt) and mysterious Indian housekeeper Ayah (Gwen Watford).

There is more to this house than meets the eye. Years before, Lawrence visited India where his wife and son were converted to a local cult, resulting in his wife's eventual suicide. He returned to England with his Indian servant Ayah, and his son who had become a ghoul-like creature, craving human flesh and blood in order to survive. The Ghoul now lives in the attic of his father's house, guarded by the ever-vigilant Ayah who, with Lawrence's help, sates the unfortunate young man's bloodlust with unwary travelers who get lost in the area. So the scene is set for a tale of misery and horror as, one by one, Daphne and her friends meet grisly fates at the hands of the Ghoul and those who try to keep his existence a secret.

There is no escaping the fact that *The Ghoul* is a slow film and its plot, what there is of it, surprisingly light. Even so, it is imbued with a marvelously creepy ambience, and the viewer is left feeling sullied by a relentlessly shock-filled and downbeat denouement. The film perfectly evokes a bygone era, adding to the musty atmosphere that permeates events. Making excellent use of a minimal number of sets, most of the film's pivotal scenes are restricted to two main rooms. The grand lounge of the house in which the opening house party takes place marks the location from which the young couples set out on their fateful race, while the sitting room-cum-study of Lawrence's gloomy mansion makes a deceptively hospitable environment in which he lures his perspective victims to their deaths. That these rooms are fun-filled and homely respectively emphasizes the terrors housed several floors above, the comfort and attention to detail of the lower quarters standing in stark juxtaposition with the claustrophobic air of the attics and their approaching staircases.

Little is actually seen of the interiors of the attics. They mostly appear in semi-darkness, as does the room where Daphne proves her mettle during Billy's macabre game, or not at all, as in the case of the place where Ayah keeps watch over her unfortunate charge, and where you get the impression Lawrence himself seldom ventures. That we never see inside the Ghoul's abode plays into the belief that less is more, particularly where effective horror is concerned. The imagination is often more powerful than anything which can be shown on the screen, and here the viewer is left to put meat on the bones of what actually happens in the lair where Geoffrey confronts the Ghoul, with suitably grotesque results.

This minimalism also plays in the film's favor, allowing the cast to lend a sense of depth and feeling to the central characters not often associated with the horror genre: Cushing in particular brings Lawrence alive with a deep and heartfelt performance. By the end of the film, with the exception of Tom the gardener who has few if any redeeming qualities, it is Lawrence and his household with whom the viewer has the most sympathy. Daphne and her unfortunate friends may not deserve their fates but neither are they particularly pleasant people, with the result that those watching are left unmoved by their fates at the hands of the Ghoul in his attic lair.

Burnt Offerings (1976)

Like you do to her room?

Director: Dan Curtis
Written by: William F. Nolan, Dan Curtis (screenplay, based on the novel by Robert Marasco)
Starring: Bette Davis, Oliver Reed, Karen Black, Burgess Meredith, Eileen Heckart, Lee H. Montgomery, Dub Taylor, Anthony James

Despite everyone's best efforts, director Dan Curtis' infamous 1970s shocker *Burnt Offerings* never quite manages to live up to its promises. Emerging shortly before the period when possessed-house features—like *The Amityville Horror* (1979) and *The Changeling* (1980)—became all the rage, the film is little more than a series of wonderfully inventive set-pieces, held tentatively together by long periods of introspective soul-searching on the part of several not particularly pleasant central characters. It's just as well then that the Allardyce house where the story plays out—which belongs to a suitably creepy brother and sister played by Burgess Meredith and Eileen Heckart—is a superbly well-rounded and fleshed-out character in itself. The place comes complete with rambling grounds, dodgy swimming pool, grand staircases and, of course, a foreboding attic; it'd be hard for any cast—even one including Oliver Reed and Bette Davis—to hope to compete with a house which exudes such an air of brooding, unspoken menace.

It's difficult to lay the blame for all the troubles that haunt the Allardyce house on just one room. The film follows the Rolf family—Ben (Reed), Marian (Karen Black), their son Davey (Lee H. Montgomery), plus old aunt Elizabeth (Davis)—as they rent a dilapidated Californian mansion one long, hot summer, with tragic results. Though perhaps best known for featuring two of cinema's greatest hell-raisers Reed and Davis, the real villain of the piece turns out to be the house, feeding off its inhabitants in order to magically transform itself into a rejuvenated vision of its former Victorian glory. Every part of the house is like a character, offering up some diabolical secret, each worse than the last.

Each room conjures up a veritable cornucopia of devilish "accidents"—from turbulent swimming pools to crumbling chimney stacks—which might just prove to be the death of the Rolf family. Despite all this, it seems to be the absent owners of the house—Arnold and Roz Allardyce (Meredith and Heckart)—and their mother, whom they leave in the care of the Rolfs, and who lives in the attic—who hold the secret to the whole terrible affair. Though the old woman herself is never actually seen, the sitting room where Marian leaves her meals is imbued with a sense of unease and melancholia. Littered with collections of framed photographs—which turn out to feature a rogue's gallery of previous victims—and a strange music box, the room and everything about it is colored by the claustrophobic sense of Victoriana which weighs heavily on all aspects of the house.

The room where the final, horrific confrontation between Ben and the reclusive Mrs. Allardyce takes place could only be the old lady's attic aerie. Complete with typical small window set beneath the eaves at the front of the house, commanding the perfect view of its driveway and ex-

10. The Attic

Is there anybody there?: The Allardyce family mansion is the focal point of a poster for director Dan Curtis' "possessed house" chiller *Burnt Offerings* (1976).

tensive lawns, it forms the ideal vantage point from which Mrs. Allardyce can watch all that happens within the vicinity of her beloved home.

Despite the best efforts of the rest of the house to dispatch the various members of the family, the only person to come to a sticky end before the finale is poor old Aunt Elizabeth. Most of the deaths come during its closing scenes, as a result of things that happen in the attic room at the top of the house. A room which dispatches its victims in the most spectacular of manners: throwing one from its window onto a car on the drive below, or crushing another by a chimney falling from the roof.

The film ends on an ambiguous note. At least one character's fate is left open, while that of the house and the secrets it holds in the room at the top of the twisting staircase, remain to be discovered by yet another new group of house-sitters.

11

The Conservatory and Greenhouse

The Greenhouse was a magnificent structure. It stood with its back against a wall and rose to more than three times the height of a man. Inside, tall fluted, cast-iron columns decorated with acanthus leaves stretched up to its glass, where they were reflected upwards until they joined the earth to the sky.'
—*The Greenhouse*, Susan Hillmore (1988)

Though frequently on a grand scale, as suggested by Susan Hillmore, a greenhouse is generally far enough removed from a residence as not to be overly obtrusive. Conservatories, on the other hand, protrude from the main building, spreading across flagged terraces or eating into the perimeter of beautifully manicured lawns. Extensions of a house's living area, conservatories evolve seamlessly from sitting rooms, kitchens and hallways, providing places where family and friends meet to eat, socialize or simply while away a pleasant autumn evening. Greenhouses, however, are enhanced potting sheds, workrooms, glorified incubators for nurturing all manner of flora and vegetation, before they're cast adrift to fend for themselves in the garden.

In horror films, these edifices of glass and ornate Victorian-esque metalwork, steel and even plastic sheeting, can also be harbingers or instruments of death: a meeting place where the seeds of mistrust in a relationship are cast, as in Spanish director José Ramón Larraz's insidious 1974 chiller *Symptoms*, or a breeding room from which alien beings hatch their plans for world domination *à la* 1956's *Invasion of the Body Snatchers*. Read on and you'll discover these variations on the glasshouse theme prove anything but a rejuvenating environment.

Invasion of the Body Snatchers (1956)

> "They weren't people. It was more of them. They're growing thousands of pods in greenhouses. We've got to get away."

Don't Go Upstairs!

Director: Don Siegel
Written by: Daniel Mainwaring (screenplay), Jack Finney (from his *Collier's* magazine serial)
Starring: Kevin McCarthy, Dana Wynter, Larry Gates, King Donovan, Carolyn Jones, Jean Willes, Ralph Dumke, Virginia Christine, Tom Fadden, Kenneth Patterson, Guy Way, Eileen Stevens, Beatrice Maude, Jean Andren, Bobby Clark, Everett Glass, Dabbs Greer, Pat O'Malley, Guy Rennie, Marie Selland, Sam Peckinpah, Harry J. Vejar, Whit Bissell, Richard Deacon, Frank Hagney, Robert Osterloh

"It has always been easier to recognize a film noir than to define the term. One can easily imagine a large video store where examples of such films would be shelved somewhere between gothic horror and dystopian science fiction: in the center would be *Double Indemnity*, and at either margin *Cat People* and *Invasion of the Body Snatchers*."[1]

In his essay, James Naremore highlights a characteristic of the cult classic *Invasion of the Body Snatchers* which has enhanced its longevity, namely the difficulty of categorizing it within the parameters of a specific

The invasion of Southern California by seeds of giant plants which exude "blank" human forms that drain the emotional life of people threatens to destroy the world, in **"Invasion of the Body Snatchers"** to be telecast Saturday, December 3 from 8-10 pm, ET with repeats from 12 midnight-2 am, ET, Sunday, December 4 from 4:30-6:30 pm, ET and Saturday, December 10 from 4:01-6:01 pm, ET. Stars Kevin McCarthy and Dana Wynter.

Contact: Chris Creed, 212/408-3695

Seed bank: Becky (Dana Wynter), Jack (King Donovan), "Teddy" (Carolyn Jones) and Miles (Kevin McCarthy) make a four-pronged attack in *Invasion of the Body Snatchers* (1956).

genre. Doubtless a horror–sci-fi hybrid, the film, with its underlying tones of social hysteria and gritty suburban mystery, could just as easily pass as an example of 1950s American noir.

During a Hollywood career in which he directed some of cinema's most iconic thrillers, including cult Clint Eastwood dramas *Dirty Harry* (1971) and *Escape from Alcatraz* (1979), Don Siegel also made *Invasion of the Body Snatchers*, a film which changed horror – sci-fi cinema forever. This is all the more impressive because *Invasion* contains none of the gore on which such genre films generally rely, its lack of such visceral qualities being one of its most unnerving aspects.

The film's story involves the takeover of the Californian community of Santa Mira by alien beings who possess and replicate the locals. It takes place in various homes and buildings throughout the town. However, though appearing only briefly, the home of local doctor Miles Bennell (Kevin McCarthy) and particularly his greenhouse form an unacknowledged core from which the film's action radiates. As with so many films in which a greenhouse—or, in the case of this film, greenhouses plural—play an integral part, the building here is given relatively brief screen time. But what it *does* get is utilized to maximum effect.

It's the normality of the greenhouse, tucked along the edge of Miles' compact backyard-cum-garden, which makes it all the more chilling. This is not some ornate Victorian monstrosity made from glass and steel, of the kind associated with country mansions or fancy city townhouses. A narrow, rectangular room, separated from the main house by a veranda and patio where Miles treats friends to cookouts during the long Californian evenings, this greenhouse is deceptively large. It is first seen when Miles goes to find some fuel for the barbecue: His entrance to the building is shot from a distance and at an angle, lending it an elongated appearance which adds to its sinister air.

The alien incubation pods are surrounded by a myriad of plants, vines, flowers and vegetables, so it's understandable that Miles initially misses seeing them hidden in the back of the greenhouse. Only when he is already halfway out is he startled by the sound of the giant, cabbage-like pods as they burst, spewing forth embryonic replicas of him and his friends. At this early stage in their development, the creatures are clearly incapacitated, but they nonetheless exude menace from every steaming pore, and the looks of horror on the faces of Miles and his friends as they stand transfixed, watching the birth of their hideous doppelgängers, are chilling. The close proximity within the confines of the greenhouse between the humans and the alien creatures is enough to make the viewer scream at them to run for their lives.

Later, towards the film's climax, the horrors in Miles' greenhouse are multiplied a hundredfold as he happens across rows upon rows of the glass buildings in a market garden on the edge of town, housing hundreds of grotesque alien pods. Though seen only fleetingly as Miles and his girlfriend Becky (Dana Wynter) make a last desperate attempt to escape the invading creatures, the sight of dozens of hothouses churning out extraterrestrial lifeforms on an industrial scale leaves an indelible image on the viewer's mind.

Invasion of the Body Snatchers was made at a time during the 1950s when Americans were obsessed to the point of paranoia about their communities being infiltrated by "foreign bodies," both imaginary and real. Morris Dickstein explains: "The politics of this film are exceptionally ambiguous. In one sense these lookalikes embody an anti–Communist vision of an invisible fifth column undermining the American way of life, a belief that They are gradually taking over."[2] The premise that sometimes you can't even trust your own friends or family remains as true today as then, and is probably the most disturbing horror of all.

Die, Monster, Die! (1965)

> *But, Steve, no one ever goes into the greenhouse at night!*

Director: Daniel Haller
Written by: Jerry Sohl (screenplay), H.P. Lovecraft (from the story "The Colour Out of Space")
Starring: Boris Karloff, Nick Adams, Suzan Farmer, Freda Jackson, Terence de Marney, Patrick Magee, Paul Farrell, Leslie Dwyer, Harold Goodwin, Sydney Bromley, Billy Milton, Sheila Raynor, Gretchen Franklin, George Moon

There is no escaping the fact that some films, no matter how you look at them, aren't terribly good. That is not to say their various components in and of themselves don't impress. It is simply that they fail to come together as a whole. Take, for instance, the horror–sci-fi curiosity *Die, Monster, Die* (aka *Monster of Terror*), which in theory should have had so much in its favor. Based on H.P. Lovecraft's classic tale of cosmic terror "The Colour Out of Space," it featured a stunning rural English setting (shot in authentic Home Counties locations) and showcased the talents of Hammer leading ladies Freda Jackson and Suzan Farmer. Top this off with the presence of the king of chills himself, Boris Karloff in one of his final film roles, and the resultant film should have had class written all over it.

Unfortunately it doesn't. The film, which follows American Stephen Reinhart (Nick Adams) as he visits his English girlfriend Susan Witley (Farmer) and her father Nahum (Karloff) in their country mansion, only to discover the house hides a terrible secret of cosmic proportions,

11. The Conservatory and Greenhouse

Going to pot: Stephen Reinhart (Nick Adams) and Susan Witley (Suzan Farmer) make a shocking discovery in *Die, Monster, Die!* (1965).

never manages to shake itself free from the mood of a second feature. In fact, as Chris Wood observes, though the producers were clearly trying to infuse it with a touch of "English class," the result is more new world than old:

> [It] is a very American film, and not just because it's (loosely) based on an H.P. Lovecraft tale. Although set in Britain, with a mainly British cast, somehow it has more in common with the drive-in movies being made across the pond at the time than anything by Hammer or Amicus. In fact, the town of "Arkham" could quite easily be in New England (apart from the "oo-arrr" accents which proliferate).³

All this said, the film does contain scenes which, on their own, work, not least those set within the greenhouse of the Witleys' sinister country house. If ever a building exuded unease from its first appearance, this one does.

Stephen initially encounters the greenhouse under less than ideal circumstances, and from there, things go downhill. Following the accidental death of the Witleys' butler Merwyn (Terence de Marney) at dinner, Stephen follows Nahum and watches him bury the dead man in the garden. Next he sees Nahum enter the isolated greenhouse, which is emitting a strange green light. Stephen later explains to Susan that he recognized the light as the result of radiation.

The couple decides the next day, in typical chiller mode, to investigate the house of glass and steel shrouded in swirling mists and overgrown shrubbery, despite copious warning signs *not* to. As if Susan's earnest admonition that "no one ever goes into the greenhouse at night" isn't enough, there is the fact its windows are whitewashed. After finding the greenhouse door padlocked, they get in by climbing through some loose paneling at the side of the building.

Inside they find an oasis of sub-tropical wonders, plants as big as trees, giant flowers and vegetables, before venturing into a laboratory—or what Stephen refers to as a "zoo in Hell"—located in what used to be a potting shed at the back of the building. Here, a brazier-like stand emits glowing rays of radiation while cages against the walls hold bizarre, Lovecraftian creatures with octopus-like tentacles and large, heavy, hooded eyes, which give out strangled, dinosaur-like cries. Needless to say, the couple leaves quickly. Back in the main greenhouse, they discover stones embedded in the soil which again give off the strange glow. Stephen deduces that they come from some larger rock. They are so engrossed in their discoveries that they fail to notice vines hanging from the ceiling, vines which appear to have a life of their own, vines which make a grab for the unwary Susan. She and Stephen only just escape, never to return to the horror of the greenhouse again.

Though seen for only a few minutes, the greenhouse is by far the film's most atmospheric location, exuding an air of otherworldliness. Like the plants and creatures within it, the building appears much more disturbing than many of the other more intentionally horrific elements of the film. Why? Probably because it captures marvelously the feel of many greenhouses, an intangible sense of the melancholy which lingers around them, shrouded with a forgotten air. The Witley greenhouse is no exception. The sense that it's removed from the main house and reality—often, as here, across the garden or crouching behind a wall—is never far away.

Ultimately the explanation for all the hokum lies behind a slightly prosaic storyline spun around a fallen meteorite, the main body of which has been hidden in the basement of the Witley house for generations. Both here, and in the greenhouse, pieces of the meteorite are used to produce the radiation that has been causing the horrors—barren landscapes, strange lights and mutated plants and animals—which have given the house its unsavory reputation amongst the local people.

On reflection, the events which play out within the confines of the greenhouse exude more energy than those that take place in the main Witley mansion. The result is a crystal edifice which positively glows amongst its more drab and lackluster surroundings.

Frogs (1972)

> *Suppose nature gave a war, and everybody came. The snakes, the birds, the lizards and frogs. And suppose that the polluters, the specie on Earth called man, were the enemy in that war. And then suppose that the human race lost!*

Director: George McCowan
Written by: Robert Hutchison and Robert Blees (screenplay), Robert Hutchison (story)
Starring: Ray Milland, Sam Elliott, Joan Van Ark, Adam Roarke, Judy Pace, Lynn Borden, Mae Mercer, David Gilliam, Nicholas Cortland, George Skaff, Lance Taylor, Sr., Hollis Irving, Dale Willingham, Hal Hodges, Carolyn Fitzsimmons, Robert Sanders

Films dealing with the revolt of animals and nature against human aggressors saturated the horror market during the 1970s. The likes of *Night of the Lepus* (1972)—killer rabbits—*Squirm* (1976)—man-eating worms—and particularly *Frogs*—perhaps one of the most stylish entries in this sub-genre—left little doubt in viewer's minds as to which camp they were meant to side with.

Frogs featured the dysfunctional Crockett family, overseen by the egotistical Jason (Ray Milland), who hasn't cared about what of nature's bounty he laid waste to in his rise to the top. Things are about to change, however, as his extended family gathers at his mansion in the Florida swamps for their annual combined celebration of his birthday and the Fourth of July. Over the years, the chemicals which Jason has pumped into the surrounding area, in his bid to make a paradise out of his little corner of the Sunshine State, have had a devastating effect on the native wildlife. This holiday weekend, the victims of Jason's actions have decided to take their revenge.

> *Frogs* (1972) is typically issue-conscious: Floridian swampland creepy-crawlies exterminate the family of Ray Milland, a polluting industrialist. The alliance of frogs, snakes, birds, turtles, leeches and spiders gracefully excludes the ecology-minded hero and a few other innocents from the massacre.[4]

Frogs, despite its admirable subtext, never quite lives up to its promise: You can't help feeling that it wants to be more horrific than it actually is. Though its set-piece moments are genuinely disturbing, its overarching storyline is lackluster, draining any life which it may have had overall.

Slippery character: Kenneth Maltindale (Nicholas Cortland) and some friends in *Frogs* (1972).

The characters are either overbearing (Jason Crockett), ineffectual (most of his offspring) or mere window dressing (his staff).

Despite a lack of depth, the film more than compensates for the shortfall with a palpable sense of unease permeating throughout. From the opening credits to the final reel, the proceedings play out against a cacophonic symphony of amphibian song from the ever-increasing congregation of frogs, along with hundreds of newts, lizards, spiders, snakes and crocodiles which emerge from the surrounding lakes and swamps to encroach upon Jason's plantation mansion and its overgrown grounds. The resultant sense of decay from which nothing and nobody escapes is tinged with the feeling something could happen at any moment. Forget that you're a good halfway into the film before the real horrors kick in. The following onslaught leaves ten members of the 16-strong cast dead by the end. While some are killed off-screen, the deaths of those shown in their full-blooded glory leave little to the imagination.

All the deaths take place in the open air—either on the grounds of the house, or the swamps—save for Jason's climactic demise, and one other which, though more restrained than the rest, is undoubtedly the most atmospheric. When the horrors do strike, they are effectively unsettling, in particular the demise of Jason's nephew Kenneth (Nicholas Cortland). He's sent by his mother Iris (Hollis Irving)—Jason's sister—to the greenhouse to pick some flowers for a table setting; it's clear before he leaves the assembled guests that something nasty is going to happen.

Set well apart from the main house in an area surrounded by trees and vegetation, the greenhouse is not what you might expect for a structure associated with a classical, colonial mansion such as the Crockett family home. Instead of an ornate mix of glass and wrought-iron, or brick with leaded panes which usually makes up the greenhouse of a large estate, here we have the arched frame with stretched polythene cover more often associated with a market-garden set-up or inner-city allotment. What the outside of the structure lacks in finesse is made up for with its wild, exotic, downright sinister interior. Hidden from prying eyes by the clouded polythene, there are rows of fantastical plants and hothouse flowers alongside empty pots and tubs of potting soil, as well as the incongruous presence of an occasional container of acid or bottle marked POISON.

Then there are the creatures: an array of neon-colored lizards, snakes and popeyed toads, as well some outsized dragon-like reptiles which make their way into the greenhouse, somehow managing to close the door with their tails. All hell is then literally let loose as the creatures crawl, swing and drop from every conceivable surface before knocking over the containers of noxious oxides which combine in a lethal gas that spells the end for Kenneth. As with most of the deaths that take place in the film, Kenneth's death—the lizards upsetting the bottles which combine to create the gas that asphyxiates him—could be explained away as an accident. But consider the glint in the lizard's eyes as they nudge the containers from the shelves, and their readiness to swarm over Kenneth's prostrate body the moment he collapses...

Frogs has any number of glaring shortcomings for the horror connoisseur to pick on, not least its total lack of characters for whom the viewer feels the slightest sympathy. Fortunately Kenneth's greenhouse death scene and a genuinely creepy open ending, with an effective shock twist, save the film. It's a memorable if not necessarily classic exercise in eco-horror.

Symptoms (1974)

> *I couldn't find you when I got up this morning, so I wandered 'round the house and discovered this. It's the perfect setting for getting down to work, so here I am.*

Don't Go Upstairs!

Director: José Ramón Larraz
Written by: José Ramón Larraz and Stanley Miller (screenplay), Thomas Owen (story)
Starring: Angela Pleasence, Peter Vaughan, Lorna Heilbron, Nancy Nevinson, Ronald O'Neill, Marie-Paule Mailleux, Mike Grady, Raymond Huntley

What did lovers of obscure cinema do before YouTube? In those not-so-faroff days, if you couldn't get a film on DVD or video, you had to hope you'd be lucky enough to catch it on a late-night television rerun. Which also meant many little-known, independent films were seldom seen after their initial, often limited cinema release. Take for instance *Symptoms*, a strange delight I bet you never heard of.

Anne (Lorna Heilbron) is invited by her friend Helen (Angela Pleasence) to stay at an isolated mansion deep in the English countryside. During their time together, Anne becomes increasingly unsettled by Helen's temperamental moods. However, as they go back a long way, she's used to her friend's eccentricities and not unduly perturbed by her behavior. Anne begins to realize they may not be alone in the house, as she was initially led to believe. Something, or someone, is prowling the gloomy corridors

Not my type: Helen (Angela Pleasence, left) and Anne (Lorna Heilbron) discuss their feelings over tea in *Symptoms* (1974).

11. The Conservatory and Greenhouse

of Helen's home and its lonely grounds—someone who intends that Anne become a permanent guest.

Symptoms is the perfect example of a film which builds palpable unease and disquiet through inference and suggestion, as opposed to in-your-face gore. Not that it doesn't have its share of graphic murders. What twisted psycho thriller from this period would be complete without a vicious and frenzied knife attack to spice things up? The real beauty of the film, and the reason it works so well, is that it doesn't depend on visceral horror to create an impact. Here, a room bathed in early morning sunlight, or a leaf-strewn garden avenue dappled in late afternoon shadow, is as capable of provoking chills as any visible bogeyman.

Nowhere is this better embodied than in the scenes which take place in Helen's conservatory. Like some hybrid of a greenhouse and Victorian hothouse, the conservatory has a tranquil, sinister beauty which steals the breath away. Classical Roman statuary, wicker armchairs, potted plants and enormous ferns. A paneled ceiling is supported by ornate metal columns while through the clouded French windows a wild garden encroaches upon the glass structure. And everything, both inside and out, is shrouded in warm, damp mist.

Other moments may top those seen here for gruesomeness but none are infused with the same chill and unspoken malice as that emanating from Helen in the glass house, when she thinks she is being slighted by the woman she believes to be her best friend. Though never actually spelled out, there are plenty of none-too-subtle moments clearly pointing to Helen's lesbian tendencies. When her close female friends—both Anne and another called Cora (Marie-Paule Mailleux), whose spirit may or may not haunt the house—start showing interest in anyone else, particularly men, it triggers Helen's darker side.

This becomes clear when Helen encounters Anne on her first morning following her arrival. Having woken early, Anne—a journalist or writer of some kind—has ensconced herself at a makeshift desk in the conservatory. By the time Helen appears, Anne is typing away, surrounded by books and papers, sipping from an outsized teacup and dragging on an ever-present cigarette. Their ensuing conversation consists mainly of innocuous pleasantries amongst two people between whom there's obviously some form of underlying tension. It's clear from the outset that Helen places more store by their friendship than Anne, resulting in a sense that Helen idolizes her, resenting Anne's more confident approach to life, an infatuation which ends up in disaster.

The second and final time the conservatory appears, there's an even terser exchange between the women after John (Ronald O'Neill), a friend of Anne, turns up unannounced to persuade her to return to London.

Clearly upset by John's visit, Helen is monosyllabic in her communication. Potting plants in the conservatory when Anne finds her, she virtually stabs them into their containers as her friend tries to explain the presence of her previously unmentioned boyfriend.

Things are never quite the same between the friends following their final showdown in the conservatory. Anne's concerns about Helen's fragile state and suspicions that someone else is in the house finally prove right with tragic results. None of the visual horrors which follow however, come close to repeating the psychological malice which seeps from Helen in the conservatory.

It's not hard to see why Spanish director José Ramón Larraz cast the actresses he did, and in particular Pleasence in the central role. Considering her appearance, Pleasence was ideal as the brittle Helen. With her waif-like fragility, she embodied perfectly a person living on the edge of sanity. Helen was happy in her own private kingdom, but ultimately found difficulty sharing either it—or anyone she became close to—with the outside world. The sight of her mournful features greeting you over the breakfast table would be enough to make anyone question their sanity, and without doubt plays a part in forcing the otherwise feisty and independent Anne to question her own grip on reality.

Add to this the heavily gothic influences: down-at-heel country houses, lonely country lanes and apocalyptic storm-lashed nights. These were Larraz's trademarks, and the result is a film which haunts you long after the final credits have died, like the fading autumn sun which dapples the forgotten corners of Helen's bewitching glass house.

The Hand That Rocks the Cradle (1992)

The hand that rocks the cradle is the hand that rules the world.

Director: Curtis Hanson
Written by: Amanda Silver
Starring: Annabella Sciorra, Rebecca De Mornay, Matt McCoy, Ernie Hudson, Julianne Moore, Madeline Zima, John de Lancie, Kevin Skousen, Mitchell Laurence, Justin Zaremby, Eric Melander, Jennifer Melander, Ashley Melander, Brian T. Finney, Stephen West, David Scully, Julie Clemmons, Joseph Franklin, Tom Francis, Jeff Conkel, Patrick Ryals, Charles Lucia, Rachel Glenn, Valerie Masterson, Chuck Riley

It's clear from the outset that the greenhouse in *The Hand That Rocks the Cradle* will be the instrument of death. It's one of the most unpleasant murders to rear its stylishly ugly head from the plethora of slick chiller thrillers turned out during the early 1990s. From the moment you're in-

11. The Conservatory and Greenhouse

troduced to Claire (Annabella Sciorra) and Michael (Matt McCoy) Bartel who, with their young family, live the picture-perfect suburban America life, you know the glass and steel structure at the bottom of their garden will play a major role in the proceedings. Built as a project to keep Claire, a botanist, busy after the birth of their son Joey, the structure soon takes on a life of its own.

This thriller works despite, or perhaps because of, it being obvious immediately who is behind all the skullduggery. It emerges early on that Peyton (Rebecca De Mornay), the Bartels' new live-in nanny, is the wife of a Dr. Victor Mott (John de Lancie) who violated Claire during a traumatic ante-natal checkup, the aftermath of which indirectly leads to his suicide and her fragile state. As Peyton plots revenge for her husband's untimely death, she poses as a nanny and infiltrates the Bartel household, slyly turning family and friends against each other. And all the time the greenhouse sits glinting in the background, biding its time until it comes into play as the ultimate tool of Peyton's destruction.

During the film's early stages, it feels like it's working towards the spectacular greenhouse denouement. Claire is an asthmatic with an al-

Suspicious minds: Peyton Flanders (Rebecca De Mornay, left) and Marlene Craven (Julianne Moore) have an uneasy first encounter in *The Hand That Rocks the Cradle* (1992).

most obsessive dependency upon her medical inhalers (which of course fail just when she needs them most). She devotes every spare moment to the building and fine-tuning of her glass palace. Her falling-out with her oldest friend Marlene (Julianne Moore), orchestrated by Peyton, conveniently allows for a twist in which Claire—the intended victim—avoids the grisly garden accident, but succumbs to a possibly worse demise.

It's Peyton's instigation of and reaction to the accident which is as chilling if not more chilling than the incident itself: the way in which, with clinical precision, she rigs the greenhouse roof to collapse on the next person who enters. (Though she intends the trap for Claire, there is always the possibility that anyone might be unfortunate enough to enter.) Her cool-as-ice demeanor when Marlene arrives at the Bartel home looking for Claire, and then confronts Peyton about her true identity. Or her emotionless reaction when, after directing Marlene to the greenhouse, she eats an apple, while watching from the lounge window as the unfortunate woman is shredded by the falling glass roof.

In true Grand Guignol tradition, the horrors don't finish there. The shock of Marlene's death is merely emphasized when Claire returns home with bedding plants for the garden, heading straight for the greenhouse where the sight of her friend's lacerated remains is enough to instigate a violent asthma attack. The now-absent Peyton anticipated such a scenario, doctoring Claire's inhalers accordingly. The following scene as Claire stumbles gasping from the greenhouse into her kitchen only to find all her medication destroyed is second only to Marlene's death for shock factor. The sight of her lying choking on the front veranda, a side-on close-up of her face reminiscent of Janet Leigh's on the bathroom floor in *Psycho* (1960), is as harrowing as any full-on bloody attack.

Disturbing as the film is, watching it raises several questions, not the least being why the Bartels need a nanny in the first place. Though it's inferred that Claire is in a volatile state following the unpleasant experiences in the run-up to Joey's birth, nothing implies that, as a woman who is under no financial pressure to work, she cannot take a few months off to devote herself to the care of her new son. Or perhaps, as *The Los Angeles Times*' Peter Rainer pointed out in his appraisal of the film, Claire and Michael simply see the hiring of a live-in nanny as another requirement for every modern, successful couple: "But the film isn't just a well-made TV-style thriller either. It's on to something—the way upwardly mobile parents, hoping to make their lives more professionally fulfilling, unwittingly bring the danger of the unknown into their lives."[5]

The premise also stretches the viewer's credulity, asking the question why the Bartels would employ the too-good-to-be-true Peyton with scant regard for her experience or credentials. However, bearing in mind that their shortsightedness allows for the appearance of one of the best demonic childcare performances since Mrs. Baylock in *The Omen* (1976), this failure could be forgiven.

Since its release, *The Hand That Rocks the Cradle* has built a reputation as an understated classic of the yuppie horror genre, alongside such features as *Basic Instinct* (1992) and *Sliver* (1993). And this despite the fact that, as a whole, the film never quite equals the shock or originality of its infamous greenhouse murder.

12

The Grounds

> *The wind howled round Motley Hall. It blew the dead leaves along the moss-covered terraces and sent them spinning down the steps to lodge in the long grass of the overgrown lawn.*
> —*The Ghosts of Motley Hall*, Richard Carpenter (1977)

What is more atmospheric, more enticing (or sometimes off-putting) than the grounds or gardens of a house? In his 1977 novelization of popular British children's television series *The Ghosts of Motley Hall*, Richard Carpenter captured perfectly the feel of the forlorn stately home at the center of the story, in his description of its neglected surroundings.

The grounds which surround a house sometimes act as a foretaste of what lies within the dwelling itself. Think of the skeleton-infested backyard of the Freeling family's suburban new-build in *Poltergeist* (1982). However, the horrors that the grounds contain can often be much worse, as the storm-lashed acres which lie round and about the Karswell mansion prove in *Curse of the Demon* (1957). The results, as we will see in the following films, are far from the tranquil environments we've come to expect from such outside spaces.

The Beast with Five Fingers (1946)

> *"The print of a hand. It broke the window and climbed through. And walked away ..."*

Director: Robert Florey
Written by: Curt Siodmak (screenplay), William Fryer Harvey (story)
Starring: Robert Alda, Andrea King, Peter Lorre, Victor Francen, Charles Dingle, John Alvin, J. Carrol Naish

Variety's December 1945 review of director Robert Florey's atmospheric "dark house" mystery *The Beast with Five Fingers* said the film gave "more credit for intelligence than the average thriller."[1] Considered now,

Sleight of hand: (Top to bottom) Robert Alda, Andrea King, Peter Lorre, Victor Francen and J. Carrol Naish on a poster for Warner Bros. *The Beast with Five Fingers* (1946).

one can see what they meant: Here is a genre example which has outlasted many others from the period, appearing as disturbing today as when it was first released. The title of this disquieting film is probably the most troubling aspect of what is, in fact, a remarkably restrained exercise in inference and suggestion.

Following the death of the renowned concert pianist Francis Ingram (Victor Francen), his relations and employees gather at his desolate residence to find out who will benefit from the dead man's estate. Those present have designs on Francis' fortune, but he appears to have had other ideas, proceeding to take revenge from beyond the grave upon the assembled misfits in the most bizarre of manners.

Shadows—particularly in films of the pre-color era—speak more strongly than any amount of verbose dialogue ever could. Heightening the viewer's senses, making them more susceptible to suggestion, shadows conceal a multitude of sins, allowing filmmakers to infer much more than they can show—a tactic some present-day horror practitioners might learn from. This approach is used to great effect in *The Beast with Five Fingers* which, like many "horror" entries of the period, is in fact more thriller than chiller, despite a story whose disturbing premise allows for plenty of unsettling imagery.

Much of the film plays out within the confines of Francis Ingram's gloomy mansion. However, the parts which take place outside the house, particularly in and around the Ingram family's garden crypt, are amongst the film's most unnerving. To have a private mausoleum in the grounds of your home probably says as much about your attitude about the Afterlife as it does about your undoubted wealth and privilege in the here and now. In films, these ornate temples to the dead frequently give the impression that they are merely stopping-off points, until the dead inhabitants can return to make their presence felt in the real world.

The mausoleum features comparatively briefly in the film. However, when it does, it more than makes up for such brevity through its ostentatious appearance. Here is a building which, in the best horror film tradition of such edifices, drips with melodramatic menace, its exterior surrounded by crooked stone crosses and sunken tombstones swathed in mist and moonlight. Though set well apart from the main house, it is still conveniently enough placed for the inhabitants to notice what happens inside. When members of Francis' domestic staff see a light in the supposedly empty building, it is enough to make them vacate the house post-haste. This initial introduction of the mausoleum, and the resultant speedy exit of the servants, provides the proceedings with one of those brief moments of comic relief inserted within many horror films in order to leaven their more unpleasant elements.

When the interior of the building is revealed—first, as Francis' greedy brother-in-law and nephew investigate the light, and later when they, along with the dead maestro's colleagues and the local police, inspect the building—the viewer is confronted with an environment of suitably gothic sensibilities. Once inside, it's easy to imagine all kinds of evil lurking in the dark recesses of the heavily pillared alcoves, bathed in shade and festooned with cobwebs. These fears are confirmed when Francis' coffin is opened to reveal that he has severed his own right hand, and (it seems) sent it forth to exact a grisly revenge.

Florey, born in Paris at the dawn of the twentieth century, was not particularly well known for horror films. In his entry in the 1976 edition of *The Oxford Companion to Film*, he is somewhat unjustly dismissed as a filmmaker of "prolific" though largely "unmemorable"[2] output. The entry does, however, highlight *The Beast with Five Fingers* as an exception in a directorial career spanning over 30 years, encompassing everything from comedies and gangster flicks, to musicals and television films.

On occasional forays into the macabre—including Universal's 1932 classic of Edgar Allan Poe's *Murders in the Rue Morgue* with Bela Lugosi—Florey drew heavily on stylistic and expressionist sensitivities, influences which again came to the fore in *The Beast with Five Fingers*. The family mausoleum and later Francis' library—the settings for several pivotal scenes—rich in decay and decadence, were mirrored by the severe minimalism of the mansion's extended hallway and living room. It is here, in a room dominated by a sweeping staircase at one end and a grand piano in stark isolation at its center, that Francis, and later his disembodied hand, hammers out the haunting strains of Brahms' left-hand arrangement for Bach's "Chaconne in D Minor": a melody which is the precursor to disaster when heard throughout the film.

The luridly titled Warner Brothers shocker marked their sole genre entry during the 1940s. It was also the final appearance at the studio for their regular collaborator Peter Lorre, who gave a characteristically theatrical portrayal of Conrad's put-upon librarian. Indeed, of all the film's human cast, it is Lorre's character who stands out, an appearance equaled only by the "beast" itself.

As noted previously, the film retains its ability to frighten because it infers more than it actually shows. When the "hand" eventually puts in an appearance—a good third of the way into the story—it appears disconcertingly authentic. As Ed Naha puts it in *Horrors: From Screen to Scream*, "the only aspect of the film equal to Lorre's crazed performance is the sporadic clever effects seen whenever the hand makes a personal appearance on the screen...."[3]

Curse of the Demon (1957)

It's in the trees, it's coming.

Director: Jacques Tourneur
Written by: Charles Bennett, Hal E. Chester (screenplay, based on the short story "Casting the Runes" by M. R. James)
Starring: Dana Andrews, Peggy Cummins, Niall MacGinnis, Maurice Denham, Athene Seyler

It's strange to think, unless you're a horror film aficionado, that the cult British shocker *Curse of the Demon* is probably best known for the snatch of dialogue which English singer Kate Bush incorporated into her 1986 hit ballad "The Hounds of Love." The essence of this unsettling film is succinctly captured in the six words, "It's in the trees, it's coming," uttered, just prior to his death, by a victim of its titular monster. Though the demon itself is seen periodically as the story unfolds, for the most part this

Clowning around: Karswell (Niall MacGinnis in top hat) is about to show John Holden (Dana Andrews) and some young guests (uncredited) a few tricks at a garden party in *Curse of the Demon* (1957).

film works as much by insinuation as through anything portrayed physically on the screen.

The tone of unease running throughout the film is established early on. One of several featured deaths—occurring because of a disagreement between fusty Prof. Harrington (Maurice Denham) and the villain of the piece, Dr. Julian Karswell (Niall MacGinnis)—takes place at night, outside and amongst trees. The opening scenes see Harrington drive through pitch-black forests, the road ahead lit only by the beam of his car's headlights, before he arrives at Karswell's secluded mansion; there he confronts the occultist about the curse he's placed on Harrington. The results are amongst the best examples of cinematic suspense, created purely through setting and suggestion.

A break with this pattern allows for one of the film's most memorable sequences, and one which brings the outside of the house into full play within the film's context. It takes place on a deceptively tranquil afternoon, and everything about it lulls both viewer, and characters, into a false sense of security, before all Hell is literally let loose through the will of the diabolical Karswell. John Holden (Dana Andrews), a visiting American psychologist, has joined forces with the professor's niece Joanna (Peggy Cummins) to investigate her uncle's death. At the invitation of Karswell, Holden drives out to the wicked doctor's country estate, in the hope of discovering more about Harrington's untimely demise. What the couple are confronted with is a scene so "English" in its tranquility, that it is virtually impossible to imagine what is about to take place.

The couple arrives in the midst of a Halloween garden party for local children, being held in the grounds of their home by Karswell and his doting mother. (Character actress Athene Seyler gives an eccentric performance as Mother. Having made a career of such roles, Seyler would appear in "The Man-Eater of Surrey Green" [1965], one of the most bizarre episodes of the cult TV show *The Avengers*.) Suddenly interrupting the festivities, Karswell conjures a storm of Biblical proportions quite literally from thin air, to convince the doubting Holden of his dark powers. Garden furniture is tossed across the beautifully manicured lawns, while mad oceans of autumn leaves engulf terrified guests, who run for the safety of Karswell's house. Once within the storm-free confines of his study, Karswell allows himself a brief moment of false self-deprecation, admitting fleetingly to the unnerved Holden that he might have slightly overdone it with his example.

Various characters find themselves inside Karswell's mansion during the film. But it's very much its exterior, and in particular the surrounding grounds, which tell us about the occultist and his mother. As Holden exclaims to Joanna as they drive across an ornamental bridge and the house first comes into view around a bend, whatever it is that Karswell does for a living, it must certainly pay well. Everything about his home's outer appearance—from the cars in the drive, to the obvious respect with which he is held within the local community through the staging of his annual children's party—speaks volumes about Karswell's social standing. It also sets the scene perfectly for the horrors to come.

The garden party scene creates an impact in two ways: through the storm's visual ferocity, as well as by being one of the few places in the film where devilry and evil is depicted during daylight. We have become used to seeing the Devil's works taking place at night, or in the shadowy corners of some lonely, forgotten churchyard. As a result, when we see them burst forth on a sunny afternoon, on the grounds of a country house which plays host to a throng of innocent children, the effect is all the more disturbing.

Curse of the Demon's emphasis on atmosphere over visceral gore should come as no surprise. Uncharacteristically even for the period in which it was made, the film depicts very little violence on screen. In his 1967 book *Horror Movies: An Illustrated Survey*, Carlos Clarens refers to director Jacques Tourneur's understanding of "real horror" as "a fragile, glass-boned thing." Though Tourneur directed more than 70 films in a career spanning over four decades, few were actually genre entries. Three, however—made for RKO in the 1940s and produced by the king of classic chills, Val Lewton—were archetypal examples of suggestive horror: *Cat People* (1942), *I Walked with a Zombie* (1943) and *The Leopard Man* (1943) perfectly encapsulate the style of restraint and intimation which Tourneur went on to utilize so effectively in *Curse of the Demon*, especially during the sequence set in the garden. For a scene deriving its horror purely from natural sources and the environment, it remains a startlingly effective piece of shock cinema.

The film involves few occasions when the "demon" is actually revealed, which is fortunate as these are amongst its most disappointing. The old adage "less is more" was never truer, as the monster here appears as little more than a cuddly teddy bear, albeit a 50-foot one. Consequently, the edge of an otherwise wonderfully disturbing exercise in the macabre is blunted by a creature the substance of which would have been better left to the viewer's imagination.

The Ballad of Tam Lin (1970)

I'll swallow anything as long as it's illegal.

Director: Roddy McDowall
Written by: William Spier (original screenplay)
Starring: Ava Gardner, Ian McShane, Richard Wattis, Cyril Cusack, Stephanie Beacham, David Whitman, Fabia Drake, Sinéad Cusack, Joanna Lumley, Jenny Hanley, Madeline Smith, Bruce Robinson, Victoria Fairbrother, Rosemary Blake, Michael Bills, Virginia Tingwell, Peter Hinwood, Hayward Morse, Julian Barnes, Norman Oliver, Salena Jones, Delia Lindsay

The slow-witted Sue (Madeline Smith) seems to have been game to try most things once, but even she may find that, if watched now—without the benefit of a late 1960s and early 1970s hippie haze—*The Ballad of Tam Lin* (known in the U.S. under the less romantic title *The Devil's Widow*) stretches credibility to the limit. Which is a shame as here is a film that, although frequently ponderous, possesses a magic that would have done justice to the Scottish legend which inspired it.

Much of its appeal—and any possibly horrific elements it may contain—are more inferred than physical as Tom Milne pointed out in the June 1977 issue of *Monthly Film Bulletin*: "McDowall builds a broodingly enigmatic sense of menace out of stray allusions and apparitions that hover without ever really being explained or over-exploited."[4] Indeed, if you lack a vivid imagination, the film's true essence may well be lost on you.

12. The Grounds

In the shade: Tom Lynn (Ian McShane) ponders his fate in *The Ballad of Tam Lin* (1970).

The film concludes with a swampland chase to the death featuring its hero and heroine Tom Lynn (Ian McShane) and Janet Ainsley (Stephanie Beacham), which is about as shocking as it gets. As we all know, however, the most effective horror doesn't always have to be visceral. What *Tam Lin* may lack in terms of in-your-face frights, it more than compensates for with an air of dreamlike menace. From the pre-credit sequence when Michaela Cazaret (Ava Gardner) is first seen, diminishing a would-be addition to her group as she departs London for her country retreat, you realize that here is a woman who disregards anyone and anything who fails to excite her interest.

Nothing here is as it seems, from the characters' relationships, to the true identity of Michaela herself. The only solid thing appears to be the baronial fortress where she and her young devotees recline in decadent splendor. But what a house it is: The expansive gray frontage rises in regal grandeur, surrounded by manicured lawns, protected by black, wrought iron gates and patrolled by peacock sentries. A sweeping gravel driveway plays host to the various limousines and open-top sports cars used by

Michaela and her horde to drive up from London, as they descend en masse upon the Scottish Borders, disrupting the tranquility with their fevered gathering of louche debauchery.

If the front of the house gives a deceptive appearance of discreet gentility, then the back of the building—with its cascading terraces and expanse of pristine grass, dissolving into acres of woodland, mountains and forest glades—reflects the true identity of the estate's owner and those she gathers around her. Here is the home of a woman who likes to surround herself with understated luxury and the attention of fawning acolytes, hanging on her every word and spending their days in the pursuits of the idle rich—drinking, reading, conversing, playing games and making music. Anything that keeps their minds from focusing on the humdrum reality of everyday life.

Here is where Janet, the guileless daughter of the local vicar who has brought a puppy for the childlike Sue to buy, first encounters a lifestyle so alien to her own. Here too is where she meets a group of characters who includes the man who will change her life forever: Michaela's lover, the broody Tom. And here is where everyone present treats her with aloof disregard: the vague flick of a wrist with which a girl called Georgia (Joanna Lumley) directs Janet to where Sue may be suggests a complete lack of interest in anything and everything but herself.

The great facade of the house also creates the perfect backdrop against which Michaela introduces herself to Janet, as she floats from a doorway above in a cloud of orange chiffon. Its stone-like appearance and the cool green pastures which surround the house stand in stark juxtaposition with its comfortable, wood-paneled interiors which are later revealed as the film's action flits intermittently through its rooms. All of which is the opposite of Michaela, whose warm and welcoming exterior hides a steely cold and brittle inside.

The Ballad of Tam Lin stands out in the memory for several reasons besides its unsettling, ethereal essence. One of the last big-screen appearances of screen goddess Ava Gardner—her acting roles afterwards were mainly television appearances—the film also featured a host of minor names who went on to bigger and better things. McShane, Smith, Lumley and Beacham, along with Sinéad Cusack, Jenny Hanley and Bruce Robinson, all found greater fame than their roles here might have suggested. These things aside, the fact the film was the only directorial effort by Hollywood legend Roddy McDowall should alone give it special precedence in the pantheon of uncanny and bizarre cinema horrors. McDowall's lightness of touch was considered by many critics to be one of the film's saving graces, as highlighted in *The Overlook Film Encyclopedia, Horror*:

After the boring opening and the syrupy freeze-frame depiction of McShane and Beacham's blossoming romance, McDowall's direction, together with inspired dialogue alluding to Robert Burns' "The Ballad of Tam Lin"—about a young man held in thrall to the queen of the fairies—begin to bring the picture to life.[5]

Which simply emphasizes the fact that this is a film unjustly overlooked by filmgoers whose feet are planted too firmly in the real world.

Vampyres (1974)

Every lesbian vampire should own a castle.

Director: José Ramón Larraz
Written by: Diana Daubeney (screenplay)
Starring: Marianne Morris, Anulka Dziubinska, Murray Brown, Brian Deacon, Sally Faulkner

John Stanley's description of this obscure 1974 erotic horror may have appeared somewhat dismissive.[6] However, when the castle in question is Oakley Court, the faux-gothic pile by the River Thames near Bray, Berkshire, which frequently showed up in British horror films during the 1960s and 1970s, one could indeed see what he meant. It's a veritable symphony of crenelated turrets, hotchpotch gables and mullioned windows; the mere sight of the Victorian architectural meringue conjures up all manner of frightful fairy tale visions.

This made it the perfect setting for the story of Fran (Marianne Morris) and Miriam (Anulka Dziubinska), bewitching young lovers who prowl the lonely mansion, luring unwitting travelers to a grisly end within its shadowy corridors and dusty rooms.

Not being English may have allowed Spanish filmmaker José Ramón Larraz a degree of objectivity, with which he captured a sense of the country's spirit that a native couldn't have. Whatever it was, the director—who had a successful career in the horror genre—had a knack for bringing the vibe and spirit peculiar to 1970s Britain alive on the screen. In the early years of the decade, he made several films in the U.K., including *Scream ... and Die!* (1973) and *Symptoms* (1974). Though his films covered a wide variety of subjects—from good old-fashioned exploitation in *Deviation* (1971), to the supernatural in *Vampyres*—everything he did was tinged with a sense of the surreal and horrific. Despite this—and perhaps unexpectedly, considering their subject matter—many of his films retained a remarkably serious tone: The moody thriller *Symptoms* featured early roles for industry-revered players Angela Pleasence and Peter Vaughan, while *Vampyres* was spotlighted on the June 1976 cover of the authoritative British film journal *films and filming*.[7]

Larraz had a thing for placing action in isolated country settings, often in an out-of-the-way mansion, lonely, remote and seemingly cut off from society. In *English Gothic: Classic Horror Cinema 1897–2015* (Signum Books, 2015), critic-author Jonathan Rigby's revised edition of his in-depth study of British horror cinema, he quoted a review of the film from a contemporary issue of *Films Illustrated*, which praised Larraz's direction as "showing a taste for the somber visual."[8] Much of *Vampyres*' mayhem happens within the house itself: The horror here is gloriously visceral, kicking in before the opening credits and sustained to a surprisingly high level until the film's climax.

The exterior of the house—its grounds, surrounding country lanes and an adjacent churchyard—are equally important to the developing story. The entrance and exit of many of Fran and Miriam's victims takes place outside the house, meaning its environment plays a key role in events, often acting as a unifying factor in the proceedings: Whoever the character, or for whatever reason they appear, virtually everyone in the film passes through the grounds of the house at some stage.

The immediate environs of the house provide the opportunity for Larraz to express his creativity. That there is an idyllic country church, with suitably decayed graveyard, adjacent to the property should come as little surprise; you can't have vampires without a graveyard nearby. A strong sense of otherworldliness overwhelms the approach to the house, a sense of the surreal which Larraz captured in many of his films, as though those who discover the place are entering another dimension. The road to the house itself is little more than an overgrown path cut through towering hedges and unrestrained rhododendron bushes.

What is strange—even slightly disorientating—is the apparent size of the grounds themselves, which seemingly continue forever. Once they appear in all their sweeping glory, they are as large and rambling as the house itself. In real life, the mansion's paved terraces and manicured lawns lead within a few hundred feet to the banks of the River Thames. In the film, however, Larraz has surrounded the house and gardens with woods and copses, as well as an isolated lake, all of which create the perfect environment to extend the horrors outside the mansion, providing the film with some of its most surreal and disturbing imagery. Though much of the mayhem takes place within the confines of the house, the bodies of the victims are often found abandoned in the grounds or on nearby roads, appearing as casualties of apparent car accidents.

The viewer is also periodically confronted with the sight of Fran and Miriam—in full-length, low-cut evening gowns and all-enveloping velvet capes—silently flitting through swirling morning mists and dancing eddies of autumn leaves, as they flee through the woods and churchyard to escape the encroaching dawn. Or they hide amongst the trees bordering their property, as they wait to flag down the next hapless person who happens to drive past. It is in scenes such as these that Larraz reveals his ability to let silence speak much louder than words, and in the process create images as memorable as many of the film's more gore-soaked visions. As Julian Upton explains, Larraz was "a director unafraid of silence or stillness (even his more attention-seeking follow-up, *Vampyres*, which boosted the sex and gore to grind house levels, builds much of its atmosphere from an entrancing wordlessness)...."⁹

Continuity is not something which concerned Larraz greatly. In the best vampire tradition, Fran and Miriam initially appear to have a severe aversion to daylight: They can't get away quick enough following their nights of unbridled debauchery, staying one step ahead of the first rays of morning light as they lurk amongst the tombstones of the graveyard looking for somewhere to lie low. However, it's no time before they're out and about again in the afternoon sun, hitching a lift from their next unwary victim. Still, without the light, Larraz could not have shown off the grounds to their best advantage, making them all the more atmospheric, dappled in the first rays of dawn, or cast in the long shadows of late afternoon sunlight.

The Shining (1980)

> *Has it ever occurred to you that I have agreed to look after the Overlook Hotel until May the first?*

Director: Stanley Kubrick
Written by: Stanley Kubrick, Diane Johnson (screenplay, based on the novel by Stephen King)
Starring: Jack Nicholson, Shelley Duvall, Danny Lloyd, Scatman Crothers, Barry Nelson, Philip Stone, Joe Turkel

Not long into director Stanley Kubrick's psychological shocker *The Shining*, a big-budget production based loosely on Stephen King's cult novel, Jack Torrance (Jack Nicholson) reminds his wife Wendy (Shelley Duvall) of the obligation he has taken on as caretaker of the remote Overlook Hotel over five long winter months. In doing so, he coveys in a few words the sense of isolation, exile and mental suffocation which slowly engulfs him and his family as the story unfolds.

A brief glimpse of the Overlook Hotel should be enough to tell you it is not the ideal environment for those who are, like Jack, troubled by their own company. But then it doesn't take the viewer long to realize all is not right with Jack. Family problems and miserable job prospects abound:

Clearly irritated by his wife and understandably bored son, he struggles as a writer, with an employment outlook that is far from rosy.

From the opening scenes where the camera tracks a lone car through spectacular mountain scenery, past wide glacial lakes and deep mountain ravines, it is clear *The Shining* is all about scale and visual impact. As film historian David J. Skal pointed out, "Since King's work is so image-based, it was inevitable it would be adapted for film," though, unfortunately, as he also pointed out, none of the films "even approached a commercial success equivalent to that of his books."[10]

Even so, Kubrick's reimagining of the Overlook Hotel packed a punch in every way. From its cavernous reception area to the endless hallways and warren-like kitchens, everything about the interior is big, a feeling emphasized after the staff members finish for the season, leaving Jack and his family alone in the hotel's echoing, empty shell.

Outside, Kubrick continues the feeling of confinement with which he so skillfully paints the interiors of the building—despite their seemingly exaggerated size. The hotel is about as far removed from civilization as possible, with the building itself standing alone in an open patch of land at the foot of a towering mountain range. Nonetheless, a strong sense of claustrophobia pervades every aspect of the structure

Amazing: Jack Torrance (Jack Nicholson) loses it in the grounds of the Overlook Hotel in *The Shining* **(1980).**

and the area around. Once at the hotel—whether a guest or staff—there is no easy escape. All of this comes into play during the film's frenzied conclusion.

Mazes—both psychological and physical—are a recurring theme. The film's three primary characters, Jack, Wendy and Danny, are a tangled knot of neuroses. Danny has a lot going on in his young head, his gift of the "shining"—which enables him to see things not everyone else can—proving the least of his problems. The Torrance family's internal complexities are mirrored by the maze-like themes Kubrick plays with in the hotel's appearance and setting. Its labyrinthine interior with a myriad of bedroom suites and public rooms—empty during the winter season. The kitsch 1970s orange, red and green carpet, which runs a hexagonally shaped pattern through endless rows of deserted corridors, connecting each floor with a sense of unspoken cohesion.

Garden mazes have featured frequently throughout cinema's long history. Seldom, though, has the frustration and slow mounting panic you feel when trapped in one, been captured so effectively as here. The version in the hotel's grounds—created to entertain guests bored with the area's natural attractions—proves an instrument of both grace and death, mostly resulting from Wendy and Danny's attempts to escape Jack's increasingly erratic and violent behavior. It is also—indirectly—the medium which brings each parent, individually, together with their son, though unfortunately with different end purposes in mind. It first appears when Wendy and Danny, in an attempt to break free from the confines of the hotel, become lost within those of the ornate maze. During the climactic scenes, a deranged Jack hunts his terrified son through the maze, now a series of bizarre snow-covered shapes looming from shadowy corners thanks to the attraction's floodlight system.

Though the hotel in King's book—as well as the real-life Stanley Hotel on which he based it—are located in Colorado, the building which features as the exterior of the Overlook in the film is the Timberline Lodge in a mountainous winter sports area of Oregon. The isolation of the Timberline Lodge's location was better suited to the sense of removal from the real world which permeates all aspects of Kubrick's film: In reality, the grand Stanley Hotel is within hailing distance of the popular Estes Park ski resort, which lacks the remoteness inferred in King's story. King is said to dislike Kubrick's vision of his book, while the film was not a resounding success with many critics. Kubrick edited large sections from the finished work even after its initial American release, including an ending completely different from the now familiar one. The November 1980 edition of the *BFI Monthly Film Bulletin* devoted its back page to a list of 18 cuts Kubrick made before the film's

The real thing: The Stanley Hotel, Estes Park, Colorado, as seen today. The Colonial Revival building was Stephen King's inspiration for the Overlook Hotel in his cult novel *The Shining* (author's photograph.)

U.K. release, amounting to almost 30 minutes of deleted footage. One deleted scene involved the hotel's manager showing the Torrances the "famous hedge maze" and warning them "not to go in unless they have an hour to spare to find their way out,"[11] a scene which—in the light of the significance of the said topiary garden puzzle—it might have been better to have retained.

13

The Spare Room

> *Then he came to the passage which led to the shuttered room—Aunt Sarey's hideaway—or prison—he could now never learn what it might have been, and, on impulse, he went down and stood before that forbidden door. No snuffling, no whimpering greeted him now—nothing at all, as he stood before it, remembering, still caught in the spell of the prohibition laid upon him by his grandfather.*
> —*The Shuttered Room*, August Derleth (1959)

There's always one room in the house which is surplus to requirements. As a result, it often takes on a role that is not essential to the running of a normal home. Music rooms, laboratories, artists' studios are not to be found in everyone's house, but could become a quirky selling point if you ever considered putting yours on the market.

They may occasionally be used to hide dark family secrets, such as in the shuttered room from the story by writer August Derleth, inspired by the writings of H.P. Lovecraft. Nonetheless, these rooms frequently become no-go areas, as the purposes they're used for may require solitude—such as the locked art studio at the top of the lonely Cornish mansion in the Hollywood classic *The Uninvited* (1944); secrecy—like Henry Hull's garden laboratory in *WereWolf of London* (1935); or simply the space to accommodate the owner's bizarre collections—like the dungeons beneath Boris Karloff's fortress home in *The Black Cat* (1934). With this in mind, visitors are well advised to steer clear of spare rooms, however innocent they may appear, as you can never be sure what nefarious purposes they're really being used for.

The Black Cat (1934)

> "You know ... this is a very tricky house. The kind of place where I'd like to have company."

Don't Go Upstairs!

Strung up: Dr. Vitus Werdegast (Bela Lugosi) and arch-enemy Hjalmar Poelzig (Boris Karloff, right) discuss the cutting-edge design of the Satanist's chamber of horrors in *The Black Cat* (1934).

Director: Edgar G. Ulmer
Written by: Peter Ruric (screenplay), Edgar G. Ulmer and Peter Ruric (story), Tom Kilpatrick (contributing writer, uncredited), Edgar Allan Poe (suggested by a story by)
Starring: Boris Karloff, Bela Lugosi, David Manners, Julie Bishop (as Jacqueline Wells), Egon Brecher, Harry Cording, Lucille Lund, Henry Armetta, Albert Conti

Watching the Universal classic *The Black Cat*, it is easy to see why the film has consistently raised a perplexing question since its release in 1934. As Andre Sennwald noted in his *New York Times* review (May 19, 1934), "The acknowledgment which the producers of *The Black Cat* graciously make to Edgar Allan Poe seems a trifle superfluous, since the new film is not remotely to be identified with Poe's short story."[1]

The film—as Sennwald also points out—makes play of the presence of a black cat in the house of the story's evil protagonist Hjalmar Poelzig (Boris Karloff), and the repeated mention of the fear Poelzig's houseguest and adversary Dr. Vitus Werdegast (Bela Lugosi) has of the animal. "[Hjalmar] usually carries a black cat up his voluminous sleeve because his enemy, Dr. Werdegast, rolls his eyes and froths at the mouth when he sees black cats, and that suits Hjalmar."[2] Other than this, one can't really see the point of the moviemakers' attempts to associate the film with the story. Admittedly there are other similarities, the most obvious being Poelzig's secreting of Werdegast's dead wife (whom he'd fooled into marrying him after her separation from Werdegast following his imprisonment in a notorious Siberian prison camp) in the basement of his house: Poe's tale involves a man who walls his dead wife up in the basement of his house. However, most of these links are tenuous at best, resulting in the film's misleading title detracting from an otherwise remarkably atmospheric, creepy and effective Golden Age chiller.

Proceedings are lent impetus by the presence of several additional characters, including young American honeymooners Peter and Joan Alison (David Manners and Julie Bishop), who find themselves guests at Poelzig's house, following a road accident. However, the crux of the proceedings is clearly Poelzig and Werdegast's relationship—the association between the men during World War I and what happened in the years following this—and how this led to their meeting at the time of the story. However, the building in which they have their reunion and ultimate showdown—with its futuristic appearance and setting atop a hill overlooking a war-ravaged no-man's-land—overshadows everything and everyone, save the two central characters. The house comes alive in a profusion of glass walls, sliding electronic doors and a great sweeping staircase dominating the main open-plan reception room and hallway. As well as this, the most significant part of the house—outside of the diabolical dungeons beneath—is the makeshift Satanic temple where Poelzig holds regular black masses, along with his group of devout followers. Poelzig's role as head of a mystical devil cult brings yet another distasteful angle to a plot already brimming with torture, brutality and the inference of incest and necrophilia.

The Black Cat is an exquisite example of how to make something from nothing. The sets, given life by art director Charles D. Hall, are nothing short of a triumph of minimalist design. As little as a single spiral staircase—the only connection between Poelzig's main house and its basement where he performs his atrocities—stands in stark relief against a blank, concrete wall, emphasizing the film's various characters, as they repeatedly traverse its steps in a mad dash from top to bottom and back.

And it's when proceedings relocate to the chambers beneath the house that things take a turn for the worse. Upstairs, though the scenarios which play out are none too pleasant, everything is gilded with a surface of civility and good manners. But all such pretensions are forgotten downstairs. Here amongst a warren of secret rooms and sterile corridors, Poelzig's worst perversions are revealed, in a chamber of glass cabinets where the embalmed bodies of numerous ethereal beauties (including that of Werdegast's wife) are suspended for his pleasure. Where Poelzig has acquired these lifeless embodiments of pulchritude is anyone's guess, though probably the less said on this, the better. When Werdegast eventually discovers what Poelzig has done to his wife—and also plans for his (Werdegast's) daughter, having subjected her to the same fateful marriage and subsequent death as her mother—his revenge is without mercy, providing one of the most disturbing and haunting images of classic horror cinema. Chaining him to an embalming rack, Werdegast proceeds to flay Poelzig alive, peeling his skin, bit by bit, in a scene almost as harrowing to watch as it is for the victim to endure.

It goes without saying that the villains of the piece—for both Werdegast and Poelzig, in their own way, are equally twisted—meet their just ends, and the Alisons escape with their lives. However, the final scenes where Werdegast detonates a stash of explosives, upon which the house is built, by flicking switches and pulling levers upon a giant electrical grid (without which no horror outing of the era was complete), provide a fitting finale for a torture chamber as good as any from the period.

Despite its largely unnecessary connection with Poe, *The Black Cat*—and in particular its realization of Poelzig's house with its subterranean horrors—remains a classic example of art deco–Expressionist terror. A hybrid which, as writer Jerry Tillotson pointed out in 2017, has lost none of its power to shock:

> This masterful little gem ... gets better with the passage of time. The whole movie moves along like a dream with bizarre settings, art deco interiors and wardrobe, with Bela Lugosi and Boris Karloff playing arch-types, rather than living beings. Made on a small budget, director Edgar Ulmer shows what can be done if you're gifted and a genius.[3]

WereWolf of London (1935)

> "The werewolf is neither man nor wolf, but a Satanic creature with the worst qualities of both."

Director: Stuart Walker
Written by: John Colton (screenplay), Robert Harris (story), Harvey Gates and Robert Harris (adaptation—uncredited), Edmund Pearson (contributing writer—uncredited)
Starring: Henry Hull, Warner Oland, Valerie Hobson, Lester Matthews, Lawrence Grant, Spring Byington, Clark Williams, J.M. Kerrigan, Charlotte Granville, Ethel Griffies, Zeffie Tilbury

In the fifth edition of *Halliwell's Film Guide*, esteemed critic Leslie Halliwell was, like many authorities, somewhat scathing in his appraisal

Mixing it up: Dr. Glendon (Henry Hull) makes novel use of his botanical laboratory in *WereWolf of London* (1935).

of the genre classic *WereWolf of London,* referring to it as a "patchy horror film which lurches from excellent suspense scenes to tedious chunks of superfluous dialogue."[4] Watching it now, you can't help feeling Halliwell may have been a little harsh, as many films from Hollywood's Golden Age of Horror retain their appeal today as much for their idiosyncratic charm as for any ability to chill. What unsettled those who first saw the film in 1935 is unlikely to do more than raise the occasional nostalgic thrill amongst modern gore-hardened audiences. What the film lacks in the chiller department, it more than makes up for with understated style and elegance, as well as being, as Halliwell also pointed out, "in many ways a milestone in the history of its kind."[5] Officially the first werewolf film was the silent short *The Werewolf* (1913); and not until Universal's Lon Chaney Jr. vehicle *The Wolf Man* (1941) was lycanthropy firmly established on the movie map; but *WereWolf of London* is still considered the film which really brought the werewolf to film fans' attention.

While searching for the mariphasa plant in Tibet, respected botanist Wilfred Glendon (Henry Hull) is attacked by a wolf-like man in a remote mountain pass. Returning to London with specimens of the rare plant, Glendon finds that, as a result of the attack, he has succumbed to the curse of lycanthropy. The only remedy is from the juice of the mariphasa plant, which he has yet to get bloom under laboratory conditions. As the phase of the full moon approaches—when the mariphasa will flower, and he will be transformed into a werewolf—Glendon discovers that someone has followed him to England and will stop at nothing to get the plant for himself.

Throughout the film, sets were mostly used to recreate a remarkably authentic setting of 1930s London, surprising considering that everything was shot at Universal in Hollywood—bar the opening scenes for which the Vasquez Rocks Natural Area Park in Agua Dulce, California, doubled as mountainous Tibet. However, despite the action skipping between gentrified townhouses and sumptuous country estates, Glendon's laboratory stands out, appropriately so considering how many pivotal scenes take place within that room. Here is a private workshop—set across the garden from the house which Glendon shares with his wife Lisa (Valerie Hobson)—that would make your average botanist green with envy.

Though spartanly furnished, the room nonetheless has the usual trappings of scientific laboratories of the genre during the 1930s and 1940s. Here we have benches laden with flasks, tubes and apparatus prepared for Glendon's next experiment. Electricity-generating machines crackle to life at the pull of a lever and illuminate the darkened room with the flickering light so typical of Hollywood horror of the era. An early prototype video security camera alerts Glendon of unwanted guests at the laboratory door. And the centerpiece of Glendon's equipment is his moon lamp, a monstrosity of technical wizardry which produces the artificial moonlight he requires to grow the rare mariphasa. The fact that he lets no one but his trusted assistant enter the laboratory adds to the air of mystery surrounding Glendon and his activities; even the feisty and spirited Lisa gets no further than the threshold. Only a mysterious visitor, Dr. Yogami (Warner Oland), who requires the mariphasa for his own lycanthropic plight, eventually manages to enter the room uninvited, an intrusion which ultimately leads to tragedy.

Hull's werewolf transformation was the work of legendary makeup artist Jack Pierce, who had been responsible for Boris Karloff's iconic Monster in *Frankenstein* (1931), and would later turn Chaney Jr. into a lycanthrope in *The Wolf Man*. In *WereWolf of London*—though Pierce's work is (considering the era) remarkably effective, creating a look for Hull which is somewhere between man and beast—it is the way that Hull's transformation unfolds on screen which lends his animal state credibility. Though later Hull's metamorphosis is achieved by a lap dissolve effect in full view on-screen, his initial transmutation is brought about as he stalks across the garden between his house and laboratory: sporadically hidden behind trees, bushes and walls, he re-emerges each time more wolf-like, until he appears fully transformed when entering his scientific lair.

Certain aspects of the film may appear unnecessary, and—in the eyes of modern audiences—slow things down. Take, for instance, the addition of regular bouts of light-hearted humor. The "music hall" banter between two gin-addled old East End landladies adds little to the proceedings. The opening sequence also seems somewhat laborious. Though integral to the storyline, the segment—featuring Glendon and a companion searching the mountains of Tibet for the fabled mariphasa, followed by an attack by a werewolf (later shown to be Dr. Yogami) which leads to Glendon's own infliction with the curse—is melodramatic and ponderous, and could easily have been condensed with little detriment to the film.

These weaknesses aside, however, once the action is relocated to London and the viewer introduced to Glendon's in-house laboratory, there is little doubt that that room is one of vintage horror's most atmospheric scientific sanctuaries.

The Uninvited (1944)

And you'd not be nervous in such a lonely house? Or of the wind at nights. It plays odd tricks in old houses.

Director: Lewis Allen
Written by: Dorothy Macardle (novel), Frank Partos, Dodie Smith (screenplay)
Starring: Ray Milland, Gail Russell, Ruth Hussey, Donald Crisp, Cornelia Otis Skinner, Dorothy Stickney, Barbara Everest, Alan Napier

What was it with 1940s Hollywood and spooky houses set on the wild, coastal stretches of England's West Country? Whatever the attraction, just such a place acted as the perfect backdrop for *The Uninvited*, one of horror cinema's most effective yet criminally neglected ghost stories. Despite an excessively exaggerated trailer (done in the best 1940s melodramatic style), this is, in fact, a classic example of the power of atmospheric suggestion over in-your-face shocks: The seeping unease emanates from the room at the top of the stairs, saturating the house at the center of the story and haunting every aspect of the film.

As often is the case with the most effective chillers, *The Uninvited* relies as much on ambience as full-on, visceral frights, which are few and far between. In his *New York Times* review (February 21, 1944), Bosley Crowther warned audiences to:

Hold tight: Ray Milland protects Gail Russell in a stylized poster for Paramount's ghost classic *The Uninvited* (1944).

> Proceed at your own risk ... if you are at all afraid of the dark. For this fiction about two young people who buy an old seaside house in England, only to discover that a couple of banshees have taken up residence first, is as solemnly intent on raising gooseflesh as any ghost story weirdly told to a group of shivering youngsters around a campfire on a dark and windy night.[6]

Adapted by prolific Hungarian screenwriter Frank Partos and Dodie Smith (of *101 Dalmatians* fame) from Irish author Dorothy Macardle's novel *Uneasy Freehold* (a deliciously suggestive title!), *The Uninvited* still works, even in today's age of CGI wizardry. The haunting atmosphere of Windward House—the desolate mansion where the ghostly proceedings play out—was beautifully realized by Charles Lang, one of the archetypal cinematographers of Hollywood's Golden Age. It has everything one could want from a haunted house. Empty, dusty rooms—many locked for years; a grand staircase majestically sweeping the height of the house, lighting that works sporadically, meaning those in the house must revert to candlepower at the most inopportune of moments—and a room on the top floor which remains cold even on the warmest of summer afternoons. All of this sitting amongst gardens which roll down to the cliff edges, sitting dramatically above the jagged rocks and crashing waves of the Atlantic.

The fact that the film's cast is sparse—only eight people feature in main roles—enforces the feeling of Windward House as the story's central character. From the moment brother and sister Roderick and Pamela Fitzgerald (Ray Milland and Ruth Hussey) come across the deserted building while walking their dog along a remote coastal path, to their meeting with its austere owner, Commander Beech (Donald Crisp) and his beautiful but timorous granddaughter Stella (Gail Russell), until their confrontation with Windward's vengeful ghost during the dramatic finale, the Cornish mansion drives and influences every aspect of the proceedings. For make no mistake, Windward House is the star and its spirit lingers long after the closing credits.

Though the house as a whole may be wonderfully sinister—in a shadowy, half forgotten fashion—it is the room at the top of its winding central staircase, its wide, floor-to-ceiling windows overlooking the dramatic Atlantic coast, which is by far the most romantically realized. The black-and-white cinematography of Lang (Oscar-nominated for his efforts) makes the mid-afternoon shadows and candlelight late at night play tricks on the fevered imaginations of viewers as well as those of the film's characters. Here, as Roderick and his sister first encounter it—having let themselves into the house to have a furtive snoop around—is a room cut off, separate from the rest of the building. With its wall of windows providing panoramic views of the rocks and sea far below, and an eerie feeling of self-contained isolation, it's no surprise that Roderick—a musical composer—should commandeer the room for his music studio. Nor that it is the center for the house's paranormal activity, and where the couple find Stella after she's gone exploring when visiting them for dinner shortly after they've moved in.

The *Uninvited* posters hailed it as being "From the Most Popular Mystery Romance since *Rebecca*," which one can understand: With its haunted mansion like a virtual character, and the overbearing presence of a previous female owner, *The Uninvited* shares more than a passing resemblance to what is widely considered one of Hitchcock's masterpieces. But linking the two films does director Lewis Allen's brooding supernatural drama an injustice, as his Cornish cliffhanger surpasses the better known Hollywood hit for its sense of disquiet and unease. As pointed out in the film's entry in *The Overlook Film Encyclopaedia / Horror*, what few manifestations of spookiness that actually take place—in the form of "several shots of ectoplasmic apparitions"—had been included by Paramount in order to provide a supernatural explanation in favor of any Freudian reasoning. Fortunately, the British censors, for once, saw sense and, "removed the shots of the ghosts and so the film won much praise from the critics for having the courage to make a ghost film without ghosts!"[7]

Unlike many chillers from the period, *The Uninvited* is far from being a set-bound melodrama. The Pacific coastline in California effectively doubled as Cornwall, while other locations included San Francisco further upstate and Phoenix, Arizona. Despite this, it is Roderick's haunted music room to which the film's characters (human and otherwise) as well as its action keep returning, and which haunts your memory long after the film has finished.

The Black Cat (1981)

> "The air conditioning is not working. Please find the key, I'm frightened."

Director: Lucio Fulci
Written by: Lucio Fulci and Biagio Proietti (screenplay), Edgar Allan Poe and Biagio Proietti (story)
Starring: Patrick Magee, Mimsy Farmer, David Warbeck, Al Cliver, Dagmar Lassander, Bruno Corazzari, Geoffrey Copleston, Daniela Doria, Vito Passeri, Lucio Fulci (deleted scenes)

"Like so many Italian horrors, this one's a wacky, virtually plotless exercise in style—mediocre as it is—over substance."[8] Never one to pull a punch, Mike Mayo made this less-than-glowing commentary on director Lucio Fulci's feline frightfest *The Black Cat* in his *Videohound's Horror Show* movie guide (Visible Ink Press, 1998), and it seems rather ruthless. Okay, the acting is creaky and the multi-stranded plot hard to decipher, but there is no denying the film is a beautifully lush and evocative viewing experience. It is hard to totally write off what must be the only film to feature an idyllic Thames side boathouse as a place for gory murder.

Few in this day and age can either afford, or require, the luxury of a place to moor their motor-cruiser. For a start, even the concept of one conjures visions of someone wealthy and privileged, whose house backs onto a quiet stretch of the Thames. Which is where Lucio Fulci's *The Black Cat* is set. Though the story's location is never actually disclosed, it is obvious from the village setting and its proximity to a river that the story takes place somewhere in London's Home Counties: many of the outdoor locations were shot in Buckinghamshire and Hampshire, where picture postcard villages lend themselves perfectly to Fulci's vision of an English country idyll.

This vision of tranquility, conjured up by a rural hamlet straight

13. The Spare Room

from an Agatha Christie novel—complete with village green, post office, honey-colored cottages and grand houses on the riverbanks—emphasize the blood and gore when it sporadically raises its ugly head. This is a Fulci film, after all. The film concerns the unpleasant dealings of Robert Miles (Patrick Magee), an eccentric medium who believes he can communicate with the dead, and forces his pet cat through mind control to kill off his enemies in various nasty ways. There is little cohesion in the plot, save to connect one over-the-top death scene with the next.

The horrors here (a car crash, impaling, and burning amongst others, all instigated by the cat) are far-fetched. That doesn't mean they are any less effective, just slightly more restrained than Fulci's usual take on viscerally graphic violence; perhaps he thought that a subtler approach was more in keeping with the story's gentrified setting. The exception here is the death in the boathouse, which has all the slow-boil tension and graphic unpleasantness which fans expect from the director.

The moment you see the young couple, indulging in illicit sex in the bottom of a boat moored on the riverbank, you know things won't end well—such scenarios always flag a shock set-piece in this type of film. When they take their craft further along the river, mooring it in the grand if slightly down-at-heel boathouse, things really kick off. They lock themselves in a side room off the main area. All pointers to trouble are there: being somewhere they shouldn't; the girl wanting to leave, but being coerced into staying by her randy boyfriend; the lights failing; and a dodgy-looking air-conditioning system, which is the only means of ventilation in the room. Our titular feline, who just happens to be prowling in the vicinity, ensures that it breaks down, with stifling results.

There's nothing more frightening than being trapped somewhere within hailing distance of help, but you can't draw the attention of anyone in the outside world. Which is just the case with the boathouse here: Beautiful to behold, it is nonetheless removed just far enough from the outside world for people not to know what goes on inside. Palatial in stature—the owners of Thames side boathouses seldom skimp on exteriors—this is a building which commands the attention of anyone passing it on the river.

The interior is another story: Apart from the main section of the building where the boats are moored, the only other place is the dodgy-looking side room where the kids meet their fate. Furnished with work benches, a table, chair and—for some inexplicable reason—a bed, this is clearly an establishment seldom visited for any extended period, all of which is perfect for allowing the kids to go undiscovered for some time. Once locked in—with the key conveniently gone missing and the air conditioning broken down—it's just a matter of time before the inevitable happens, with gruesome results. By the time the girl's mother, and the local police, manage to get into the room, there's little left of them worth saving. Clearly days have elapsed (though this is never actually said) since the kids went missing, and what with the warm summer weather, an airless room and the inevitable addition of some rats, the kids have been reduced to little more than a pulpy mass, depicted in suitably Fulci-ish close-up. Blood and scratches seen on the walls and door add to the viewer's horror of what the young man and woman must have endured as they became increasingly desperate.

The film's finale is a typically frenzied Fulci affair, containing one of its few similarities to Edgar Allan Poe's story "The Black Cat" from which it supposedly takes inspiration. However, aside from this and a somewhat ambiguous conclusion, the film is worth watching simply for its setting, and in particular the scenes in the boathouse which conjure a macabre-tinged portrait of a bucolic British countryside.

The Hidden Face (2011)

> "The bunker is a place isolated from everything. A box within a box. One-sided bulletproof mirror. Impossible to detect."

Director: Andrés Baiz
Written by: Andrés Baiz (screenplay), Arturo Infante and Hatem Khraiche (story), Hatem Khraiche (writer)
Starring: Quim Gutiérrez, Martina García, María Soledad Rodríguez, José Luis García, Marcela Mar, Humberto Dorado, Julio Pachón, Juan Alfonso Baptista, Marcela Benjumena, Clara Lago, Alexandra Stewart, Mozad, Manuel Antonio Gómez

Classical conductor Adrián (Quim Gutiérrez) and shoe designer Belén (Clara Lago) have a somewhat shaky relationship, not helped by the fact that Belén is convinced that Adrián is having an affair with a member of his orchestra. When Belén discovers the secret of the country house they've just rented outside Bogotá in Colombia, she decides to test Adrián's true feelings towards her. Once owned by a Nazi war criminal, the house has a secret room where the German planned to hide should his past catch up with him. Complete with two-way mirror and concealed entrance, the room makes the perfect lair where Belén can hide and spy on Adrián, and watch his unfolding reactions to his girlfriend's disappearance. Through an unfortunate mistake, Belén finds herself trapped in the room and realizes that she is now confined within a living tomb with no means of escape.

As stated above in the entry for *The Black Cat* (1981), there must be no worse death than to be trapped in a room where you can see the outside world and those in it, but have no way of escape. Such is the premise of *The Hidden Face*, a beautifully atmospheric and taut chiller, largely overlooked since its release. That's unfortunate as this film achieves a feat seldom realized in horror cinema: a genuinely unnerving and disquieting viewing experience, which achieves its aim without the aid of gratuitous violence.

None of the film's characters are particularly pleasant. Because of Adrián's moodiness and duplicity in his relationship with Belén—is he, or is he *not*, having an affair with a member of his orchestra behind her back?—the viewer has little sympathy for him. And it's hard to feel empathy for Belén. Though her actions and the trick she hatches to test Adrián are perfectly understandable, her ultimate reaction to and treatment of Fabiana (Martina García)–a young waitress Adrián starts seeing after Belén's disappearance—make Belén no better than the woman she believes to have wronged her. Even Fabiana, the heroine of the piece, is less than honest, leading to a twist in the tale and an unexpected finale which will leave viewers questioning what they've just seen.

The human characters, however, are only subsidiaries to the central focus and essence of the film: the house in which the story unfolds. Though the action intermittently floats wider than the confines of the rambling country mansion and its grounds, the building remains the most arresting image in the viewer's mind after the film concludes. Against a background of classical music which Adrián both plays and conducts throughout the proceedings, a house is revealed which is both expansive and large, yet intimate and inspiring.

Both Adrián and Belén are artists in their own right (Adrián a conductor and Belén a designer), and one can understand why they would find the beautifully bohemian yet understated grandeur of the house appealing. Its unassuming exterior—from the outside, the house has the look of a somewhat bland stone farmhouse—belies an interior which combines majestic grandeur and understated opulence.

The brightness, beauty and simplicity of the main house is ideal to emphasize the horror and gloomy squalidness of the secret room behind the master bedroom. Whether or not the hidden chamber was originally intended to be as basic and threadbare as it appears when Belén becomes imprisoned in it, isn't made clear. It was designed as a refuge for the house's original owner, and it emerges that he was involved in wartime atrocities the results of which he believed might overtake him at any time. It is never revealed if the room was actually used for its intended purpose. But it's obvious that he did use it to hide the trappings of his sordid past, and Belén's discovery of these items adds to her mounting horror and that of the viewer as she discovers that she has become trapped in the room. Her entrapment in the room—with her ability to see Adrián, and later his new girlfriend Fabiana, and their activities in the bedroom by means of a one-way mirror—and her increasing frustration and horror as she realizes she is likely to die in it, makes for a truly nerve-grinding viewing experience; this is similar to the experience of being buried alive, yet with the added element of being able to see those on the outside and unable to communicate with them. Can you imagine the mounting terror Belén feels as the hours and days build?

Several plot twists lead to a conclusion you don't expect, with the viewer questioning how they might react if they found themselves in a similar situation.

Like all the best horror films, *The Hidden Face* works because you feel that it could actually happen. The fact it all plays out within the confines of such a seedy and claustrophobic environment, hidden in turn behind a facade of tranquil and understated beauty, makes it all the more disturbing.

Appendix: Abner Pastoll on the Importance of the House as a Film Character

Director Abner Pastoll is a filmmaker whose work challenges its audience, constantly providing a unique, unexpected and richly rewarding cinematic experience. This embodies itself perfectly in his 2015 psychological chiller Road Games.

Jack (Andrew Simpson) and Véronique (Joséphine de La Baume) meet while hitchhiking in rural France. After getting a lift from a man called Grizard (Frédéric Pierrot), the young couple reluctantly accepts his offer of a room for the night at the manor house he shares with his wife Mary (Barbara Crampton), deep in the French countryside. As the evening progresses, Jack and Véronique begin to realize there is more to their seemingly genial hosts and the mysterious mansion they call home than meets the eye.

The characters in Pastoll's films come in many forms and he feels that a house, like that in Road Games, *can be as twisted and multifaceted as any human.*

Where did you get the idea for Road Games?

I first came up with the idea when I was traveling in the north of France in the summer of 2001. I stayed at a very peculiar house that was filled with unusual, quirky artwork. It was incredibly inspiring. I've always been fascinated by language barriers and miscommunication between people, so I knew I'd draw on that in my work at some point. Being an English speaker traveling in the French countryside, it all sort of evolved from there. I wrote an initial story about a young man hitchhiking across France, trying to get home to England, who finds himself totally lost, and he ends up at this weird house with strange but interesting people and becomes inexplicably entangled in a mystery out of his control or full understanding. It wasn't until many years later though that I rediscovered the idea, literally by hard copy pages falling out of a drawer during a move,

Maison Grizard: The St. Clere Estate, Heaverham, Kent, doubles for the French chateau of eccentric couple Grizard and Mary in *Road Games* (2015) (courtesy Abner Pastoll).

and that's when I pursued developing it further as a feature screenplay, which is also when I added the love story angle.

Do you look at a house differently as a writer and a filmmaker, and what do you see as the role that houses play in films, particularly in the horror genre?

Houses can, in general, be crucial to telling a story in how they represent the characters who inhabit them. I find this especially applies to the horror genre. Many factors, including the size and layout, are key elements to influencing mood, atmosphere and tone. When looking at houses, there is also a strong sense of feeling I draw from to figure out if it's the right fit. It's a very similar process to casting an actor in a role.

When seeking a house to use as a location, what are the key elements a filmmaker is looking for?

What can be difficult is that we might find the perfect house in terms of look and feel yet it could be completely impractical to shoot in. Or it may just not be available. You need a space that can work for the story and the budget. Mood and atmosphere of the location are key and finding a

The camera crew prepares a shot on the set of *Road Games* (2015) (courtesy Abner Pastoll).

"connection" to the right house is just as much based on a feeling, as is the perfect look.

In Road Games, *Grizard and Mary's house is like a character in itself. When writing the film, how real was the house in your mind, and how important was it in the development of the story?*

The house was the first character I came up with: Maison Grizard. It was initially based on a real location, so in terms of drawing from that inspiration, it did help plan out scenes and elements of the story. Having a layout in mind just simplifies the writing process. I never expected to be able to shoot at the same location, though, so I was prepared for having to adapt the script when time came to shoot, but I'm talking very minor tweaks that mostly only really apply to my own visualization in my head. It's part of the process.

Had you seen the physical house you used before you started writing the story? What involvement did you have personally in the process of choosing the film's locations, including the house?

The filming location was sourced a long time after the script had been

Appendix: Pastoll on Importance of House as Character

Dream world: The St. Clere Estate's real rooms were dressed to evoke an air of shabby chic, touched with French decadence in *Road Games* **(2015) (courtesy Abner Pastoll).**

completed, so it didn't influence the initial writing in any way. It had been many years between the birth of the idea, concept and story, the writing of the script, and then the shoot itself, but indeed the house location ultimately affected the shooting script because without a set build where you can create something exactly as envisioned, you need to adapt to the space available. We were very lucky in the location we eventually shot in because it was so absolutely huge that there was plenty of space to work with.

I was of course very involved in the process of choosing all the locations. My location managers utilized their expertise to seek out various locales to fit the description of what we were looking for; and during the pre-production period, we viewed a good number of options before settling on the ones featured in the film.

Road Games is set in France, yet the house you used for filming was in England. Why did you do this and how did you go about finding the house which is very typical of a rural French manor house in appearance?

Shooting the house scenes in England was from a practicality standpoint, based on the way the film was set up as a U.K.–France co-production. It was cost-effective and turned out to be more efficient to double the house in Kent [England], which we discovered to have an interchangeable landscape with Picardie in the North of France, where the film is set and also where a lot of the exterior scenes were filmed. So it was a perfect fit. The production went through various formations during the lengthy pre-production period, though. At one point, it looked like it would be a co-production with Belgium, whereby the whole film would be shot there. It went as far along as me location-scouting in the rural Belgian countryside and actually even finding a house location that would have been magnificent. It certainly would have changed the feeling of the film but was in the same vein. I do believe that things happen for a reason, so when the production became delayed and restructured over the course of nearly another year, it enabled us to find the final location featured in the film. I can't quite imagine it having been elsewhere.

How much of the actual house did you use in the film? Does it look the same in reality?

I'd say a lot less than half of the actual real house location is featured in the film. It's a huge mansion on the St. Clere Estate in Sevenoaks, Kent. Several rooms were designed and completely made from scratch because there were empty floors at the top of the house that were out of use. That worked significantly to our advantage and is really rare to be able to do. The house looks pretty much the same in real life as it does in the film with a few exceptions: Grizard's study, Véronique's bedroom and the attic space were all designed specifically for the film. So while these rooms exist in the house, they do not look the same. The entrance hallway looks exactly the same, as does Jack's bedroom and the dining room. Some interesting trivia: The pianoforte that Jack touches in the living room belongs to the location and was once played on by Mozart.

The four main characters—Jack, Véronique, Grizard and Mary—are all distinctly individual, even isolated, characters. In the same way, the house is represented as being remote, singular and unique. Did you sense this mirroring of the characters with the house and was it deliberate?

I've always seen the house as one of the characters, and much of the mirroring is completely intentional. Each character is harboring secrets and that very much includes the house.

When it came to shooting in the house, did the building have any effect on the physical filmmaking process? Did you change anything in the story or script to accommodate the house, or vice versa?

You always have to tweak the shooting script if you're using a real location. It comes with the territory. You have to find the right angle and approach to make the story work. Nothing changed in a major way as we

Grand entrance: Jack (Andrew Simpson) and Véronique (Joséphine de La Baume) make their escape through the paneled hallway of Maison Grizard in *Road Games* (2015) (courtesy Abner Pastoll).

had plenty of space available to us. It would have been interesting had we ended up shooting the film in the house in Belgium as it had two staircases, one on each side of the house, and both went all the way up to the attic. That would have been fun to play with.

Is the house you used inhabited in real life, and how did its owners feel about their property appearing in a horror film?

The family was still living in the house during the shoot, but we scheduled filming so as not to be in their way and didn't impose too much on their living space. The house is huge so we never felt like we were in each other's way. There is still a weight on your shoulders knowing that the owners are present and could be watching your every move, no matter how supportive they are. They did go away on holiday for the second week we were at the house, which was a relief, but also spent a few moments here or there watching us shooting with intrigue. My lead actor Joséphine became very good friends with one of the young girls who'd occasionally be peeking from around the corner. The only other feature film to have shot in the house before us was the 1980 Agatha Christie mystery *The Mir-*

ror Crack'd, starring Angela Lansbury, Elizabeth Taylor, Tony Curtis and Rock Hudson. The owner recalled being a young girl during that shoot and befriending Elizabeth Taylor while she was in the makeup chair, so there was a wonderful sense of synergy between that and of her daughter doing something similar with Joséphine.

What condition was the house in and how much freedom did you have to do what you wanted in it?

The house has interesting mixes of well-kept and completely run-down, depending on what floor you're on or which room you're in. That's what made it so perfect. The owners mostly inhabited rooms on the ground and first floors and we couldn't change too much in these areas other than having the freedom to redress and move furniture around—as long as it could be returned to its original state. There were plenty of other rooms on the upper floors and in the attic, however, where we had total freedom to repaint and pretty much do as we needed, as there were large areas of the house where they had plans for refurbishment. It's very rare to have that kind of freedom in a real location. They just let us loose.

The St. Clere Estate and its grounds—as they appear in *Road Games* (2015)—also featured in *The Mirror Crack'd* (1980), based on Agatha Christie's novel and directed by Guy Hamilton of Bond film fame (courtesy Abner Pastoll).

210   Appendix: Pastoll on Importance of House as Character

What are the day-to-day difficulties of making a film in what is in many cases someone's actual home?

You have to be conscious not to damage anything and be respectful of the fact that it's actually someone's home. Be aware you need to return it to them intact. We were lucky that the house was so big because we didn't get in their way.

Watching the film, it is clear that it was filmed in an actual house. As a filmmaker, what kind of freedoms, or restrictions, does using a real (sometimes inhabited) house have over filming on a sound stage?

Building a set gives you the creative freedom to make a space exactly from imagination. It also comes with more flexibility in terms of lighting and using certain filming equipment. Shooting in a real location means you have to adapt to what exists, and you might encounter restrictions

Make-believe: Joséphine de La Baume, Andrew Simpson (seated) and a crew member (center) prepare for a dramatic attic scene in *Road Games* (2015) (courtesy Abner Pastoll).

with equipment and space, but it can also inspire new ideas in the story or in the technical approach. There are pros and cons to both. It really comes down to the project, and then the location and budget options you have available.

When making a film, how attached do you become with the house or building where you're filming? In the same way as an actor will say they like working with certain directors, or directors with certain actors, does this happen with the location where you're working?

There is a connection in a sense and I have fond memories of some locations I've filmed in but otherwise I don't usually become that attached to houses or places in the same way. It's different with people because you make a human connection.

Did anything strange happen in the house when you were filming, or were there any particular incidents involving the house which stand out in your memory?

The night before our first shooting day, *The Mirror Crack'd* played on TV. Being the only other film to have shot in the same house, it was

Up to their necks: As *Road Games* (2015) crew members stand by, Andrew Simpson and Joséphine de La Baume take a dip in the lake in the grounds of the St. Clere Estate (courtesy Abner Pastoll).

quite surreal to see the entrance hallway and grounds, and to recognize several other rooms. The timing could not have been more perfect. Several of the crew saw it on TV in their hotel rooms that night so there was much excitement and conversation about it the next morning while we were setting up our first shot, which just so happened to be in the entrance hallway.

There were various strange things that happened during filming but the most significant was when we were in the attic. We had been told stories by the groundskeeper of a ghost in the house but never thought much of it over the course of the shoot, despite some items occasionally moving from positions they had been left in. The art department had almost finished dressing the attic and left the room unattended, for a lunch break. A mirror that was to be hung on the wall was placed securely on padded bedding. When they returned not 30 minutes later, the mirror was all the way on the other side of the room, smashed, in pieces on the floor. Nobody had access to the attic during the break, so we decided it had to have been the ghost. What else could it have been? In any case, we decided to assemble the broken shards and piece them together on the wall—so that is the reason why Mary has a cracked mirror on the wall of her attic art room. Literally, the mirror crack'd...

What are the key elements of a haunted house and what role, if any, do these have in the making of a good horror film?

Having a live-in ghost certainly helps!

What is your favorite room of a house and do you have a favorite representation of that room in a horror film?

This is a very tricky question. I'm not sure that I have a favorite room. I think, when you use a room in an interesting way, that is what can make it memorable, like the bathroom at the Bates Motel in *Psycho*, or Norman's mother's bedroom in their mansion up the hill. And of course the basement! I think for the most part, at least for me, it's the scenes that take place—and what the characters do within them—that makes the rooms memorable. Dining rooms lend themselves to wonderfully tense dinner scenes, and bedrooms can hold all kinds of secrets. I like it when a room is shown or used in an unexpected way. For example, the way the living room is used in *The Snorkel* is rather magnificent, and so I'd have to say that's right up there as one of my all-time favorites.

Which are your favorite houses in horror films and what effect have any of them had on you and your career as a filmmaker?

The list could potentially be endless, but a few memorable houses off the top of my head would be from *Psycho, A Nightmare on Elm Street,*

Appendix: Pastoll on Importance of House as Character 213

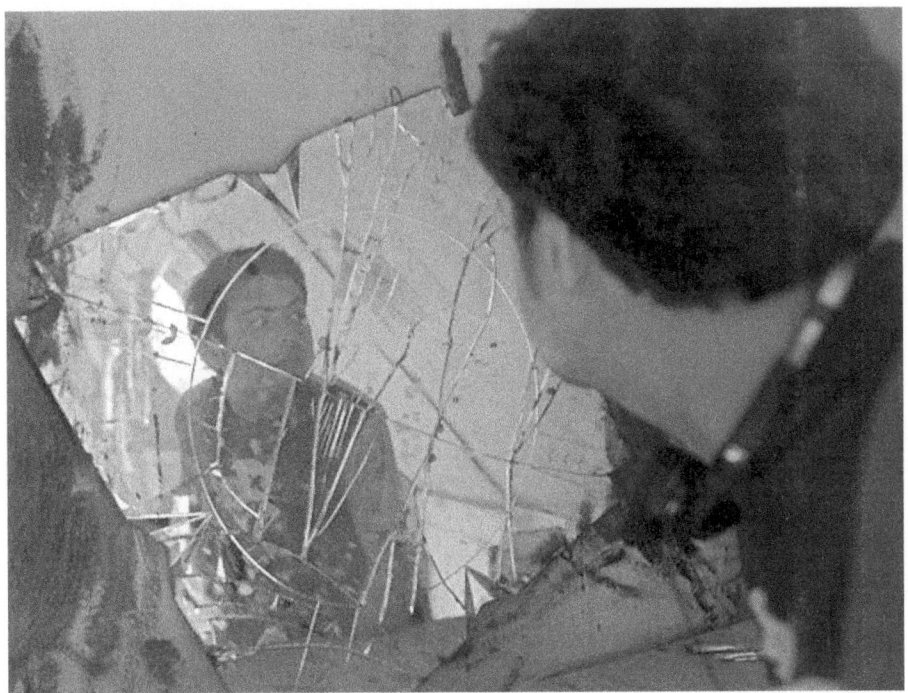

Broken image: Director Abner Pastoll contemplates his reflection in the cursed mirror on the wall of Mary's attic studio in *Road Games* **(2015) (courtesy Abner Pastoll).**

Texas Chain Saw Massacre, The Exorcist, Paranoiac, Taste of Fear [Scream of Fear], Burnt Offerings, Poltergeist, The Nanny and of course The Snorkel. They've certainly provided a lot of inspiration to draw from but I can't say they've specifically had an effect on my career.

Is there any house—famous or otherwise, anywhere in the world—where you'd really like to make a horror film, and why?

I'd love to shoot on my father's farm in South Africa. There are a few houses, a couple of which he's built himself out of mud. I've always wanted to make a horror film about the Tokoloshe, a Zulu myth about a mischievous, dwarf-like water sprite that can become invisible by drinking water, because it was such an influential story to me growing up. The only way to keep the Tokoloshe away at night is to put a brick beneath each leg of one's bed, although it still doesn't fully protect you. It's super creepy. There have finally been a few films made about this in recent years, so I'll probably not tackle that story specifically unless I have a nice and unique angle. But I believe the mud houses would lend themselves to an intriguing horror story. Watch this space.

214　Appendix: Pastoll on Importance of House as Character

Nightmare vision: The remains of one of Mary's forgotten projects lies discarded in an empty room at Maison Grizard in *Road Games* (2015) (courtesy Abner Pastoll).

Chapter Notes

Chapter 1

1. "The Omen." *The Variety Movie Guide '96*. Ed. Derek Elley. London: Hamlyn, 1995. 707.
2. "The House by the Cemetery." *The Overlook Film Encyclopaedia / Horror*. Ed. Phil Hardy. New York: The Overlook Press, 1994. 370.
3. Head Cheeze (James F. Reilly). "Opera." *Horrorview*. www.horrorview.com/movie-reviews/opera.

Chapter 2

1. Hall, Mordaunt. "The Invisible Man." *The New York Times*, 18 November 1933. www.nytimes.com/1933/11/18/archives/claude-rains-makes-his-film-debut-in-a-version-of-hg-wellss-novel.
2. "The Invisible Man." *The Oxford Companion to Film*. Ed Liz-Anne Bawden. Oxford: Oxford University Press, 1976. 354.
3. Tarratt, Margaret. "Tales from the Crypt." *Films and Filming* 19.1 (1972): 53.
4. Alexander, Chris. "Tales from the Crypt / Vault of Horror, Scream Factory Blu-ray Review." *Fangoria*, 28 November 2014. www.fangoria.com.
5. Newman, Kim. "The Beast Must Die." *Nightmare Movies* (updated edition). London: Bloomsbury, 2011. 34.
6. Annett, Paul. "Directing the Beast." *The Beast Must Die*. Dir. Paul Annett. Amicus, 2013. DVD.
7. Eder, Richard. "From Beyond the Grave." *The New York Times*, 4 March 1976. www.nytimes.com/1976/03/04/archives/film-beyond-the-grave4-episodes-delve-into-a-nether-world.
8. Campbell, Bruce. *If Chins Could Kill*. London: Aurum Press, 2009. 98.
9. "The Evil Dead." Variety, 31 December 1982. www.variety.com/1982/film/reviews/the-evil-dead-1200425402.
10. "The Evil Dead." The Overlook Film Encyclopaedia / Horror. Ed. Phil Hardy. New York: The Overlook Press, 1994. 376.

Chapter 3

1. A.D.S. "Murders in the Zoo." The New York Times, 3 April 1933. www.nytimes.com/1933/04/03/archives/an-imaginative-killer.
2. Everson, William K. "Murders in the Zoo." Classics of the Horror Film. New York: The Citadel Press, 1974. 113.
3. Nugent, Frank S. "The Cat and the Canary." *The New York Times*, 23 November 1939. www.nytimes.com/1939/11/23/archives/the-screen-paramount-finds-comedy-in-the-cat-and-the-canary-return.
4. Everson, William K. "The Wolf Man." *Classics of the Horror Film*. New York: The Citadel Press, 1974. 214.
5. Conrad, Derek. "The Mummy." Films and Filming 6.2 (1959): 23–24.
6. Ibid.
7. Riley, Clayton. "A Clockwork Orange." *The New York Times*, 9 January 1972. www.nytimes.com/1972/01/09/archives/-or-a-dangerous-criminally-irresponsible-horror-show-a-clockwork-or.
8. McDowell, Malcolm. "McDowell on 40th Anniversary of *A Clockwork Orange*." *BBC Breakfast News*, 23 May 2011. www.youtube.com/watch?v=cbktMGs0meI&t=120s.

Chapter 4

1. "Son of Frankenstein." *The New York Times*, 30 January 1939. www.nytimes.

com/1939/01/30/archives/the-screen-son-of-frankenstein-with-boris-karloff-seen-at-the.

2. Halliwell, Leslie. "Son of Frankenstein." *The Dead That Walk*. London: Grafton Books, 1986. 152.

3. Skall, David J. "Son of Frankenstein." *The Monster Show* (revised edition). London: Faber and Faber, 2001. 206.

4. Cocteau, Jean. "La belle et la bête." *Diary of a Film*. Trans. Ronald Duncan. London: Dennis Dobson, 1950. 164–165.

5. Eyles, Allen. "Dracula: Prince of Darkness." *Films and Filming* 12.6 (1966): 55–56.

6. McGillivray, David. "Twins of Evil." *Films and Filming* 18.4 (1972): 61–62.

7. Weiler, A. H. "Twins of Evil." *The New York Times*, 14 July 1972. www.nytimes.com/1972/07/14/archives/screen-2-chillers-for-the-hot-weather.

8. Kay, Jeremy. "You're Next." *The Guardian*, 13 September 2011. www.theguardian.com/film/2011/sep/13/youre-next-toronto-festival-review.

Chapter 5

1. Hanks, David. "Corruption." *eofftv.com*. www.eofftv.com/index.php?title=Corruption_(1967).

2. *Ibid.*

3. Ebert, Roger. "Images." *RogerEbert.com*, 10 December 1974. www.rogerebert.com/reviews/images-1974.

4. Bacon, Charles. "Poltergeist." *Film Review* 32.10 (1982): 6–7.

5. Perkins, Anthony. "Psycho II." Interview by Barbara Paskin. *Film Review* 33.10 (1983): 10–11.

6. Gunz, Joel. "Original Psycho House—Found." *Alfred Hitchcock Geek*, 25 March 2010. www.alfredhitchcockgeek.com/2010/03/original-psycho-house-found.

7. Button, Simon. "Psycho II." *Films and Filming* 3.11 (1983): 42–43.

8. Gordinier, Jeff. "Scream." *Entertainment Weekly*, 17 January 1997. www.ew.com/article/1997/01/17/scream.

Chapter 6

1. Harrison, Jack. "Psycho." *The Hollywood Reporter*, 17 June 1960. www.hollywoodreporter.com/review/psycho-review-1960-movie-1014164.

2. Baker, Peter, "Psycho." *Films and Filming* 6.12 (1960): 21.

3. Stanley, John. "The Pit and the Pendulum." *Creature Features Movie Guide Strikes Again* (4th revised edition). Pacifica, CA: Creatures at Large Press, 1994. 299.

4. Clarens, Carols. "The Horror Revival." *Horror Movies: An Illustrated Survey*. London: Panther Books, 1971. 216.

5. Stuart, Alex. "Asylum." *Films and Filming* 19.2 (1972): 50–51.

6. Rabinowitz, Mort, and Hooper, Tobe. "Salem's Lot." Interviews by Bill Kelley. *Cinefantastique* 9.2 (1979): 11–13.

7. *Ibid.*

Chapter 7

1. Rushford Greason, Alfred. "Frankenstein." *Variety*, 7 December 1931. www.variety.com/1931/film/reviews/frankenstein-2-1200410509/.

2. Newman, Kim. "Frankenstein." *1001 Movies You Must See Before You Die*. London: Cassell Illustrated, 2004. 94.

3. Frank, Allan. "The Devil Doll." *Horror Films*. London: Spring Books, 1983. 39.

4. Nugent, Frank S. "The Devil Doll." *The New York Times*, 8 August 1936. www.nytimes.com/1936/08/08/archives/hollywood-opens-its-bag-of-tricks-for-the-capitols-the-devil-doll.

5. Hutchings, Peter. "The Horror Man: 1957–62." *Terrence Fisher / British Film Makers Series*. Manchester: Manchester University Press, 2001. 113.

6. Stanley, John. "The Brides of Dracula." *Creature Features Movie Guide Strikes Again* (4th revised edition). Pacifica, CA: Creatures at Large Press, 1994. 59.

7. Brosnan, John. "The Abominable Dr. Phibes." *The Horror People*. London: Macdonald and Jane's, 1976. 271.

8. Peary, Danny. "Theatre of Blood." *Guide for the Film Fanatic*. London: Simon & Schuster, 1986. 428.

Chapter 8

1. Crowther, Bosley. "Dead of Night." *The New York Times*, 29 June 1946. www.nytimes.com/1946/06/29/archives/the-screen-dead-of-night-a-britishmade-film-is-premiere-at-winter.

2. Crowther, Bosley. "The Innocents."

The New York Times, 26 December 1961. www.nytimes.com/1961/12/26/archives/screen-the-innocentsfilm-from-james-tale-is-at-two-theatres.
 3. Clarke, Cath. "The Innocents (rerelease)." *Time Out*, 9 December 2013. www.timeout.com/london/film/the-innocents.
 4. Castell, David. "The Changeling." *Films Illustrated* 10.109 (October 1980): 27.
 5. *Ibid.*
 6. *Ibid.*
 7. Puig, Claudia. "The Woman in Black." *USA Today*, 2 February 2012. www.usatoday.com.
 8. Rutherford, Ed. "The Ones Below." *Screen Daily*, 13 September 2015. www.screendaily.com/reviews/the-ones-below-review/5092223.article.

Chapter 9

 1. Weiler, A. H. "Hands of the Ripper." *The New York Times*, 14 July 1972. www.nytimes.com/1972/07/14/archives/screen-2-chillers-for-the-hot-weather.
 2. McGillivray, David. "Hands of the Ripper." *Films and Filming* 18.4 (1972): 61.
 3. Fox, Julian. "Squirm." *Films and Filming* 23.1 (1976): 34–35.
 4. "A Nightmare on Elm Street." *The Variety Movie Guide '96*. Ed. Derek Elley. London: Hamlyn, 1995. 681.
 5. Addiego, Walter. "Final Destination." *San Francisco Examiner*, 17 March 2000. www.sfgate.com/news/article/Final-Destination-3068640.php.
 6. Gonzalez, Ed. "*What Lies Beneath*." DVD release. 2 May 2001. www.slantmagazine.com/film/review/what-lies-beneath.
 7. Graham, Bob. "What Lies Beneath." *San Francisco Chronicle*, 21 July 2000. www.sfgate.com/movies/article/Chilled-to-the-Bone-The-past-haunts-Harrison-2747764.php.

Chapter 10

 1. Elley, Derek. "Frightmare." *Films and Filming* 21.6 (1975): 38–39.

Chapter 11

 1. Naremore, James. "American Film Noir: The History of an Idea." *The Film Studies Reader*. London: Arnold, 2000. 106.
 2. Dickstein, Morris. "The Aesthetics of Fright." *Flesh and Blood: The National Society of Film Critics on Sex, Violence, and Censorship*. San Francisco: Mercury House, 1995. 144.
 3. Wood, Chris. "Die, Monster, Die!" *British Horror Films*, 22 February 2010. www.britishhorrorfilms.co.uk/diemonsterdie.
 4. Newman, Kim. "Frogs." *Nightmare Movies: Horror on Screen Since the 1960s* (revised edition). New York: Bloomsbury USA, 2011. 89.
 5. Rainer, Peter. "The Hand That Rocks the Cradle." *Los Angeles Times*, 10 January 1992. www.articles.latimes.com/1992-01-10/entertainment/ca-1450_1_cradle-movie-family.

Chapter 12

 1. "The Beast with Five Fingers." *Variety*, 31 December 1945. www.variety.com/1945/film/reviews/the-beast-with-five-fingers-1117788929/.
 2. "Florey, Robert." *The Oxford Companion to Film*. Ed. Liz-Anne Bawden. Oxford: Oxford University Press, 1976. 256.
 3. Naha, Ed. "The Beast with Five Fingers." *Horrors: From Screen to Scream*. London: Futura, 1976. 19.
 4. Milne, Tom. "The Ballad of Tam Lin." *Monthly Film Bulletin* (June 1977). www.old.bfi.org.uk/sightandsound/feature/49693.
 5. "The Devil's Widow." *The Overlook Film Encyclopaedia / Horror*. Ed. Phil Hardy. New York: The Overlook Press, 1994. 231.
 6. Stanley, John. "Vampyres—Daughters of Darkness." *Creature Features Movie Guide Strikes Again* (4th revised edition). Pacifica, CA: Creatures at Large Press, 1994. 421.
 7. "Vampyres." *Films and Filming* 22.9 (1976): cover.
 8. Rigby, Jonathan. "Vampyres." *English Gothic: Classic Horror Cinema 1897–2015* (revised edition). Cambridge: Signum Books, 2015. 256.
 9. Upton, Julian. "Symptoms." *Offbeat: British Cinema's Curiosities, Obscurities and Forgotten Gems*. London: Headpress, 2012. 297.
 10. Skall, David J. "The Shining." *The*

Monster Show (revised edition) London: Faber and Faber, 2001. 366.
    11. "Shine On ... and Out." *Monthly Film Bulletin* (November 1980): 228.

Chapter 13

1. A.D.S. "The Black Cat." *The New York Times*, 19 May 1934. www.nytimes.com/1934/05/19/archives/not-related-to-poe.html?module=inline.
2. *Ibid.*
3. Tillotson, Jerry. "The Black Cat." TCM, 2017. www.tcm.com.
4. Halliwell, Leslie. "Werewolf of London." *Halliwell's Film Guide* (5th edition). London: Guild, 1986. 1063.
5. *Ibid.*
6. Crowther, Bosley. "The Uninvited." *The New York Times*, 21 February 1944. www.nytimes.com/1944/02/21/archives/the-screen.
7. "The Uninvited." *The Overlook Film Encyclopaedia / Horror*. Ed. Phil Hardy. New York: The Overlook Press, 1994. 87.
8. Mayo, Mike. "The Black Cat." *Videohound's Horror Show*. Detroit: Visible Ink Press, 1998. 29.

Bibliography

Blu-Ray / DVD

Annett, Paul. "Directing the Beast." *The Beast Must Die*. Dir. Paul Annett. Amicus, 2013. DVD

Books

Bawden, Liz-Anne, ed. *The Oxford Companion to Film*. London: Oxford University Press, 1976.
Brosnan, John. *The Horror People*. London: Macdonald and Jane's, 1976.
Campbell, Bruce. *If Chins Could Kill*. London: Aurum Press, 2009.
Clarens, Carlos. *Horror Movies: An Illustrated Survey*. London: Panther Books, 1971.
Cocteau, Jean. *Diary of a Film*. Translated by Ronald Duncan. London: Dennis Dobson, 1950.
Dickstein, Morris. "The Aesthetics of Fright." *Flesh and Blood: The National Society of Film Critics on Sex, Violence, and Censorship*. San Francisco: Mercury House, 1995.
Elley, Derek, ed. *The Variety Movie Guide '96*. London: Hamlyn, 1995.
Everson, William K. *Classics of the Horror Film*. New York: The Citadel Press, 1974.
Frank, Allan. *Horror Films*. London: Spring Books, 1983.
Halliwell, Leslie. *The Dead That Walk*. London: Grafton Books, 1986.
Halliwell, Leslie. *Halliwell's Film Guide*, 5th ed. London: Guild, 1986.
Hardy, Phil, ed. *The Overlook Film Encyclopaedia / Horror*. New York: The Overlook Press, 1994.
Hutchings, Peter. *Terrence Fisher / British Film Makers Series*. Manchester: Manchester University Press, 2001.
Mayo, Mike. *Videohound's Horror Show*. Detroit: Visible Ink Press, 1998.
Naha, Ed. *Horrors: From Screen to Scream*. London: Futura, 1976.
Naremore, James. *The Film Studies Reader*. London: Arnold, 2000.
Newman, Kim. *Nightmare Movies*, updated ed. London: Bloomsbury, 2011.
Peary, Danny. *Guide for the Film Fanatic*. New York: Simon & Schuster, 1986.
Rigby, Jonathan. *English Gothic: Classic Horror Cinema 1897–2015*, rev. ed. Cambridge: Signum Books, 2015.
Schneider, Steven Jay, ed. *1001 Movies You Must See Before You Die*. London: Cassell Illustrated, 2004.
Skall, David J. *The Monster Show*, rev. ed. New York: Faber and Faber, 2001.
Stanley, John. *Creature Features Movie Guide Strikes Again*, 4th rev. ed. Pacifica, CA: Creatures at Large Press, 1994.
Upton, Julian. *Offbeat: British Cinema's Curiosities, Obscurities and Forgotten Gems*. London: Headpress, 2012.

Magazines

Bacon, Charles. "Poltergeist." *Film Review*, vol. 32, no. 10, Oct. 1982: 6–7.
Baker, Peter. "Psycho." *Films and Filming*, vol. 6, no. 12, Sept. 1960: 21.
Button, Simon. "Psycho II." *Films*, vol. 3, no. 11, Nov. 1983: 42–43.
Castell, David. "The Changeling." *Films Illustrated*, vol. 10, no. 109, Oct. 1980: 27.
Conrad, Derek. "The Mummy." *Films and Filming*, vol. 6, no. 2, Nov. 1959: 23–24.
Elley, Derek. "Frightmare." *Films and Filming*, vol. 21, no. 6, March 1975: 38–39.
Eyles, Allen. "Dracula: Prince of Darkness." *Films and Filming*, vol. 12, no. 6, March 1966: 55–56.

Fox, Julian. "Squirm." *Films and Filming*, vol. 23, no. 1, Oct. 1976: 34–35.

McGillivray, David. "Hands of the Ripper." *Films and Filming*, vol. 18, no. 4, 1972: 61.

McGillivray, David. "Twins of Evil." *Films and Filming*, vol. 18, no. 4, 1972: 61–62.

Perkins, Anthony. "The Long Wait for 'Psycho II' Ends. Interview by Barbara Paskin." *Film Review*, vol. 33, no. 10, Oct. 1983: 10–11.

Rabinowitz, Mort, and Hooper, Tobe. "Salem's Lot. Interviews by Bill Kelley." *Cinefantastique*, vol. 9, no. 2, Winter 1979: 11–13.

"Shine On ... and Out." *Monthly Film Bulletin*, Nov. 1980.

Stuart, Alex. "Asylum." *Films and Filming*, vol. 19, no. 2, Nov. 1972: 50–51.

Tarratt, Margaret. "Tales from the Crypt." *Films and Filming*, vol. 19, no. 1, Oct. 1972: 53.

"Vampyres." *Films and Filming*, vol. 22, no. 9, June 1976: cover.

Television

McDowell, Malcolm. "McDowell on 40th Anniversary of A Clockwork Orange." *BBC Breakfast News*, 23 May 2011. www.youtube.com/watch?v=cbktMGs0meI&t=120s.

Websites

Addiego, Walter. "Final Destination." *San Francisco Examiner*, 17 Mar. 2000. www.sfgate.com/news/article/Final-Destination-3068640.php.

A.D.S. "The Black Cat." *The New York Times*, 19 May 1934. www.nytimes.com/1934/05/19/archives/not-related-to-poe.html?module=inline.

A.D.S. "Murders in the Zoo." *The New York Times*, 3 Apr. 1933. www.nytimes.com/1933/04/03/archives/an-imaginative-killer.html.

Alexander, Chris. "Tales From the Crypt / Vault of Horror, Scream Factory Blu-ray Review." *Fangoria*, 28 Nov. 2014. www.fangoria.com.

"The Beast with Five Fingers." *Variety*, 31 Dec. 1945: www.variety.com/1945/film/reviews/the-beast-with-five-fingers-1117788929/.

Clarke, Cath. "The Innocents (rerelease)." *Time Out*, 9 Dec. 2013. www.timeout.com/london/film/the-innocents.

Crowther, Bosley. "Dead of Night." *The New York Times*, 29 June 1946. www.nytimes.com/1946/06/29/archives/the-screen-dead-of-night-a-britishmade-film-is-premiere-at-winter.

Crowther, Bosley. "The Innocents." *The New York Times*, 26 Dec. 1961: www.nytimes.com/1961/12/26/archives/screen-the-innocentsfilm-from-james-tale-is-at-two-theatres.

Crowther, Bosley. "The Uninvited." *The New York Times*, 21 Feb. 1944: www.nytimes.com/1944/02/21/archives/the-screen.html.

Ebert, Roger. "Images." *RogerEbert.com*, 10 Dec. 1974: www.rogerebert.com/reviews/images-1974.

Eder, Richard. "From Beyond the Grave." *The New York Times*, 4 March 1976: www.nytimes.com/1976/03/04/archives/film-beyond-the-grave4-episodes-delve-into-a-nether-world.html.

"The Evil Dead." *Variety*, 31 Dec. 1982: www.variety.com/1982/film/reviews/the-evil-dead-1200425402/.

Gonzalez, Ed. "What Lies Beneath." DVD release, 2 May 2001: www.slantmagazine.com/film/review/what-lies-beneath.

Gordinier, Jeff. "Scream." *Entertainment Weekly*, 17 Jan. 1997: www.ew.com/article/1997/01/17/scream/.

Graham, Bob. "What Lies Beneath." *San Francisco Chronicle*, 21 July 2000: www.sfgate.com/movies/article/Chilled-to-the-Bone-The-past-haunts-Harrison-2747764.php.

Greason, Alfred Rushford. "Frankenstein." *Variety*, 7 Dec. 1931: www.variety.com/1931/film/reviews/frankenstein-2-1200410509/.

Gunz, Joel. "Original Psycho House—Found." *Alfred Hitchcock Geek*, 25 March 2010: www.alfredhitchcockgeek.com/2010/03/original-psycho-house-found.html.

Hall, Mordaunt. "The Invisible Man." *The New York Times*, 18 Nov. 1933: www.nytimes.com/1933/11/18/archives/claude-rains-makes-his-film-debut-in-a-version-of-hg-wellss-novel.html.

Hanks, David. "Corruption." *eofftv.com*: www.eofftv.com/index.php?title=Corruption_(1967).

Harrison, Jack. "Psycho." *The Hollywood Reporter*, 17 June 1960: www.hollywood

reporter.com/review/psycho-review-1960-movie-1014164.
Hunter, Allan. "The Ones Below." *Screen Daily*, 13 Sept. 2015: www.screendaily.com/reviews/the-ones-below-review/5092223.article.
Kay, Jeremy. "You're Next." *The Guardian*, 13 Sept. 2011: www.theguardian.com/film/2011/sep/13/youre-next-toronto-festival-review.
Milne, Tom. "The Ballad of Tam Lin." *Monthly Film Bulletin* (June 1977). www.old.bfi.org.uk/sightandsound/feature/49693.
Nugent, Frank S. "The Cat and the Canary." *The New York Times*, 23 Nov. 1939: www.nytimes.com/1939/11/23/archives/the-screen-paramount-finds-comedy-in-the-cat-and-the-canary-return.html.
Nugent, Frank S. "The Devil Doll." *The New York Times*, 8 Aug. 1936: www.nytimes.com/1936/08/08/archives/hollywood-opens-its-bag-of-tricks-for-the-capitols-the-devil-doll.html.
Puig, Claudia. "The Woman in Black." *USA Today*, 2 Feb. 2012: www.usatoday.com.
Rainer, Peter. "The Hand that Rocks the Cradle." *Los Angeles Times*, 10 Jan. 1992: www.articles.latimes.com/1992-01-10/entertainment/ca-1450_1_cradle-movie-family.
Reilly, James F. (Head Cheeze). "Opera." *Horrorview*: www.horrorview.com/movie-reviews/opera.
Riley, Clayton. "A Clockwork Orange." *The New York Times*, 9 Jan. 1972: www.nytimes.com/1972/01/09/archives/-or-a-dangerous-criminally-irresponsible-horror-show-a-clockwork-or.html.
"Son of Frankenstein." *The New York Times*, 30 Jan. 1939: www.nytimes.com/1939/01/30/archives/the-screen-son-of-frankenstein-with-boris-karloff-seen-at-the.html.
Tillotson, Jerry. "The Black Cat." TCM, 2017: www.tcm.com.
Weiler, A. H. "Hands of the Ripper." *The New York Times*, 14 July 1972: www.nytimes.com/1972/07/14/archives/screen-2-chillers-for-the-hot-weather.html.
Weiler, A. H. "Twins of Evil." *The New York Times*, 14 July 1972: www.nytimes.com/1972/07/14/archives/screen-2-chillers-for-the-hot-weather.html.
Wood, Chris. "Die, Monster, Die!." *British Horror Films*, 22 Feb. 2010: www.britishhorrorfilms.co.uk/diemonsterdie.shtml.

Index

Numbers in **_bold italics_** indicate pages with illustrations

ABC-TV 114
The Abominable Dr. Phibes (1971) 111, ***112–113***, 114
Absolutely Fabulous (TV) 96
Adams, Nick 162, ***163***
Addiego, Walter 139
Albright, Ivan 146
Alda, Robert 174, ***175***
Alien (1979) 6, ***8***
Allan, Michael 119–120
Allen, Lewis 195, 197
Altman, Robert 71, 75
Alvin, John 174
American International Pictures (AIP) 90
Amicus 24, 27–31, 33–36, 87, 93–95, 123, 153, 163
The Amityville Horror (1979) 4, ***7***, 156
And Then There Were None (book) 31, 68
Anders, Luana 90, 92
André, Marcel 59
Andrews, Dana 177–178, ***178***
Ankers, Evelyn 46, 48
Annett, Paul 31, 33
Archibald, William 121
Architectural Digest (magazine) 143
Argento, Dario ***21***, 22–23
Arquette, David 83–84
Art Institute of Chicago (museum) 146
Asher, Jack 110
Asylum (1972) 28, 87, 92–93, ***93***
Attic 145
Atwill, Lionel 40–41, ***42***
Auberjonois, Rene 75, ***75***
The Avengers (TV) 97, 114, 179

Baiz, Andrés 200
Baker, Peter 89
Baker, Rick 136
Baker, Roy Ward 92
Balderston, John L. 103
The Ballad of Tam Lin (1970) 7, 180–183, ***181***
Barbarella (1968) 65
Baron, Lynda 131
Barrett, Simon 68
Barrymore, Drew 83–85, ***85***

Barrymore, Lionel 85, 105–106
Basic Instinct (1992) 173
Bastedo, Alexandra 153–154
bathroom 131
Bayldon, Geoffrey 27–28, 92
BBC Breakfast News 54
BBC Films 128
Beacham, Stephanie 180–183
Beal, John 44, ***45***
The Beast in the Cellar (1971) 2
The Beast Must Die (1974) 30–32, ***31***
The Beast with Five Fingers (1946) 174, ***175***, 176–177
bedroom 102
Bell, Keith 131, 133
La Belle et la Bête (1946) 56, 59–60
Bennett, Charles 177
Bevan, Stewart 153
Birn, Laura 128
Bishop, Julie 190–191
Black, Karen 155–156
The Black Cat (1934) 189–192, ***190***
The Black Cat (1981) 198, 200
Black Narcissus (1947) 67
Black Park Country Park, Wexham, England 66
Blair, Linda 10, 83
Blakely, Ronee 136, 137
Blatty, William Peter 10
Blees, Robert 165
Blish, James 31
Bloch, Robert 34, 80, 87, 92–93
Boddey, Martin 27
Boles, John 103–104
Bozzuffi, Marcel 75
Breakfast at Tiffany's (novel) 123
The Brides of Dracula (1960) 49, 62, 108–110, ***109***
Briganti, Elisa Livia 18
Brolin, James ***7***
Brosnan, John 114
Brown, Murray 183
Browning, Tod 105–106
Bryan, Dora 131
Bryan, Peter 108

223

Burgess, Anthony 52
Burke, Kathleen 40, *42*
Burnham, Edward 111–112, *112*
Burns, Marilyn 12–13
Burnt Offerings (1976) 155–156, *157*
Burstyn, Ellen 10, *10*
Bush, Kate 177
Butcher, Kim *4*, 150, *151*, 153
Byington, Spring 192
Byron, Kathleen 65, *66*

Callas, Maria 23
Campbell, Bruce 36
Campbell, Neve 83–84
Campbell Moore, Stephen 128
Cannes Film Festival 77
Capote, Truman 121, 123
Carbone, Antony 90–91
Carlson, Veronica 153
Carmichael, Ian 33–34, *34*
Carpenter, Richard 174
Carradine, John 25
Castell, David 124
Casting the Runes (story) 177
The Cat and the Canary (1939) 39, 43–44, *45*
Cat People (1942) 160, 180
Cavalcanti, Alberto 119
cellar 87
Chadbon, Tom 31, *31*
Chaney, Lon, Jr. 46–47, 193–194
The Changeling (1980) 123–125, 156
Charleson, Ian 22
Chelsea Embankment, London, England 116
Chester, Hal E. 177
Chetwynd-Hayes, R. 33–34
Chitty Chitty Bang Bang (1968) 120
Christie, Agatha 31, 68, 199, 208, *209*
Christodoulou, Raymond 33
Clarens, Carlos 92, 179
Clark, Marlene 31, *31*
Clarke, Cath 123
Clarke, Mae 103–104
Clarke, Robin 33
Clarke, Warren 52, *53*
Clayton, Jack 118, 121–122
Clive, Colin 103
Cliver, Al 198
The Clock (2010) 2
A Clockwork Orange (1971) 52–53, *53*, 68, 74
Coates, Darcy 145
Cocteau, Jean 59–60
Coles, Michael 95
Collier's (magazine) 160
Collins, Joan 1, 27, *28*, 29–30, 34
Collinson, Madeleine 65, *66*, 67
Collinson, Mary 65, *66*, 67
The Color Out of Space (novel) 162
Colton, John 192

The Company of Wolves (1984) 107–108
Conrad, Derek 51–52
conservatory 159
The Cook (novel) 71
Cooper, Willis 56
Corman, Roger 90–91, *90*
Corri, Adrienne 39, 52–53, *53*
Corruption (1968) 2, 71–72, *72*, 74
Cortland, Nicholas 165, 167
Cox, Courtney 83–84
Craig, Johnny 27
Crampton, Barbara 68, 203
Craven, Mimi 136
Craven, Wes 80–83, 136–137, *137*
The Crazies (1973) 134
Crisp, Donald 195, 197
Crosby, Floyd 92
Crowther, Bosley 119–120, 122, 195
Culver, Roland 119
Cummins, Peggy 177, 179
Cundey, Dean 82
The Curse of Frankenstein (1957) 150
Curse of the Demon (1957) 174, 177, *178*, 179–180
The Curse of the Werewolf (1961) 107
Curtis, Dan 155–156, *157*
Curtis, Tony 209
Curtis, Tony (art director) 30, 94
Cusack, Sinéad 180, 182
Cushing, Peter 27–28, 31–34, *31*, 48–49, *49*, 63, 65, *66*, 67, 72–73, *72*, 92, 95–96, 108, 110, 114, 153–155, *154*

Dahl, Roald 131
Dane, Alexandra 71–72, 74
Danziger, Allen 12–13
Daubeney, Diana 183
Davidson, Lewis 131
Davies, Rupert 150
Davis, Bette 155–156
Dawley, J. Searle 103
Day, Josette 59
Deacon, Brian 183
Dead of Night (1945) 118–120
Deathtrap (1976) 101
DeLeon, Walter 44
Denham, Maurice 177–178
De Mornay, Rebecca 170–171, *171*
Depp, Johnny 102, 136
Derleth, August 189
Deviation (1971) 183
The Devil Doll (1936) 85, 105–108, *106*
The Devil Rides Out (1968) 148–149, *149*
Devine, Sophie 123
Dickstein, Morris 162
Die, Monster, Die! (1965) 162, *163*
Die Screaming, Marianne (1971) 151
Dingle, Charles 174
dining room 56
Dirty Harry (1971) 161

Index 225

Dr. Cyclops (1940) 107
Dr. Jekyll & Sister Hyde (1971) 132
Dr. Phibes Rises Again (1972) 114
Dr. Terror's House of Horrors (1965) 28
Donella, Chad 139–140
Donner, Richard 15
Donovan, King 160, *160*
Doré, Gustave 60
Doria, Daniela 198
Dors, Diana 115–116, *115*
Dow, R.A. 134–135
Dracula: Prince of Darkness (1966) 56, 61–64, *62*, *64*
Dracula's Daughter (1936) 107
Duc de Richleau 148–150, 149
Dunagan, Donnie 56–57
Dunne, Dominique 77–78, *79*
Duvall, Shelley 185
Dynasty (TV) 29
Dziubinska, Anulka 183

Ealing Studios 119
Eastwood, Clint 161
Ebert, Roger 77
Eder, Richard 35
Edison Studios 103
Elley, Derek 153
Elliott, Sam 165, *166*
Endore, Guy 105–106
Englund, Robert 136–137
Escape from Alcatraz (1979) 161
Everson, William K. 41, 47
The Evil Dead (1981) 36, 38
The Exorcist (1973) 6, 9–10, *10*, 213
Eyles, Allen 62

Fairfax, Deborah 150–151
Farmer, Mimsy 198
Farmer, Suzan 62–63, *62*, 162, *163*
Farr, David 128
Faulkner, Sally 183
Feldstein, Al 27
Final Destination (2000) 139–140
Finch, Scot 31
Finney, Jack 160
Fisher, Terence 48, 61–62, 108, 110, 148, *149*
The Flesh and Blood Show (1972) 151
Flickfeast (website) x
Florey, Robert 103, 106, 174
Ford, Barry 120
Ford, Derek 72
Ford, Donald 72
Ford, Grace 105–107, *106*
Ford, Harrison 141–142
Fort, Garrett 103, 105–106
Foster, Ashley 126
Fox, Julian 135
Francen, Victor 174–175, *175*
Francis, Freddie 27, 123, 153
Frank, Alan 105

Frankenstein (1910) 4
Frankenstein (1931) 58, 102–103, 107, 194
Franklin, Pamela 121–122
Franklin, Richard 80, 82
Franklyn, William 95
Franks, Chloe 27, 29
Freud 18, 111, 132–134, 197
Friedkin, William 10
Frightfest (film festival) ix
Frightmare (1974) ix, 3, *4*, 65, 150–151, *151*, 153
Frogs (1972) 165–167, 166
From Beyond the Grave (1974) 24, 28, 33–34, *34*
Frye, Dwight 25, 103
Fuest, Robert 111, 114
Fulci, Lucio 5, 18, 198
Furneaux, Yvonne 48, 50, *51*

Gaines, William M. 27
Gambon, Michael 31, *31*, 33
García, Martina 200–201
Gardner, Ava 180–182
Gates, Harvey 192
Gates, Tudor 65
Gausman, Russell A. 58
Gavin, John 87, 89
Gein, Ed 14
Ghirardani, Paul 127
Ghost Story (1981) 124
The Ghosts of Motley Hall (novel) 174
The Ghoul (1975) 153–155, *154*
Gibbons, Cedric 1, 147
Gibson, Alan 95
Goddard, Paulette 44, *45*
Goldberg, Rube 139–140
Goldman, Jane 126
Goldstein, William 111, 114
Gonzalez, Ed 142
Grais, Michael 77
Gray, Charles 31, 33, 115, 117, 148
Gray, William 124
Greason, Alfred Rushford 104
Great Expectations (1946) 123
Greene, Leon 148
greenhouse 159
The Greenhouse (novel) 159
Greenwood, Paul 150, *151*, 152
Gregg, Clark 141
Greig, Robert 105, 107
Greville-Bell, Anthony 115–116
grounds 174
Gutiérrez, Quim 200

Hall, Charles D. 1, 27, 191
Hall, Mordaunt 26
Haller, Daniel 92, 162
Halliwell, Leslie 58, 192–193
Halliwell's Film Guide 192
Halloween (1978) 80, 102, 137

226 Index

hallway 9
Hamilton, Guy *209*
Hammer 33, 49–52, 56, 62–63, 65–67, 75, 87, 92, 96–98, 107, 109–110, 123, 126, 128, 132–134, 148–149, 153, 162–163
The Hand That Rocks the Cradle (1992) 5, 170, *171*, 173
The Hands of Orlac (novel) 56
Hands of the Ripper (1971) 131–132, *132*, 134
Hanks, David 74
Hanley, Jenny 180, 182
Hansen, Gunnar 13–14, *13*
Hanson, Curtis 170
Harris, Robert 192
Harrison, Cathryn 75–76
Harrison, Jack 88
Hartford-Davis, Robert 72, 74
Harvey, William Fryer 174
Hatfield, Hurd 145, *146*
The Haunted Realm (book) 102
The Haunting of Blackwood House (novel) 145
Hawkins, Jack 115–116, *115*
Head Cheeze 22
Heckart, Eileen 155–156
Heilbron, Lorna 168, *168*
Hendry, Ian 27, 29, 115
Henkel, Kim 12
Herbert, James 3
Heyward, Louis M. 114
Hickox, Douglas 115
The Hidden Face (2011) 4, 200–202
Higgins, Fran 134–135
Highgate Cemetery, London, England 29
Hill, Susan 118, 126
Hillmore, Susan 159
Hinds, Anthony 61, 153
Hinds, Ciarán 126–127
Hitchcock, Alfred 52, 81, 83, 87, 136
Hitchcock, Patricia 87
Hobson, Valerie 192, 194
Holland, Tom 80
Hollywood's Golden Age 4, 27, 43, 46, 48, 59, 191, 193, 196
Hooper, Tobe 12, 77–78, 98, 153
Hope, Bob 44, *45*
Horror of Dracula (1958) 49, 62, 109, 150
Hough, John 65
Houghton, Don 95
The Hounds of Love (song) 177
The House by the Cemetery (1981) 5, 18–20, *19*
The House of Hammer (magazine) ix, 134
House of Mortal Sin (1976) 2
Howes, Sally Ann 119–120
Hudson, Rock 209
Hull, Henry 189, 192–193, *193*
Hunt, Gareth 97
Hunt, Martita 108, *109*
Hunter, Russell 124

Huntley, Raymond 48–49, 168
Hurt, John 153–154
Hussey, Ruth 195, 197
Hutchings, Peter 110
Hutchinson, Josephine 65–57, *57*
Hutchinson, Robert 165

I Monster (1971) 95
I Walked with a Zombie (1943) 180
Images (1972) 71, 74–77, *75*
In Search of Unicorns (book) 75, 77
The Incredible Shrinking Man (1957) 107
Infante, Arturo 200
The Innocents (1961) 118, 120–123, *121*
Invasion of the Body Snatchers (1956) 159–162, 160
The Invisible Man (1933) 4, 24–26, *25*, 41
Irving, Hollis 165, 167
Iver Heath, Buckinghamshire, England 66

Jack the Ripper 133
Jackson, Freda 108, *109*, 111, 162
James, Anthony 155
James, Henry 121
James, M.R. 177
Jason King (TV) 123
Jaws (1975) 78, 80
Jeffrey, Peter 111, *112*, *113*
Jenkins, Megs 92, 121, 123
Jessop, Clytie 121
Johns, Mervyn 119
Johnson, Diane 185
Jones, Carolyn 160
Jones, Norman 111, *112*, *113*

Karloff, Boris 25, 56, 103, *103*, 162, 189–190, *190*, 192, 194
Kay, Jeremy 68
Keir, Andrew 62–63
Keith, Sheila *4*, 150, 151, 152
Kernochan, Sarah 141
Kerr, Deborah 121–123, *121*
Kerr, John 90–91
Khan, James 77
Khazanova, Alisa 126
Khon, John 115
Khraiche, Hatem 200
Kidder, Margot *7*
Kilpatrick, Tom 190
King, Andrea 174, *175*
King, Stephen 7, 87, 98–99, *99*, 185–187, *188*
The Kiss of the Vampire (1963) 62
kitchen 71
Kressing, Harry 71
Krueger, Freddy 84, 131, 137–138
Kubrick, Stanley 52–53, 55, 68, 185–187

La Baume, Joséphine de 203, *208*, 209, *210–211*

Index

Lago, Clara 200
Lancie, John de 170–171
landing 9
Lang, Charles 196
Langenkamp, Heather 136–137, *137*
Lansbury, Angela 145, 147, 209
Larraz, José Ramón 159, 168, 170, 183–185
Lassander, Dagmar 18, *19*, 20, 198
The Last House on the Left (1972) 84, 139
Latham, Philip 62–63, *62*
Laughton, Charles 6
Lawford, Peter 145
Lawrence, Marjie 131, *132*, 133
Lawton, Frank 105, 107
Leake, Barbara 119
Leatherface *13*, 14–15, 99
Lee, Christopher 26, 48, *49*, 50–51, *51*, 62, *64*, 95–96, 109, 148, *149*
Lee, Rowland V. 56
Le Fanu, J. Sheridan 65
Legend of the Seven Golden Vampires (1974) 96
Leigh, Janet 83, 87–88, 138, 172
Leighton, Margaret 33–36
Leopard Man (1943) 180
Leprince de Beaumont, Jeanne-Marie 59
Leroux, Gaston 23
Lewin, Albert 145
Lewis, C.S. 39
Lewton, Val 180
library 39
Lieberman, Jeff 134–136
Lippincott's (magazine) 147
living room 24
Lloyd, Sue 72–73
Lockhart, Calvin 31–32, *31*
Lodge, John 40, 42
Loggia, Robert 80, 82
Lorre, Peter 174, *175*, 177
Louis XVIII 60
Lovecraft, H.P. 18, 162–163, 189
Lugosi, Bela 25, 46–47, 56, 177, 190, *190*, 192
Lumley, Joanna 87, 95–96, *96*, 114, 180, 182
Lust for a Vampire (1971) 65

Macardle, Dorothy 195–196
MacColl, Catriona 18
MacGinnis, Niall 177–178, *178*
MacGowran, Jack 10
Macnee, Patrick 96
MacPhail, Angus 119
Madden, Ciaran 31, *31*
Maddox, Diana 124
Madhouse (1974) 95
Magee, Patrick 27, 29, 39, 52–53, *53*, 92, 162, 198–199
The Magician's Nephew (novel) 39
Mailleux, Marie-Paule 168–169
Mainwaring, Daniel 160

The Making of the Brides of Dracula (documentary) 110
Malco, Paolo 18
The Man-Eater of Surrey Green (TV - *Avengers* episode) 179
Mann, Stanley 115
Manners, David 190–191
Marais, Jean 59
Marasco, Robert 155
Marclay, Christian 2
Marcus, James 52, *53*
Mariuzzo, Giorgio 18
Mark of the Vampire (1935) 85, 107
Marney, Terence de 162, 164
Marsden, Simon 24
Marsh, Jean 124
Marsillach, Christina *21*, 22
Mary Poppins (1964) 120
Mason, James 98–99
Massey, Raymond 6
Matheson, Richard 90–91, 148
Matthews, Francis 62–63, *62*, *64*
McCarthy, Kevin 160–161, *160*
McCowan, George 165
McCoy, Matt 170–171
McCulloch, Ian 153–154
McDowall, Roddy 180, 182
McDowell, Malcolm 52–53, *53*
McGillivray, David ix, 1–3, *5*, 65, 134, 150, 152
McKern, Leo 15
McMinn, Teri 12–13
McShane, Ian 180–183, *181*
Medak, Peter 124–125
Melander, Ashley 170
Melander, Eric 170
Melander, Jennifer 170
Meredith, Burgess 155–156
Merrall, Mary 119
Merritt, Abraham 105–106
Merrow, Jane 131, 133
MGM 146
Miles, Vera 80, 82, 87–88
Millais, Hugh 71, 75–76, *75*
Milland, Ray 165, 195, *196*, 197
Miller, Jason 10–11, *10*
Miller, Seton I. 40
Miller, Stanley 168
Mills, Elliot 128–129
Mills, Joseph 128–129
Milne, Tom 180
The Mirror Crack'd (1980) 208–209, *209*, 211
Monash, Paul 98
Monlaur, Yvonne 108, *109*
Montgomery, Douglass 44, 45
Montgomery, Lee H. 155–166
Moore, Julianne 170, *171*, 172
Moran, Rob 68
Morgan, Glen 139

Morris, Marianne 183
Morrissey, David 128
Mortimer, John 121, 123
Mower, Patrick 148
The Mummy (1959) 48, *49*, 50–52, *51*, 52
Munroe, Caroline 111
Murders in the Rue Morgue (1932) 106, 177
Murders in the Zoo (1933) 2, 39–41, 42, 43, 97

Naha, Ed 177
Naish, J. Carrol 174–175
Nalder, Reggie 98–99, *99*
The Nanny (1965) 213
Naremore, James 160
Nelson, Craig T. 77, *79*
The New Avengers (TV) 114
Newman, Kim 31, 105
Nicholson, Jack 185, *186*
Nicolodi, Daria 22
Night of the Lepus (1972) 165
A Nightmare on Elm Street (1984) 84, 102, 136–138, *137*, 212
A Nightmare on Elm Street 2: Freddy's Revenge (1985) 138
Nolan, William F. 155
North, Virginia 111
Nosferatu (1922) 4
Nugent, Elliott 44
Nugent, Frank S. 108
nursery 118

Oakley Court, Berkshire, England 7, 183
O'Connor, Una 24, 26
Oland, Warner 192
The Old Dark House (1932) 4, *6*
Oleck, Jack 30
The Omen (1976) 15, *16*, 173
101 Dalmatians (novel) 196
O'Neill, Ronald 168–169
The Ones Below (2015) 2, 118, 128, 130
Opera (1987) 20, *21*, 22–23
O'Rourke, Heather 77–78, *79*
O'Sullivan, Maureen 105
The Others (2001) 120
Otterson, Jack 58
Ottiano, Rafaela 105
Owen, Thomas 168

Palance, Holly 15
Paramount Studios 42, 44, 197
Paranoiac (1963) 123, 132, 213
Parkins, Barbara 28, 92–93
Partain, Paul A. 12–13
Partos, Frank 195–196
Pastoll, Abner ix, 203, *204–206, 208–211, 213–214*
Patterson, Elizabeth 44, *45*
Pearcy, Patricia 134–135
Pearson, Edmund 192

Pearson's Weekly (magazine) 25
Peart, Pauline 95, *96*
Peary, Danny 116
Peck, Gregory 15
Peel, David 108, 110
Percy, Edward 108
Perkins, Anthony 71, 80–81, *81*, 87–88
Petrushka, Gina 10, *10*
Pfeiffer, Michelle 141–142, *142*
Phantom of the Opera (novel) 22
The Picture of Dorian Gray (1945) 1, 145, *146*
The Picture of Dorian Gray (novel) 146–147
Pierce, Jack 194
Pierrot, Frédéric 203
Pit and the Pendulum (1961) 90–91
"The Pit and the Pendulum" (short story) *90*
Pitt, Ingrid x
Pleasence, Angela 33, 168, *168*, 183
Plum, Dido 131
Poe, Edgar Allan 90–91, *90*, 177, 190, 198, 200
Poésy, Clémence 128
Poltergeist (1982) 5, 77, *79*, 82, 174
Porter, Eric 131–132, *132*, 134
Porter, Nyree Dawn 33–35, *34*
Price, Dennis 65, 67, 115
Price, Vincent 90–91, 111, 114–115, *115*
Proietti, Biagio 198
Psycho (1960) 6, 81, 87–89, 131, 143, 172, 212
Psycho II (1983) 71, 80, *81*, 82, 89, 145
Puig, Claudia 126

Rabinowitz, Mort 100
Radcliffe, Daniel 126
Raimi, Sam 36, 38
Rainer, Peter 172
Rains, Claude 24, *25*, 26, 46–47, 172
Rathbone, Basil 56–57, *57*
Rebecca (1940) 197
Reddick, Jeffrey 139
Redgrave, Michael 121–122
Reed, Donna 145
Reed, Oliver 155–156
Rees, Angharad 131, 133
Remick, Lee 15, *16*
Renard, Maurice 56
Richardson, Ralph 27, 29
Rigby, Jonathan 184
Rigg, Diana 115
Riley, Clayton 53
RKO 180
Road Games (2015) ix, 203, 205–206, *204–206, 208–211, 213–214*
Robins, Oliver 77, *79*
Robinson, Bernard 51, 110, 149
Robinson, Bruce 180, 182
Robinson, Heath 140
Rosenberg, Max 34
Rubenstein, Zelda 77, 80

Index

Ruggles, Charlie 40, *42*
Rumpole of the Bailey (novel) 123
Ruric, Peter 190
Russell, Gail 195, *196*, 197
Rutherford, Ed 129

Sacchetti, Dardano 18
The St. Clere Estate, Kent, England *204*, *206*, 207, *209*, *211*
Salem's Lot (1979) 98–99, *99*, 101
'Salem's Lot (novel) 87
Sanders, George 145
Sangster, Jimmy 48, 61, 63, 108
Sasdy, Peter 131, 134
The Satanic Rites of Dracula (1973) 87, 95–96, *96*, 98
Satan's Slave (1976) ix, 2–3, *5*, 65, 134
Sawa, Devon 139
Saxon, John 136
Scardino, Don 134–135
Schayer, Richard 105
schoolroom 118
Schubert, Bernard 107
Sciorra, Annabella 170–171
Scorsese, Martin 121
Scott, George C. 124
Scott, Randolph 40–41, 43
Scott, Ridley 6
Scream (1996) 71, 83, 85, *85*, 139
Scream ... and Die! (1973) 183
The Sentinel (1977) 124
Seltzer, David 15
Seyler, Athene 177, 179
Shakespeare, William 115, 117
Shelley, Barbara 62–63, *62*
Shelley, Mary 56, 58, 103
Sherriff, R.C. 24
Shew, Edward Spencer 131
Shingleton, Wilfred 1, 123
The Shining (1980) 185–186, *186*, *188*
The Shining (novel) 7
Shivers (magazine) x
"The Shuttered Room" (short story) 189
Siegel, Don 160–161
Silver, Amanda 170
Simpson, Andrew 203, *208*, *210*–*211*
Siodmak, Curt 46, 174
Skal, David J. 59, 186
Skyrne Castle, County Meath, Ireland 24
Sliver (1993) 173
Smith, Dodie 195–196
Smith, Madeline 115, 180, 182
The Snorkel (1958) 212–213
Sohl, Jerry 162
Son of Frankenstein (1939) 56, *57*, 58
Sondergaard, Gale 44, *45*
Soul, David 98–99
Spare Room 189
Spellbound (1945) 143
Spielberg, Steven 77–78

Spier, William 180
Squirm (1976) 131, 134–136, 165
Standeven, Guy 111, *112*
Stanley, John 90, 111, 183
Stanley Hotel, Estes Park, Colorado, USA 7, 187, *188*
Star Wars: Episode IV—A New Hope (1977) 54, 76
Starling, Lynn 44
Steele, Barbara 90–91
Stefano, Joseph 87
Stephens, Harvey 15, *16*
Stephens, Martin 121–122
Stewart, Alexandra 200
Stoker, Bram 61
Straight, Beatrice 77, 80
Stroheim, Erich von 105–106
Stuart, Alex 93
Stuart, Gloria *6*, 24
study 39
Subotsky, Milton 27, 34
Sullivan, Jean 134–135
The Sunday Times Magazine x
Suspicion (1941) *143*
Sutherland, Edward 40
Sydow, Max von 10–11, *10*
Symptoms (1974) 159, 167–169, *168*, 183
Syms, Sylvia 92–93, *93*

Tales from the Crypt (1972) 27–30, *28*
Tales of the Unexpected (TV) 29
Tarrat, Margaret 28
Taste of Fear (1961) 75, 213
Taylor, Dub 155
Taylor, Elizabeth 209
The Texas Chain Saw Massacre (1974) 1, 9, 12–13, *13*, 15, 78, 99–100, 153, 213
Thames River, London, 115–116, 183–184, 198–199
Theatre of Blood (1973) 114–116, *115*
Thesiger, Ernest 6
Thir13en Ghosts (2001) 5
Thomas, Damien 65
Tillotson, Jerry 192
Tilly, Meg 80, *81*, 82
Tingwell, Charles "Bud" 62–63, *62*
Todd, Richard 92–93, *93*
Tokoloshe 213
Tourneur, Jacques 177, 179–180
Travers, Henry 24
Travers, Susan 113
Troughton, Patrick 15
The Turn of the Screw (TV adaptation) (1974) 123
20th Century Fox 123
Twins of Evil (1971) 65, *66*, 67–68
Tyburn Films 153

Ulmer, Edgar G. 190, 192
Uneasy Freehold (novel) 196

Index

The Uninvited (1944) 7, 189, 195–198, **196**
Universal 47–48, 57, 81, 105, 177, 190, 193–194

V&A (museum) 130
Vail, William 12–13
The Vampire Lovers (1970) 65
Vampyres (1974) 183–185
Van Devere, Trish 124–125
Van Ost, Valerie 72–74, 95
Van Sloan, Edward 103–104
Vaughan, Peter 168, 183
The Vault of Horror (1973) 28
Victor, Charles 90, 92
Victor, Mark 77
Victoria and Albert Museum *see* V&A

Waggner, George 46
Walker, Pete 1–3, 150–151, 153
Walker, Stuart 192
Walls, Kevin Patrick 83, 85
Wan, James 9
Warbeck, David 65, 198
Warner, David 15, 33
Warner Brothers **99**, **175**, 177
Warren, Norman J. ix, 2–3, **5**
Watford, Gwen 153–154, **154**
We Belong Dead (magazine) ix, x
Webling, Peggy 103
Weiler, A.H. 67, 132
Wells, H.G. 24–25
The Werewolf (1913) 193
Werewolf of London (1935) 189, 192–194, **193**

The Werewolf of Paris (novel) 107
Westman, Nydia 44, **45**
Whale, James 4, 24–25, 27, 103
What Lies Beneath (2000) 131, 141–144, **142**
Wheatley, Dennis 148
White, Liz 126
Whitelaw, Billie 15, 17
Whiton, James 111, 114
Wilde, Oscar 145–147
Willard, John 44
Williams, JoBeth 77, 79
Williams, John 77
Williamson, Kevin 83–84
Winder, Michael 31
Wingard, Adam 68, 70
Winn, Kitty 10
The Witches (novel) 131
The Wizard of Oz (1939) 147
The Wolf Man (1941) 46–48, 193–194
The Woman in Black (novel) 118, 126
The Woman in Black (2012) 126–127
Wong, James 139
Wood, Chris 163
Wylie, Philip 40
Wyngarde, Peter 121–123
Wynter, Dana 160, **160**, 162
Wyss, Amanda 136

York, Susannah 71, 75, **75**, 77
You're Next (2011) 68–70

Zemicks, Robert 141–142, 144
Zsigmond, Vilmos 77
Zucco, George 44, **45**, 46

www.ingramcontent.com/pod-product-compliance
Ingram Content Group UK Ltd.
Pitfield, Milton Keynes, MK11 3LW, UK
UKHW041943140426
5217IPUK00014B/639